the Enlightened

"A revelation into the seen and unseen forces that help shape our lives."

RICARDO F. HENRY

Ivy House
Publishing Group
www.ivyhousebooks.com

Other books by Ricardo F. Henry

The Passion of a Poet

The Romanticist

Even Angels Sing the Blues

Until It's Time to Die

PUBLISHED BY IVY HOUSE PUBLISHING GROUP
5122 Bur Oak Circle, Raleigh, NC 27612
United States of America
919-782-0281
www.ivyhousebooks.com

ISBN: 1-57197-402-4
Library of Congress Control Number: 2003095718

Copyright © 2004 Ricardo F. Henry
All rights reserved, which includes the right to reproduce this book or portions thereof in any form whatsoever except as provided by the U.S. Copyright Law.

Printed in the United States of America

*Dedicated to the Messiah and all those who love him.
Special thanks to those who serve as my inspiration:
Jeanett Henry, Vassel Henry, and Mrs. Gloria Grayson.*

TABLE OF CONTENTS

	The Conception	1
1.	The Laws of Circumstances	15
2.	Universal Re-sequencing	27
3.	The Art of Meditation	33
	The First Month	
4.	The Human Soul	39
5.	The Many Faces of Beauty	45
6.	The Unison Metaphysical Theory	55
	The Second Month	
7.	Christ's Suicide	91
8.	Realism versus Spiritualism	99
9.	The Spiritual Demon	115
	The Third Month	
10.	Forgiveness and Consequences	121
11.	The Dark Souls	127
12.	The Beast Within—Is God Responsible?	133
	The Fourth Month	
13.	Beyond Redemption	141
14.	Religious Arrogance	147
15.	Spiritual Aggression versus Passivity	153
	The Fifth Month	
16.	The Transfiguration: A Hidden Mystery	159
17.	Born to Die	165
18.	Death and Pain	171

The Sixth Month

19. Trials and Tribulations — 179
20. Reassurance from God! — 189
21. In the Mind of Rage — 195

The Seventh Month

22. The Epigenetic Principles of Life — 207
23. The Two Types of Eternities — 213
24. In the Mind of God — 217

The Eighth Month

25. Facing Adversity Spiritually — 221
26. The Enlightened — 227
27. The Love that Defies Reason — 239

The Ninth Month

28. The Church — 245
29. The Metamorphosis of Love — 251
30. My Name Is Still Gandhi! — 257

The Birth

31. False Prophets — 261
32. The One Pardoned Sin! — 267
33. Heaven Is Not My Reward — 275

PREFACE

The Enlightened did not emerge from an eclectic source of inspiration that ultimately became the embodiment of what it is today. Instead it was resurrected by a single soul that has yet to find itself in this world, my dear unborn. Sometimes the bond between the unborn and a potential parent is lifeless in nature; the energy that is needed to stimulate interactions can only derive from intense focus and meditation. The voice of the unborn is frequently silent because of man's refusal to acknowledge the bond that existed between them. As the author of *The Enlightened,* my inspiration is this "voice" and the unspoken words that are seldom ever heard by the mothers and fathers of these unborn souls. *The Enlightened* does not only reflect the author's quest for spiritual enlightenment or the ability to one day embrace a state of consciousness that signifies the arrival of nirvana, but instead represents the connection between the born and the unborn and a metamorphosis that has been illuminated in the light of God. It reflects the author's urgency to prepare an unborn soul for what he perceives as a less than perfect world, only to realize that he too is in desperate need of grace. *The Enlightened* provides an avenue where two distinctive souls from different worlds can reach out and exchange the basic tenets about the quest for spiritual enlightenment. Indeed it offers insight from a perfect world, the world of an unborn soul in an effort to convey messages of hope to a father that is less than hopeful. It is a book that compels one to challenge the existence of one's being and look within oneself with the courage to confront the darkness. *The Enlightened* does not seek to find the truth or the essence of man's faith, but rather bears testimony to man's struggle with both. This is the journey of an unborn soul and the knowledge that transcends his world and finds its way in the bosom of a potential father whose notion of spirituality was uncertain until it was made clear by his dear unborn: *The Enlightened,* the journey of two souls.

INTRODUCTION

My dear unborn, as it is with people, the universe has its own psyche. It consists of a network of seen and unseen forces and principles designed specifically to influence greatly our lives through its direct and indirect impact on the universal order of things. I vehemently stress most passionately that you become familiar with as much about those factors as possible, for the simple reason that you will find that in the symphony of life the conductor is frequently the laws of circumstances and not people, as many would have you think. Indeed, comprehending the psychology of the universe is paramount in sometimes grasping an individual's psychopathology. The connection between the self and the universe creates in us a type of wholeness and must therefore be examined closely if completeness in every sense of the word is to be ensured. The misconception that man has made about himself is that it is enough to understand the psychology of the human condition with little or no attention to the psychology of the universe with respect to the laws of circumstances and cosmic energy.

The Enlightened attempts to introduce some of the more inconspicuous dynamics between the psychology of the self and the universe in hopes of showing how collectively they play a powerful force in understanding the human condition as a whole. The book also demonstrates how it is possible to manipulate these forces in order to enhance one's self-awareness and spirituality. For this reason, my dear unborn, I am compelled to make known this presentation of some of the variables that govern both the self and the universe, thus bringing your mind closer to a state of harmony.

My dear unborn, never fear the living nor the dead, but do fear the idea of one day justifying your existence to the Creator. As a psychoanalyst, success has always been to me that which I can do to assist others in feeling or thinking good about themselves. For over twenty years, a small glimpse into man's soul has served me well, for what I have seen has made me weary of hell, living my life each day as one should do as if it is the last. Because of what I have seen, I am certain of one absolute: There is a God, and he seldom sleeps. The uncertainty of life with all its predicaments sends chills up my spine when I think of you being born in the world in which we live. The bleakness intensifies when I bear witness to man's suffering, leaving me only to struggle in sweet desperation in search of some way to provide you with the little knowledge that life has afforded me in hopes that you will be sheltered from some of the catastrophic mistakes that I have made.

Although many parents rely on trial and error to teach their children many of life's valuable lessons, my wish is that the method which I have chosen, the projection of my thoughts and my experiences, will prove to be just as effective. What man would not give anything if only he could possess the knowledge at age eighteen or nineteen that he now knows at sixty or seventy? So is it with my unborn child, for if he acquires just a third of the knowledge that I have obtained throughout my lifetime at his relatively young age, my attempt would have been worth the effort.

Indeed, if you are one who thirsts for spiritual enlightenment, whether to guide your child or to ensure your own salvation, then I invite you to share in my journey by reading *The Enlightened,* a book specifically created to provide insight and revelations regarding some of the seen and unseen forces of the various entities within the universe. Socrates once challenged us to know ourselves, but knowing ourselves is only half the battle. The other half is being able to embrace cosmic consciousness, the ability to have total awareness about how the laws of circumstances influence our lives by affecting the universal order of things, because who and what we are are shaped by both the seen and unseen entities of this world and the one after.

THE CONCEPTION

My dear unborn, it is with indescribable joy and jubilation that I welcome and embrace the honor that you have bestowed on me. Not in my wildest dream did I ever imagine that one day I would be blessed with the privilege of being a father. Being a part of this earthly journey will not be easy, for life can be hard, to say the least. However, when simplified it is manageable. I am humble that our Creator has chosen me to guide you on this journey. Still, I wonder if I am suitable or even worthy.

No! I dare not tell your mother of your arrival, for in this world it is customary for her to tell me. Though in silent solitude we have been communicating for weeks now, she would not be able to comprehend the higher-level consciousness that we shared. No! It is not because I am afraid of what she might think, but then again, maybe I am. Christ once said to a group of people, "If I tell you of earthly things and you do not believe, why should you believe me when I tell you of heavenly things?" In short, your mother would not understand the clairvoyance of a simple man, much less his communicating with a soul that has not yet manifested itself, you my dear unborn.

In this realm, the gateway to happiness and long-lasting mental health is rooted in spirituality. Do not be perplexed by the extraneous variables of life. Always simplify, my dear unborn, and you will have already won half the battle. Long-lasting mental health and happiness can never be obtained unless it has a certain degree of spirituality. Indeed, while spirituality is rooted in religious principles, it seldom has anything to do with religious tenets. Spirituality is rather a heightened sense of consciousness that involves the shedding of primitive and superficial attributes. It further involves total embracing of the entities of the universe with respect to its life form and the ability to be able to identify with them in some respect. Even a cockroach's life should bring some sense of remorse to a man who is truly on the journey to spiritual enlightenment.

Spirituality and psyche are intertwined quite frequently, even inseparable. Psyche has to go through major adjustment before the journey of heightened consciousness can begin Thus, psychology is just one of the tools in which to obtain spirituality because it involves self-analysis and discovery that can cue an individual into what is needed or lacking in order to attain spirituality in its highest form. As the psyche embarks on this journey of heightened consciousness, it engages itself in a phenomenon known as spiritual purging. Spiritual purging is a process by which mental cleansing takes place. It is absolutely necessary in order for the mind to get to a point where it can be submissive to the attributes of enlightenment. In other words, without this cleansing—this spiritual purging, if you will—spiritual enlightenment cannot be achieved. The mind must go through this state of cleansing before any type of adjustment can be made in order to embrace the spiritual enlightenment. The most difficult part of this mental cleansing is to allow the mind to exercise total autonomy by allowing it to probe and project long-forgotten images that were buried in our subconsciousness. This process can be very painful because it allows us to see things or to face things that we don't wish to face or for some reason were unwilling or unable to cope with.

Spiritual purging is not a one-time phenomenon or short-term process. It is a gradual process that over a period of time can amount to many years. It is a consistent process on the part of an individual who must at times put himself into an introspective meditative state in order to go through full mental disclosure. The good news, however, is that the more frequent this episode is practiced or this phenomenon takes place, the less painful the experience. Once this mental purification takes place, paving the way for a heightened consciousness, then it is and will be the beginning of the growth of spiritual enlightenment, which ultimately serves as the premise to true happiness.

Spiritual purging is not only the gateway to happiness, but it involves transcendentalism, a concept that brings one closer and closer to the living Creator. It is important to note, however, that it is not enough to have goodwill or demonstrate the practicing of good deeds to your fellow man; rather it is more important to fully comprehend the laws of the universe and give total reverence to every thing no matter how insignificant it may appear to be. To acquire such a state of mind, one must be willing to shed the mental, physical and spiritual shackles that serve as dark clouds to our being. It is a state of mind that embodies fleeing oneself from the imprisonment of earthly ties. Here, earthly ties are defined as things that give the mind, body, and spirit the delusion that they are desperately in need of them to feel complete. The earthly ties not only stagnate positive energy, they prevent the mind, body, and spirit from obtaining homeostasis and harmony, and they dilute the hopefulness we seek for spiritual redemption.

Spiritual enlightenment cannot be obtained unless we embrace the notion that our entire lives do not follow a path of reality but rather a stream of delusions that we have convinced ourselves to be real. The more we cling to our earthly ties and experiences, the more distant the quest for spiritual enlightenment will become. The shedding of these earthly ties and experiences are absolutely necessary because the cosmic energy that drives the mind, body, and spirit are pure in all respects but will quickly become defiled by the earthly ties and experiences to which we cling. The quest for spiritual enlightenment often takes different people on relative journeys. Still, my belief is that in order to obtain spiritual enlightenment, following the biblical teachings that over the years many have been drawn to is not enough.

Although as noted earlier, spirituality is rooted in religious tenets, one cannot achieve spiritual enlightenment merely by reading the Bible. None of the inconsistencies, contradictions, indecisiveness, illogical thought, or polarization in biblical teaching can be attributed to God. God does not change views or feelings based on man's idiosyncrasies or societal changes. If there is one concrete ideology that remains constant in all shape and form, it is the teaching of God. God is omniscient, and because of this, one of his many attributes is that he has the ability to make decisions based on futuristic information that is already known to him. Hence, these inconsistencies and contradictions in the Bible can, of course, be attributed to man's own indecisiveness, which ultimately will create confusion for people who dwell on the biblical teaching as their source for spiritual enlightenment. Engaging oneself in the biblical teachings in order to obtain spiritual enlightenment is not enough. We must embrace these biblical teachings, but only through spiritual enlightenment can we know for sure just how accurate these biblical teachings are and how they apply to our lives. Only through spiritual enlightenment can we have the foresight to see the pitfalls and the nonsense of some of these verses in order to know which of them we should use to help us on the journey to spiritual enlightenment. Still, it is important for our own spirituality to develop an understanding as to why biblical teachings have so many inconsistencies. But make no mistake, without some degree of spirituality it is futile to embrace biblical teaching in hopes that it will lead to the path of enlightenment.

In order to examine the biblical teachings of the Bible with respect to knowing why it is not enough to study and learn these biblical sayings in order to gain spiritual enlightenment, we must look at it from a historical perspective. Originally man, who was inspired by God, wrote the biblical teachings and did so pure in heart. Revelations were indeed revealed to him by God, and frankly the word was God. The stability of the teaching was such that man knew exactly where he stood with God. And as time goes by and man drifts further and further from God in thoughts and in deeds, man then seeks to reconcile this gradual movement away from God by also altering the biblical writings and teachings in order for them to conform with his diluted views. The dilution of the Bible by man came about because man became lazy in regards to living up to the expectations of God. Later he concerned himself no longer with meeting God's expectations, but rather he came to the realization that he could use these revisions of biblical teachings to impose or elicit a particular type of response from his fellow man. Soon he found himself lacking in fully understanding human nature, which remains fluid and always changing. Each translation of the teaching is based on new insight into man's nature, with the intent to get man to better conform to social standards. Unfortunately, because of the fluid-like unpredictability of human nature, the revision can never be complete; as the monkey once said, just when I thought I knew all the answers, they went and changed the questions. Hence, man will forever find himself in a precarious position with God if his sole purpose for spiritual enlightenment is the biblical teachings. I am not saying that we should discount the biblical teachings. I am saying, however, that it is not enough to seek and gain spiritual enlightenment, and without some degree of spiritual enlightenment it will almost be impossible to one day stand in the presence of our Creator.

In seeking spiritual enlightenment, it is also necessary to examine one's personality, which quite often is seen as a repertoire of psychological dysfunction by some clinicians. In this context, man's greatest enemy is himself, simply because in most cases he fails miserably when it comes to controlling and dealing with these character defects or this psychological dysfunction. Therefore, in order to gain some form of spiritual enlightenment, one must work very hard on the personality, because any form of impairment in the body means some form of impairment in the spirit as well. Being conscious of any variables that may affect either the body or the spirit is important. The relationship between the body and the spirit is not only essential for good health and wholeness with respect to the personality, but it is a necessity for spiritual enlightenment as well.

The quest for spiritual enlightenment will always lead to happiness. Happiness is the reward for all the sacrifices that it took to find enlightenment. The quest for happiness has long been the primary goal for many of us. But in a world of despair, miseries, and superficial attributes, the journey for happiness has become out of reach. Individuality is lost in a world of social qualifications. Our every move must frequently experience a check-and-balance system not only by the social demons that lack the comprehension to fully grasp why we do the things we do, but amazingly enough more often than ever, by the ones we love—the ones who adore us and in some cases would even die for us. Yet, the notion of being unhappy is predicated on the very existing foundation of that magnetic love that so often has extracted our very heart and soul, linking us to our loved ones forever. Yet in a twisted sense of shared delusions we somehow convince ourselves that it must be true love, and so happiness is only but a step away. Soon reality kicks in and we're left wondering whether or not this overwhelming feeling had anything to do with love. Happiness then becomes a definition based not on our individual thoughts, feelings, or perceptions, but rather solely on these same attributes of our loved one. We feel what they feel; we think what they think, urgently trying desperately to live our lives through their eyes and as a by-product of their existence, not being cognizant of the enormous price we pay for this sacrifice. In a compelling gesture to prove our love and sincerity, we confess openly that if our loved ones are not happy, then it is somewhat unselfish for us to be happy, in an attempt to offer some consolation in these times of misery. It is as if one more unhappy person will somehow make the situation a little better, giving some peace of mind to our loved ones.

Is it our destiny to define ourselves and our happiness based on what others—especially loved ones—think, feel, and say about us? Will not the scale of love still be balanced if we do not extend so much energy ingratiating ourselves in order to be accepted by those we cherish most of all? If the love is truly unconditional, what difference does it make how you are perceived? And for those who are not content with you as a person, for whatever reason, will not the sun still shine tomorrow? An individual who cannot live an existence without the drive to be accepted by others is not living an existence at all. The need to please is then transformed into power for those whom you go at great length to be in their grace, arming them with the power to control and the power to manipulate. What we fail to realize, however, is that the need to be accepted by others is usually embedded into the psyche from childhood then later reinforced by our close friends and loved ones. We're conditioned to be controlled and manipulated, first by our parents, then by our husbands, wives, sons, daughters, and other members of the extended family. Is it any wonder then that by the time we get to establish any relationship with members of society, we're like Pavlov's dog, ready to obey and conform on signal? In the event you dispute this assertion, try and behave in a manner that is in contrast to the expectation of your loved ones by exercising total autonomy over what you think or feel about any issues that you have modified because of your love or respect for their viewpoints.

Indeed, love does involve some degree of wanting to please and be accepted by the ones we love. However, when it becomes so altruistic to the point that we genuinely cannot be happy unless they are, the road to happiness has been compromised. But more important, the possibility of experiencing any undiluted happiness is drastically cut in half, because true happiness begins and ends with self. I'm not saying that our loved ones are causes of our unhappiness, only that they are the cornerstone as to why in many cases we're not, though we may think we are. When we find ourselves molding our spirit to act and react only in accordance with their expectations, then we must ask ourselves, *Where do they stop and I begin?* because true love and happiness is remembering the unity of two without neglecting the individuality of one.

Happiness also depends on the choices we make in our lives, but more importantly the bases for these choices. Do we live our lives from a spiritual foundation or from a social one? The answer to this question can make or break us in terms of succeeding in our quest for happiness. A spiritual foundation is one in which all or most of the decisions we make in life are influenced by our metaphysical relationship with God. A social foundation, however, is one where we make our decisions based on the potential societal consequences of our actions in relation to a member or members of society. In short, the decision is made based on how it will affect our fellow man as opposed to how it will be accepted by God.

While it may be difficult to live a lifestyle that does not involve the two simultaneously, the secret is on which do we place a greater emphasis, on the spiritual or the social? A man selling insurance kept reiterating how righteous and God-fearing he is while knowingly giving me the wrong information that ultimately would increase my monthly premium. I looked at him as he dripped in perspiration from the guilt that came with his intrapersonal conflict. This man did not know it, but he was doomed to an existence of misery. True happiness is not based on such compartmentalization. One cannot claim to be a man of God and represent deeds that reflect such strong connection to social desires, and the justification for making a living is a poor one because life is about making choices and taking responsibility for our actions. The essence of happiness entails integrity not only with others but mainly with oneself.

We cannot fluctuate back and forth with respect to our values, morals, and sense of decency—which goes directly to the heart of our relationship with our Creator—merely because the circumstances suit our needs. Happiness is not always taking the easy road that would get us out of a tight spot, but rather embracing the difficulty that comes with making these hard choices, for only then can our spiritual foundation be nurtured. When one thinks back in time, all the great men and women who have impacted our society in a positive way with regards to drastically changing the way we now live our lives had to make choices that were rooted in what appeared to be hardship. The hardship, however, was nothing but a pebble being dropped in their psyches, yet from our perspective it appeared that they have carried the world on their shoulders. Quite often we even think that it would be impossible to follow in their footsteps because of this perception of hardships. Happiness based on spiritual foundation is the embodiment of hard work, hard choices, and coming face-to-face with the true meaning of one's self.

Reality is that which runs parallel to perception and conception, hence, our notion of happiness must be examined carefully to ensure that the happiness we have is indeed the real thing. People have a tendency to perceive things, confess them to be so, then exert tremendous energy trying to make these things tangible with little or no examination to determine if the things in question are only a fabrication of their minds, a mirage that stems from wishful thinking. One cannot just think happiness and be happy with no idea of what the concept embodies. But what is even further from the truth is the perception that another person can and does make someone happy. Finding happiness is not a state of mind but rather a state of being, which is not to say that to be considered happy one must walk around with a smile on their face every day. A smile or laughter is nothing but a manifestation of the mode that an individual's spirit is in at that moment in time. Happiness is the recognition of one's self-worth, one's destiny in the total scheme of this macrocosm. It is the offspring of the unification of mind, body, and spirit. It is the linkage between man and his Creator. It is the passion that allows you to cast your lonely fish back into the sea and instead choosing to die from starvation. It is impossible to obtain happiness from another person. While they may help you on a journey to self-discovery which may lead to happiness, too often this journey is confused with the happiness itself.

Because happiness cannot be obtained from another person, it seems only fitting that we take responsibility for our own happiness—a notion that escapes many of us because we sit down waiting for the right one to come along that will wave a magic wand to make us happy. Next, we drown these poor individuals in an ocean of personality defects in hopes that they can fix them and make us happy. When we realize that the poor soul is just like us, we routinely amplify their flaws in order for us to be able to say that in comparison to them I'm happy. But even worse is to embrace the notion that true happiness is only a fairy tale, something that happens only in the movies. We cloak ourselves with toxic cosmic elements, then quiver when things don't assist us on the journey to happiness. In a world of uncertainties where we can be taken away from this earth without any justification or known reasons, the degree we go to make our lives a living nightmare has always baffled me. We seldom live for today and plan for tomorrow. Instead we disburse tremendous energy in accumulating material goods with a promise that tomorrow the living will start. But the living never starts; we continue an existence of living to work as opposed to working to live. Suddenly, we find that our entire lives and self-worth is based on how successful we are in our jobs, and how much money we are able to make per year, and how much better off we are in comparison to our friends. Sometimes we are afraid to even take a vacation simply because we do not want our competitor to gain on us. Then comes the rationalizations, the notion that you are killing yourself for the sake of your family, when in reality all your family wants is just to spend time with you. And when that won't work, we reach back deep in our childhood in order to tell the story about how our father and mother had to struggle for everything they had—hence the need to do the things that you're doing so as to prevent your family from ever being in that shape. Surprisingly enough, your family buys into this garbage. Twenty years later when they're all grown up and become estranged from you, you wonder why they are not visiting you on your death bed if you should be so lucky with such longevity. My question has always been, why should they?

Happiness will always elude us as long as we're caught in this irrational way of thinking, the thinking that you have to measure your existence using a social measuring rod, and that this must be done at all cost. No amount of these toxic cosmic elements can ever lead to the path of happiness. Indeed, while it is easy to convince yourself as well as your family of this, this delusion will only serve to distance you from ever reaching true happiness. I recently saw a documentary about a woman who lived her life eating cat food three times per week and lived in an apartment that is much more inexpensive than she could really afford. She didn't take vacations and refused to help her kids through college even though she could afford to send them. She proudly admitted this, for she thought she was justified. You see, she worked for the government and therefore was confident that Social Security would not be around by the time she retired and as such she had to put away all her money for retirement. I asked myself, *What happens if she doesn't live to retire? Did somebody promise her tomorrow without promising me?* But most important, would it have been worth it to give up the fun that goes with being young, the ecstasy, the enjoyment for being sixty-five years old with a few dollars more and a life that had gone from your reach.

Fear is one of the most devastating obstacles that stands in the path of our happiness. It cripples the spirit and imprisons our potential. It drives us to the point where our lives become out of focus and our attention gets redirected to that which should be of little importance to us. The fear of death, the fear of standing up for something you believe in, the fear of not being able to live up to the expectations of others, the fear of losing your loved ones or security, and the fear of not being able to find a place in the world we live in—any variation of these fears stems from is a defense mechanism that drives one's life closer to their social roots as opposed to their spiritual one because on these elements false happiness is built. Unless you embrace these fears for what they are, obstacles, shedding your worrisome attitude and putting your faith in our Creator, you are doomed to an existence of misery and a life camouflaged as happiness. For worry comes from fear, a mind-set that is a contradiction in the eyes of God. One cannot exercise faith in God and worry in the same breath.

This is not an attempt to dismiss our fears as irrational or predicated on lack of sincere concerns; rather it's an attempt to point out that quite often our fears are misguided and based on faulty perceptions and prioritizing, The next time you cannot pay the rent, take a walk in a hospital and ask an HIV patient or other terminally ill patient if they would switch problems with you. When your journey to your happiness is blocked by any type of obstacle, remember that "now is not forever, and it too shall pass." Most of the times we defeat ourselves even before the problem we face initiates difficulties for us. We engage in a ridiculous amount of self-talk, all negative, to the point that we defeat and cheat ourselves out of happiness. A type of surrender takes the energy out of us that is needed to fight for the quest to be happy. Indeed, on occasions we fail to understand that the world will accept what it sees, more so than we are willing to do.

Realizing this would save us an enormous amount of time and energy that we now have to let the world see and accept us through our own sometimes-diluted eyes. We're more concerned about how others see our weaknesses and shortcomings, especially in a social context, than they're actually concerned with them in most cases. We create this childish concentration on ourselves, then question it when the whole world becomes our stage. Thus, we surrender the power of self and destiny to the world and wallow in self-pity when things do not work out.

"If it was not given unto you by my father, you would have had no power over me."

Paraphrasing Christ is appropriate in this context to alert us into knowing that the power one may have over us is as unreal as the circumstances from whence it came. Regardless of the intimidation factors, our fears, our need to be accepted, the true power of self and destiny lies within your hands. Seldom does our Creator allow another human being to exert that much control over another human being without good reason, reasons that may escape us at the present time. It was not intended that our happiness should solely depend on another human being. We were not created to worship each other but to worship him. A man who finds himself obtaining love and happiness from another to the degree that he does not share the same passion with respect to our Creator is no longer serving the Creator in a manner he was intended to be served. Rather he has become a servant to man and not to the Creator, and no man can serve two masters at once. Love your children, love your spouse, but choose whom you worship. More significantly, balance the love for them with the love for the Creator, always making sure the scale is tilted more toward the Creator. Love him not abstractly, but in a real sense and with the same fervor in which you love your loved ones, for he's the keeper of undying happiness. While we may always seek to be politically correct with respect to our behavior in the social context, he's more concerned that we become more spiritually correct. It is also essential that we are aware of the source of our power and growth, or else we will be like an insomniac who keeps dreaming that he's not getting any sleep.

Eternal happiness is the ultimate price we pay for nirvana. It transcends both life and death.

Recently I asked my wife whether or not she will be happy with me in death as she is with me in life. She giggled then replied, "I don't know how to answer that." "Why is the question so difficult?" I asked. "Because I don't know what to expect when I'm dead, much less whether or not I'll be happy," she said. I nodded in a gesture of empathy, but I was puzzled, for this is my wife, a woman whom I've seen walk the path of righteousness for many years. Yet, she could not say whether happiness existed in death, or even if she would get the opportunity to spend it with me. Like many, her life is rooted in spirituality. She worships the Messiah, yet her desire to know him remains a mystery. Were she able to unravel the mystery, she would have known that the Messiah is life and death and encompasses the happiness in the here and after that we all seek. She would have realized that life and death coexist in the same habitat within an eternal transition of perpetuated happiness. But the answer to my question had proven troublesome because in her mind there was a clear demarcation between life and death, a marriage that remains unconsummated and can never give birth to happiness or its offspring. My semi-fragile ego could have dealt with an answer that involved her not knowing whether or not I would still be her partner in death; hence, the question of happiness is far-fetched. Many of us take it for granted that the partner we are happy with in life we will regain in death, almost as if we expect them to wait for us before they start their life in the eternal realm. We do this because we cannot bear the thought of a loved one spending a life of eternity without us, or bear to think that their feelings for us might change in the next world.

One of the greatest misconceptions about happiness is that if we do not find it in this life we will find it in the next life, because somehow our Creator will wave a magic wand and make all our inadequacies and human baggage disappear, thus making us a new person, one who would allow us to be able to live with ourselves. For our Creator to indulge us in this misconception, it would defeat the entire purpose of the death of the Messiah. He died on earth, not in his Father's kingdom so we would be able to rid ourselves of these flaws before having access to his world, because you cannot put an imperfect person in a perfect place and expect him or her to grow spiritually. We become stronger and advance as human beings because of the presence of trials and tribulations, of which none exist in our Creator's kingdom. Second, we have to master our basic needs and desires of the self before the journey of fulfillment is considered complete. To the extent we're happy or unhappy rests entirely with us—a power no one has over us because our Creator gave us the power, and no one else. The place to purge ourselves of our defects and flaws is here, not God's kingdom. Indeed, this is where we rid ourselves of the poison that makes it impossible for us to be pure of heart.

The Conception

1

The Laws of Circumstances

The sustaining of one's existence cannot be maintained unless one is totally in sync with the laws of circumstances. The laws of circumstances compose a living, breathing force of energy, an entity whose primary purpose serves only to place individuals into predicaments that will ultimately determine their fates. Circumstances are always at opposition with the universal order of things. One of the reasons as to why the universe has random sequencing is to keep the laws of circumstances at bay in terms of being able to predict how things are ordered or set up. Therefore the universal order of things operates on a random principle; it often creates difficulties for the laws of circumstances with regards to being able to manipulate our lives, which is important in our fight against laws of circumstances. Why? Because each individual's cosmic energy is connected to certain aspects of the universe which embodies the universal sequencing of things. Because the sequencing is random, the laws of circumstances have a hard time trying to seize our cosmic energy in order to place us in situations that may be unhealthy or precarious. In actuality, the universal sequencing is saying, "I am going to protect Jimmy from the laws of circumstances by constantly making sure that his cosmic energy cycle operates randomly, thus keeping the laws of circumstances guessing as to when they will get a chance to capture him with respect to placing him in a given situation." Indeed, the universal order of things serves as a shield against the laws of circumstances. There are times, however, when people's cosmic energy is purely negative in nature; they do not associate with positive people, places, or things in order to absorb positive energy, but quite the contrary. In addition to possessing only negative energy, they themselves go at great length to defile other people's cosmic energy.

Because the universe is in the habit of engaging in behavior that entails preserving positive cosmic energy and eliminating negative energy, it has a mechanism in place to do just that. This mechanism is called the Janus Effect. What this mechanism does is to ensure the randomization of the universal sequence, thus making it impossible or even improbable for the laws of circumstances to dictate an individual's fate as a person. By this I mean making it difficult for the laws of circumstances to place an individual in a predicament that will allow the person to become a victim or a prisoner of the situation, thus creating harm to the individual. The Janus Effect operates on the principle of universal cleansing by sending the wrong signals for the laws of circumstances to follow. The universe, like other entities, will do whatever it takes to preserve itself. The Janus Effect applies to human beings and other cosmic energy as well. Indeed, while the Janus Effect deals with chronic negative energy in the universe, negative energy embedded in human beings—which manifests itself in pure evil—will sometimes gain an advantage over those human beings who embrace the positive energy. In short, occasionally evil has a tendency to overcome good with respect to human beings. One of the essential reasons for this effect is that people filled with positive energy are usually characterized as good individuals. They seek spiritual enlightenment and practice deeds that will pay tribute to such a state of mind. Even if they do not seek spiritual enlightenment, the notion of being good or doing good deeds for their fellow men has a tendency to put them in a very precarious position, because quite frequently they develop what is known as tunnel vision as far as other human beings are concerned. For example, they tend to see human beings as basically good and thus seldom develop the necessary paranoia needed to safeguard them from predicaments as far as negative people are concerned. Thus, they frequently pay a high price for their type of thinking. Because of these mind-sets, they do not fear death or consequences that can be harmful to the body but rather embrace life as an illusion that can seldom be shattered. A good-hearted person who chooses not to engage in any journey of spiritual enlightenment or try to be in sync with the laws of circumstances with respect to living their lives or trying to predict or offset the negative energy—thus walking around with their mind on autopilot—will undoubtedly eventually still become victim of the laws of circumstances. While such people may not readily accept the fact that they are more prone to be victims, they are indeed.

Negative energy manifesting itself in human beings quite frequently has a much greater chance of escaping the laws of circumstances and all the negative forces in the universe, whether they are trying to or not, because evil in its purest form is more inclined to possess tendencies for the use of the laws of circumstances. When a person tries to live in accordance with the rule of a given society, he or she is always thinking of what is right for him or her as well as others, but a person who strives on evil energy is always at war with self and society. Because of these interpersonal and individual social conflicts on the evil person's part, their mind-set cannot afford the luxury of being on autopilot for any long period of time, thus developing a heightened paranoia about people, places, and things in order for them to always escape the laws of circumstances. These conflicts further compel them to live their lives predicting and constantly being one step ahead of anything regarding society or people who they fear may have it in store for them. The fact of the matter is, they live their lives being in sync with the laws of circumstances without even being aware of it, thus always alerted to the most potential dangerous elements around them. Practically speaking, they develop a sixth sense about life and the shrewdness about their fellow man that seems to give them an edge. While they may relish having this sixth sense for awhile, which for some reasons allows them to even outlive the good, ultimately the Janus Effect will kick in, destroying the evil energy, hence destroying them by allowing the laws of circumstances to get the better of them with regard to not ensuring randomization on the part of the universe.

This is why so many people ask why the good die young, and why other people who are not making the best of their lives and frequently are unproductive seem to have a long existence. People of this nature unwillingly or unknowingly find themselves being totally in sync with the laws of circumstances as stated earlier, which is one of the ironic tenets of the laws of circumstances. It can be offset by pure evil in any shape or form. This is not to say the good is being penalized for having positive energy—hence doing relatively good deeds, therefore having a shorter existence—but rather to state the case that evil energy can sometimes serve as powerful influence with respect to how we live our lives as well as how long we serve out the remainder of the time we have on this earth. The fact remains that both good and evil provide that avenue where an individual can embrace the laws of circumstances and come out ahead in one piece. I would like to make clear, however, that the ultimate price one pays for having positive energy is spiritual enlightenment and transcendentalism with regards to nirvana and ultimately developing a personality which is known as *arahat*.

There is a very powerful association between mental energy, the laws of circumstances, and the universal order of things. The more mental energy is put forth regarding an issue, the less randomization will occur, thus increasing the likelihood of an individual becoming a victim of the laws of circumstances. In short, increased mental energy inadvertently affects the randomization of the universal order by slowing down its sequencing, making the laws of circumstances more powerful in our lives. This is one of the essential reasons as to why obsessions of any kind have often proven to have negative outcomes or dangerous elements to one's existence.

Because the mental energy that we possess is an offspring of spiritual energy, the purest of all energy, the circumstances that are likely to come about are positive ones. The way we think in our relationship to the universe can ultimately determine whether or not we will be a success or failure in this world. A child, for example, is more likely to possess this type of pure energy because he or she is not soiled by negative or subjective experiences. Thus the negative energy from these experiences will not affect the child's link to the universal order. A plane carrying a hundred children is less likely to crash than a plane carrying a hundred adults under similar circumstances. But even more importantly, a plane carrying ten children is less likely to crash than a plane carrying a hundred adults under similar circumstances. Therefore, it is obvious to assume that the more negative energy in the same place, the more probability of a negative outcome, and the more positive energy in one place, the more possibility and probability of a positive outcome.

It is also important to be mindful of cosmic fallacies, which occur when the laws of circumstances change a person's perception by letting them believe that their association with certain people, places, or things will have a negative outcome when in actuality it's quite the contrary; it's having a positive outcome. But in order to trick the individual into believing these people, places, or things—which as stated earlier bring them some type of negative consequences—the laws of circumstances create the illusion that they are bad influences on the individual. For example, a man came to me very upset. He said he loves his father and has always tried to nurture the relationship. I asked him, "What's the problem?" He said every time he gets close to his father, he noticed that he tends to lose his job. Apparently he noticed that this had happened several times, but as soon as he distanced himself from his father he always found himself another job. He was upset because the only way he could hold down a job was to avoid having any relationship with his father. He did not see that the laws of circumstances were trying to keep him from being around his father by putting another predicament in place, the loss of his job, then confusing him to the point where he drew the wrong conclusion with respect to why he was always a victim.

The body's energy also serves as a defense mechanism that can further diminish or magnify depending on one's association with negative or positive people, places, or things. The closer one gets to spiritual enlightenment, the more intense the body force field which serves to protect us also from the laws of circumstances becomes. Earlier I stated that people have the tendency to escape the laws of circumstances because of their heightened sense of awareness or consciousness around them. Here, however, an individual's body force field ultimately depends on their association with negative or positive people, places or things because the body force field is energized or reinforced based upon one's deeds and association with these people, places, or things. When the body's force field is chipped away layer by layer, then the laws of circumstances' chance of getting to the individual in order to place them in certain predicaments increases. Each layer of protective energy will be weakened or strengthened based on one's association or deeds. Each person is born with these protective layers and later develop them to become stronger or weaker over a period of time. These layers of energy are not affected as much by children who associate with negative people, places or things because most children lack a certain sense of awareness. Therefore, their force field tends to develop and maintain certain stability until they are able to decipher what's good or what's bad with respect to their association with these factors. Adults ultimately, however, have the power to groom their children with regards to their bodies' force field by exposing them to certain environments that will nurture them. In short, if you allow your children to associate with negative people, places, or things, then the body's force field will diminish. However, if you allow your child to be re-energized or reinforced by the positive energy from positive people, places, or things, then that child's force field will ultimately grow and develop and become stronger through these associations, thus decreasing the likelihood of them becoming victims of the laws of circumstances. Their body's force field will become so strong that it will serve as a shield against these laws of circumstances.

The question then becomes: why do the good die young when in actuality they should have a superb body force field or a strong protective layer? Indeed, a strong body force field is not enough to be protected from the laws of circumstances; cosmic consciousness is essential in aiding the body's force field. This is where most people fall short. They assume that human nature is basically good and as a result seldom keep their attention up for foreseeable danger. Thus, when they least expect it, danger or the laws of circumstances strike. The strength of the force field must always be rooted in cosmic consciousness in order for it to work effectively. If the cosmic consciousness and the body's protective layer still allow an individual to become a victim to some negative circumstances, then the person possesses an aiding soul. An aiding soul is destined to facilitate certain results regardless of the laws of circumstances or one's protective layers. These results frequently open the door to heartbreak and other painful experiences.

Indeed, if negative energy is the essence of one's life energy, which is the embodiment of one's body's force field, then the association with positive energy of any kind will ultimately result in the positive energy becoming negative as well. Vice versa, if one's positive life energy is associated with negative energy of any kind, then that energy will be transformed into positive energy. In short, the essence of one's life energy or force field is so powerful that it can influence this opposite. Needless to say, this depends on the degree of positive or negative energy one possesses in comparison to the association of the opposite energy. Quite frequently, when two life's energies come into contact with each other and if they are opposites, the transformation will be based on the strength of one's psyche or mental energy. The transformation of negative to positive or positive to negative with respect to one's life energy can be determined by the strength of one's mental or psychic energy. By this I mean that a strong-minded person, if you will, whether they may possess negative or positive energy will serve as a more dominant figure over someone who possesses weaker mental or psychic energy, thus influencing them to the point where the transformation of their body's force field will succumb to the essence of the dominant figure's energy, thus allowing the submissive individual to behave in accordance with the dominant figure's energy. Therefore, if the dominant figure is engaging in negative behavior, then so will the person with the weaker mental energy, and if the dominant person is engaging in positive behavior, so will the person with the weaker mental energy. The behavior that is displayed, the metamorphosis of this life energy, is totally dependent on the individual's psychic or mental energy with respect to the degree of strength

It is imperative that as individuals try to understand the rules of life, we also try to understand the rules that pertain to the laws of circumstances. We are too sophisticated to think that things happen merely because of chances or merely because they were intended to happen. The notion of predestination by birth states that God has an elaborate script of each person's life and it does not matter what an individual does in his life; his destiny is already set because God has already predicted and written down everything about his life. So many times I have heard my colleagues say something happened to them because it was just meant to be or that God wanted it to happen to them. This learned helplessness mentally absolved them of the responsibility to take control of their own destiny and to take the necessary steps needed to understand the unforeseen forces that shape their lives.

By relishing the notion of predestination by birth—that God has some elaborate script of each individual's life, and it does not really matter what he or she does—one's destiny is pretty much set because God has already predicted and written down everything about one's life. This puts one in the mind-set where if something goes wrong, it is easier to blame the Creator. If something was just meant to be or was the will of God, this approach produces a dogmatic mind-set that can no longer be open to the possibility for any other investigation into the unforeseen forces that might have influenced their lives. The cognitive response to predestination by birth is usually false. It gives the impression that our Creator has a distorted value system, creating the picture or image of him silting with the book of life saying, "Oh yes, on the next page Mary, John, and David will have a plane crash and there is nothing they can do about it." This type of learned helplessness and defeatist mentality will undoubtedly stagnate any possibility of attaining spiritual enlightenment. But even more importantly, it puts our state of mind in a state of hopelessness with respect to our goals and any other aspect of our lives that we may want to develop and challenge. It is the type of thinking that kills any type of success and produces only failure in one's life. It further creates gigantic obstacles that block our view, preventing us from seeing the true culprit, predestination by fate, an entity that is the offspring of the laws of circumstances.

Predestination by fate says that if Mary and David had a plane crash, the question should be what steps did they take to ensure that it did not happen. Did they check, for example, on-flight record and weather condition? In short, did they do everything in their power before getting on board to decrease the probability or possibility of that plane crashing? Predestination by fate asks what responsibility did I take to ensure my safety, to ensure that certain predicament does not occur that can create either embarrassment or pain in my life, as opposed to predestination by birth, which says that things are going to happen anyway because it is just written that way and there is nothing I can do about it. One absolves you from responsibility and the other reinforces that something has to be done with respect to your taking responsibility in order to offset the laws of circumstances that may rule against you in a negative way. Indeed, while fate may still cause the plane to crash, your cosmic consciousness could have drastically decreased the chance of it happening to you. Why? Because cosmic consciousness makes us more in tune with the laws of circumstances, thus decreasing the probability of things happening to us, like a plane crash, for example. Being in sync with the laws of circumstances does not offer a guarantee of the outcome of the situation, but what it does is substantially rally positive cosmic consciousness and energy as a defense or protector against the laws of circumstances and all its negative forces, putting the odds in your favor.

One may ask why would our Supreme Being allow such a powerful force to have such an influence over our lives, especially knowing that a number of people will not take the time to assess these rules that govern the laws of circumstances which will ultimately dictate what happens to them as human beings. Indeed, human beings have paid a price for being able to make choices or embark on any decision we so desire. This price is a powerful force and it is called the laws of circumstances. The laws of circumstances have a life of their own as mentioned before. They work in conjunction with the universal order, the sequence in which all things in the universe are placed. Therefore, while each human being may possess free will, indeed, it is not without a price. We should keep in mind at all times that the laws of circumstances' primary purpose is to place each individual randomly in various situations at moments when they least expect it. Some of these situations quite often are deadly, while others at times can prove to be quite challenging. Then we would have already won a large part of the battle. Free will was given to man but not without a price, the price being the laws of circumstances.

Next we must embrace the notion that when we made the decision to reject God's everlasting shield by accepting free will, we did so under the condition that the laws of circumstances would reign over our lives and the universal order of things. This is why some people find themselves in bad circumstances and others may not, frequently leaving us to ask the question, "Why me?" The answer to this question is simple: because we were not in sync with the laws of circumstances. By being in sync I mean having the instinctive ability to know the outcome or the potential of each situation before the laws of circumstances have the opportunity to place us in that predicament. Indeed, this may take practice, but it can become a vital force in determining how, when, and why something happens to you in your daily lives. If the laws of circumstances are nothing else, they are spontaneous and totally unpredictable, but exactly those factors make it predictable.

Indeed, cosmic consciousness, which is defined as having total awareness of how the universal order of things is affected by the laws of circumstances thus influencing our lives, is a powerful tool in dealing with your everyday life and why things happen to you, especially when you least expect them. While it is in our control to offset some of these predicaments that the laws of circumstances would place us in, such is not the case with cosmic balancing, a concept which states that each individual will obtain the same ratio in terms of pleasure and displeasure within his lifetime. However, through manipulation of the laws of circumstances one can ultimately decide what amount of pleasure or displeasure one will receive in a particular lifetime. The laws of circumstances explain why bad things happen to good people, but most importantly they give insight into why God should not be held accountable for all the pain and suffering within the world. Because each individual is subject to a ratio of pleasure and displeasure within a given lifetime does not mean that he or she cannot manipulate the elements of the circumstances in order to balance the ratio in his or her favor. The way to accomplish this, however, takes time and practice, something that most individuals are not willing to do. Therefore, this lack of practice and heightened consciousness has a tendency to lead to a ratio where displeasure appears to be the prevailing force. Heighten your consciousness to your surroundings with respect to all your five senses and become one with the elements, thus allowing the laws of circumstances to work for you and not against you.

THE CONCEPTION

2

UNIVERSAL RE-SEQUENCING

Life experiences when left unresolved, for whatever reason, will not just become extinct, but the process, which is a variation of cosmic balancing, will take place. Cosmic balancing will be discussed at some later date. However, when this process takes place, the unresolved issues within one's life will return, until the issue is successfully resolved within oneself. Indeed, the past never goes away, it just hides between the present and the future. Universal resequencing, a variation of cosmic balancing as stated earlier, states that any unresolved life experiences that an individual encounters will resurface in the individual's life at some later date unless it is totally resolved. These revisiting experiences may not manifest themselves in the same fashion as before, but the similarities with respect to the life experiences, unresolved ones, will place you in a position where you are compelled to find some resolution to it in a manner in which the initial experience should have resolved. In short, universal resequencing further states that cosmic forces will follow through with the cycle with regards to the order in which things are randomly placed in your life, but will randomly revisit these unresolved or aborted issues—life experiences, if you will—in a manner totally related or exactly the same as the life experience. In short, deal with me now or deal with me later.

Part of the error that is usually made by clinicians with respect to universal resequencing is to dismiss this only as synchronicity, a term coined by Jung that means meaningful coincidences. By doing this it further absolves them from taking any real responsibility with regards to taking a closer look with regards to the unseen forces that tend to influence our life experiences. Synchronicity is based on the premise of possibilities and probabilities, a chance that something may or may not happen depending on certain circumstances. Universal resequencing is more definite; it states that it is only a matter of time before "I get to a certain part of your life cycle that will allow me to dictate that you revisit that type of episode or event in your life that you were not able to deal with successfully." Unlike synchronicity, universal resequencing is not a matter of chance, but rather a matter of time.

Another phenomenon that is the offspring of universal resequencing is cosmic balancing. Cosmic balancing states that an individual will have an equal ratio of positive things to negative things regarding his or her life experience. Cosmic balancing dictates that no matter how an individual lives his or her life, in the end his life experience will amount out to be the same with respect to the ratio of pleasure and displeasure. Quite often people will say, "Well, I have certainly had my share of pain, so when will a little pleasure start?" The truth of the matter is, chances are we might have already had more pleasure than pain at that point in our lives, but we were not focusing on it while it was happening. We are quick to point out the negative things and are aware of them when they happen, but seldom do we take the time to notice the pleasure and fun, especially when it is happening to us in small quantities. Cosmic balancing is a prophetic feature because the rules of cosmic balancing state that each person will receive a ratio of 50:50 with respect to pain and pleasure before they depart from this earth. It also states that in the event that you should escape the ratio, then it is almost a certainty that you will be placed back on earth again. Once placed back on earth, then you will have to complete the pain or pleasure cycle. Hence, cosmic balancing is a prophetic mechanism that can be used as a tool to decipher whether one will revisit earth at some later date. If an inventory is done with respect to one's life and the decision is made that a person has neither suffered enough nor had the same amount of pleasure with respect to the ratio, then the conclusion can be drawn that undoubtedly there will be a second chance with respect to an equal ratio of pleasure and displeasure to fill the gap that was lacking in the prior life.

Cosmic balancing cannot be prevented or altered; it is one of the preset instruments designed by faith as well as one of the few processes that the laws of circumstances can impose on human beings that is solely fired by the universal order of things. It is unchangeable because each individual's cosmic energy is connected and interdependent on each other, meaning that we draw energy from each other, whether it may be positive or negative—a process that is necessary to feel and energize us as people or individuals. This indirect linkage of each other stems from being a part of God's holy circle of light from whence all of us came. Indeed this connection to each other is risky in terms of being exposed to cosmic balancing with respect to someone else's energy. Through the principle of association with another person we sometimes take on their energy, whether it may be negative or positive, and share the type of pleasure or displeasure in terms of the ratio they are supposed to experience. For example, an individual who associates with negative people may find himself or herself taking on some of the negative pain or displeasure to which that individual is exposed. And vice versa, if an individual associates with positive people, then they tap into that energy, thus enjoying some of the pleasure with respect to the ratio that individual might be experiencing or projecting. Because each individual is part of this cosmic interdependency that stems from the holy circle of light of which we are all a part, we are all connected and linked together; hence we must be careful of our associations.

Cosmic interdependency is more than just an interconnecting of cosmic energy. It is an avenue in which each person can channel or share painful experience or pleasure merely by their association with the other person. The residue from each person's life experience is therefore transferred to another person to a certain degree. To what degree depends on the period of time spent with that person. When an individual taps into another person's cosmic reservoir, the extraction of energy also comes with the extraction of life experiences. Cosmic reservoir is the part of us that stores the energy we get from others as well as ourselves. Indeed while we can minimize the impact of universal resequencing by making sure that we deal with each life experience openly, honestly, and from a spiritual reference point, it is useless or futile to make any attempt to eliminate cosmic balancing, for we do not control our fate as far as cosmic balancing is concerned. However, by mastering the laws of circumstances, one can drastically eliminate the amount of agony or displeasure in one given lifetime, but ultimately an individual must still experience a balancing with respect to pain and pleasure. It is still possible to minimize the amount of displeasure one receives in a given lifetime with the hope that in another lifetime, one can make up for that displeasure. Hence, while cosmic balancing may not be eliminated altogether, it is possible to negotiate through the laws of circumstances with respect to how one may live his or her life through intense manipulation of the various circumstances in which one finds oneself.

Universal resequencing also involves a phenomenon known as the Boethius complex. The Boethius complex states that people may find themselves in a position where they are at the height of success or the height of their lives and because of the laws of circumstances they come crashing down, meaning that you can be successful one day and the next minute you are unsuccessful. This goes directly to, for example, a rich man suddenly becoming a poor man or finding himself losing everything that he once had. This is the embodiment of the Boethius complex; it is a variation of cosmic balancing. In many instances cosmic balancing and the Boethius complex work simultaneously together. For example, if an individual is at the height of success and it is dictated by cosmic balancing that he has to endure more displeasure because the ratio is unbalanced, then the Boethius complex comes into play and the individual will suddenly find himself becoming a victim of circumstances where he or she may end up becoming unsuccessful or losing things that would create much more pleasure for the individual in order to balance the scale per se.

It is important to also note that one of the fundamental principles of universal resequencing is that nothing happens before its time. Quite frequently people find themselves struggling to make certain progress or to achieve certain goals and find that it is almost next to impossible to reach that goal until a certain time, or they may suddenly find themselves at the top of the mountain. This is because of the laws of universal resequencing, which simply states that nothing happens before its time. It is not only the law of nature, it is the law of the Supreme Being. Indeed, some people do have a tendency to force the issue and try to accomplish or make things happen before their time. When this happens, the rules of universal resequencing kick in and it is only a matter of time before what was built comes crashing down, allowing the universal resequencing to dictate to the individual based on circumstances what, when, and how things should take place in order for things to be successful.

3

THE ART OF MEDITATION

Meditation is a vital tool in the quest for spiritual enlightenment and happiness. It is an essential avenue for introspection, higher consciousness, and an important way of getting closer to our Supreme Being. A meditative state allows you to bring your mind, body, and spirit together as one, providing a means by which all three entities can come together in harmony with one another.

Some preliminary steps should be taken before actually attempting to meditate; these steps involve muscle relaxation and breathing techniques. While many choose to meditate in a lotus position, it is recommended that you sit in any position that feels comfortable. The environment one chooses should be peaceful or facilitated by a mood-relaxing background. Hearing any sound or activity that will drastically interfere with brain waves should be avoided. Indeed mastering mindfulness is paramount; mindfulness is a process that entails learning how to embrace all the negative impulses, abstract thoughts, and hidden demons that plague the darkest regions of the human mind, those things that inevitably will emerge through either dreams or nightmares. Mindfulness reflects all the things we have suppressed and repressed within our subconscious. It is also the embodiment of all the things that make us less than who we are or would like to be. It can be the ultimate obstacle between man and his ideal self.

You can recognize the fragmentations of mindfulness quite easily, simply because it tends to interfere with any harmonious state that one may try to reach. In times of solitude, it will be those thoughts and feelings that attempt to trigger the notion that the very idea of trying to reach a state of heightened consciousness is a waste of time. The frequency of mindfulness will arise the closer the Supreme Being finds you worthy to be a part of his holy circle of light. In any meditative state, one must conquer mindfulness if he or she is ever to master one's self, for man's greatest enemy is truly himself.

Indeed, while mindfulness may represent the "shadow" of man's harmonious state of consciousness, it possesses a positive attribute that serves as a purification methodology for all three entities: mind, body, and spirit. Coexisting as a by-product of each state of consciousness, mindfulness includes a phenomenon known as spiritual purging. Spiritual purging is the means by which the soul cleans itself by constantly attempting to secrete its toxicity. All that makes us defiled and impure, thus preventing us from being closer to the Supreme Being, is driven out during the episode of spiritual purging. Ironically enough, it is the offspring of mindfulness, the very same concept that embodies unwanted distractions as we embark on the journey of heightened consciousness. But without spiritual purging through mindfulness, the soul has no way of cleansing itself in preparation for the light of the Supreme Being.

During the process of mindfulness, urges will compel you to avoid the various distractions that will be presented to you by the mind and the spirit. It is paramount not to give in to these temptations. The secret to conquering mindfulness is not to avoid the materials that come from the purging of the spirit but rather to welcome them in total embrace. Avoidance is always counterproductive to the state of harmony. Acceptance, not denial, is the underlying principle behind the concept of spiritual purging. When one accepts one's flaws and weaknesses as opposed to remaining in denial of them, the journey to spiritual enlightenment has already started. Indeed, mindfulness is the spirit's way of purging itself from the negative energy and forces that cause an individual to worry or feel incomplete. Once a state of nirvana is reached, mindfulness also serves as a way by which the Supreme Being chooses to reveal certain revelations to the individual, especially about some of the long-forgotten variables that are just now being purged out of the spirit. The temptation will always be there to try and avoid these significant distractions, but embrace them head on and let the Supreme Being guide and grace you with his enlightenment.

When you are totally consumed by the holy light of the Supreme Being, then and only then will mindfulness and all its pitfalls cease to exist, bothering you no longer. In this moment, one's concentration is as sound and steadfast in all its forms, leaving the mind, body, and spirit to pay reverence to your being by joining together in total unison.

As the mind, body, and spirit struggle to cope with the backlash of mindfulness, the purification of the holy circle of light will entice the self to experience a metamorphosis that goes to the heart of our desire in order to seek spiritual enlightenment. Suddenly, mindfulness is transformed, and what was once an obstruction is now "vipassana" insight. But mindfulness has to be experienced before all the darkness is swept away from one's life in order to bring one closer to the bosom of the Supreme Being. *Rapassana* is a direct result of the transformation of mindfulness. It is the emergence of mindfulness out of darkness and its transition into the Supreme Being's state of consciousness. *Vipassana* is mindfulness caught in a state of grace. It is when the Supreme Being blesses you with the wisdom and the intelligence to use it wisely with respect to being able to see the meaning or significance of all the revelations that have been revealed to the individual during the process or phase of mindfulness before it is transformed. It embodies a prophetic vision in which the Supreme Being has a way of communicating things to the individual, alerting him not only to things that have happened in the past, but also to things that he needs to deal with by resolving them before he can complete another epigenetic principle of higher consciousness. It is a holy channel provided by the Supreme Being and aided by him in terms of what is needed to successfully bring further issues to peaceful resolution. Indeed, *vipassana* forces an individual to confront the depth of all revelations while in a meditative state in addition to showing one a way in which one can apply the new insight into one's life.

Once the art of meditation goes through the metamorphosis with regards to its epigenetic principles of mindfulness and *vipassana,* a higher level of consciousness is at hand—a level of consciousness that makes an individual not only one with the Creator but also one with entities of the universe. Here the art of meditation rests its pillar at the zenith of nirvana, the ultimate goal of consciousness. It is the goal as well as the mightiest of all conquests over self—a state of consciousness in which the mind, body, and spirit function in total harmony while maintaining their respective homeostasis within their domains. In a state of nirvana, the three entities not only function as one, but they provide a natural flow of energy that serves as a blocking mechanism for all negative forces that sometimes camouflage themselves in past, present, and future experiences. In a state of nirvana, one thinks of nothing yet is a part of everything. The mind, body, and spirit suddenly become enmeshed with a minute fraction of God's circle of light. In this state of mind, the Supreme Being allows the entities of the universe to pay tribute to one they can finally call their own—a tribute that will manifest itself in its own way. However, one thing is for certain: the presentation of the tribute will be such that it will undoubtedly impress upon you that you have arrived with respect to the higher state of consciousness, nirvana.

The art of meditation is frequently equated as a silent prayer to the Creator. This gesture initiates the notion that one talks to the Supreme Being as he listens. It's a passive notion that rings half true in the overall scheme in the art of meditation. The primary role in the art of meditation is to become actively involved in the quest for "oneness" with the Creator. It involves many epigenetic principles—for example, the dissociation of thought and feelings (detachment), humility tempered by firmness, channeling, revisiting, self-control, the recognition of character defects, the unification of the extension of self, the calling, fasting, and the acceptance of reverence for all things. While the process involves more tenets, I would briefly like to turn my attention to the epigenetic principles of fasting and the calling.

Fasting is the denial of bodily needs in order to intensify the strength and endurance of the spirit. It has been my contention that the personality is nothing but a repertoire of psychological dysfunctions built on a few functional traits. This is primarily why man's greatest enemy is himself, simply because in most cases he fails miserably when it comes to controlling and dealing with these character defects because any form of impairment in the body means some form of impairment in the spirit. You cannot separate the two in this regard because both are connected by the same energy solidifying the relationship between the two. Fasting is a process that strengthens the connection between the spirit and the body. But more importantly, it conditions the body to be able to tap into the energy stored by the spirit in a time of need. It is a means by which the body is constantly reinforced to draw on the strength and courage of the spirit when it falls short with respect to its need for endurance and fortitude. It's a blatant tribute to the Supreme Being in a manner that has been embraced by many personalities. It's a discipline that deemphasizes man's needs in substitution for the Supreme Being. Once the body is conditioned to rely on the energy of the spirit, which can be very crucial during certain circumstances, fasting provides an absolute: if the spirit is strong and the body is weak with regards to dealing with some situations, then during these moments of weakness, the body would have already been conditioned to sustain itself by drawing from the strength possessed by the spirit, which can make all the difference when it comes to being able to handle particular circumstances.

The art of meditation is a powerful tool that serves many purposes. One of these purposes involves telling an individual when some form of contact is needed between an individual and the Creator. The phenomenon is known as "calling." This inescapable force compels someone who has bathed in the holy circle of light to return to the said place of destination in order to be reenergized by the light of the Supreme Being. The "calling" can be described as a severe discomfort and uneasiness between the mind, body, and spirit. This discomfort and uneasiness allows an individual with heightened consciousness to gravitate toward the holy circle of light in order to be reanointed by the Supreme Being. It can be further described as a request by the Supreme Being for your presence as well as the essence of your thoughts. It does not go away; instead the urgency will intensify until you have answered the calling. Indeed, the calling is God's way of letting us know that the spiritual connection between him and us is weakened and that the energy that binds us together needs to be replenished. One replenishes or answers the calling through meditation or through one's own devices for worship. Meditation provides an avenue where one can actually become intertwined with the Supreme Being, as opposed to other religious teachings that stress faith as a way of showing one's closeness to the Supreme Being.

THE FIRST MONTH

4

THE HUMAN SOUL

My dear unborn, the human soul is the entity, the one part of our existence that makes it possible for us to be linked with our Creator. The human soul comprises two types of energy, one that is linked directly to our Creator and the other that is linked directly to the universe. The energy that is linked to the universe is called cosmic energy. Cosmic energy is divided into positive and negative types of energy. The energy that is linked to our Creator is sometimes referred to as life's energy or the chi or even the soul. Therefore, half of our soul is built of life energy and the other is made up of cosmic energy. The life energy is pure in nature. It has no negative components to it, and even when we engage in negative types of behavior, the residue does not affect our life energy, but rather our cosmic energy. Life energy is part of the soul that is quite often referred to as the spirit. It is a myth that the entire soul is a spirit. It is only that part of us that is directly connected to God that is called the spirit. The other part of the soul which is made up of cosmic energy is not the spirit, and although collectively both are referred to as the soul, this is one of the greatest myths surrounding the concept of the human soul.

My dear unborn, one may ask if this distinction is of any importance when one is striving for spiritual enlightenment, and the answer is yes. It is essential to know what aspect of the soul you are channeling to or from with regards to the quest for nirvana. Frankly, it is like going to a particular destination: one direction might help you get there, but another may help you get someplace else. The cosmic portion of our soul is linked to the universal order of things. The laws of circumstances frequently try to influence this link in order to place us in various predicaments or precarious situations. When we embrace cosmic consciousness, which is defined as total awareness of how the laws of circumstances influence the universal order of things thus affecting our lives, then we are better able to handle the cosmic aspect of our souls.

My dear unborn, the spiritual portion of our soul is strengthened through relationship with our Creator when engaging in our individualistic style of worship and faith. There are also preconceived notions that when the soul leaves the body with respect to its spiritual and cosmic portion, collectively both will rejoin our Creator. This is incorrect. The spiritual portion of our soul, the link between God and man, will rejoin our Creator. But the cosmic aspect, the link between man and the universe, will go back to the universe. Both aspects of the soul will be united as one again, but only the Supreme Being decides that you should be placed back in the womb. So with respect to the soul, in death the Supreme Being claims his own and so does the universe.

My dear unborn, it should also be mentioned that while the human soul comprises two distinct portions, the Supreme Being uses the soul not only as a link between man and himself, but also as a means to show us or bring us some significant meaning to our lives—hence the term "aiding souls." Aiding souls are souls that the Supreme Being sends to play a role in someone's life, directly or indirectly. These souls are sent in the form of a human being. The purpose is to help others find some purpose or some meaning to their existence, in addition to helping them find the direction they need to follow in their lives. The aiding souls are sometimes instigator or motivator for a much broader, everlasting meaning in someone's existence. Aiding souls are always characterized as good people because they are filled with positive energy and devote just about all their lives to the benefit of others. Aiding souls tend to manifest themselves in the shape of a friend, a relative, or even a perceived enemy. They will stay among us for as long as needed to influence our lives in the direction our Creator intended it to go. Aiding souls can be a brand-new baby who dies in the days after birth or a son or a daughter who departs from us in their teens. The two primary common denominators with aiding souls are, first, that their time on this earth is never long relative to their purpose. Second, they have an impact on our lives before they leave this earth. The drawback to this, of course, is that when they leave we miss them very, very much because they leave an irreplaceable void in our lives. Aiding souls are in this world for only one purpose: to serve. The goal is to teach us or to help us give some meaning to our lives, and then they move on. During their stay on this earth, they can often touch many lives that God intended for them to touch. Upon meeting their destiny, which as mentioned before is to aid another person in their lives, then the soul moves on. Unfortunately, one of the main problems is that there is no certain way to identify an individual who is an aiding soul. Death serves to be the only way to find out whether or not this person is an aiding soul. It's like the air we breathe. You know it's there, but you just cannot put your hands on it.

My dear unborn, quite often a man's conscience is a reflection of his soul. Unfortunately, his conscience tends to experience certain interpersonal conflicts as a result of anxiety and other external factors; he then is torn often between doing the right or the wrong thing for whatever the reasons. When this happens then the soul needs to go through certain transformation. It needs to once again embrace the fundamental principle of transcendentalism.

My dear unborn, transcendentalism is a system of beliefs that engages people on the journey to spiritual enlightenment by embracing and foregoing certain earthly ties and experiences that bind them to the world in which we live. An individual who practices will undoubtedly be seen as strange, eccentric, or someone who is even irresponsible, but the power comes from knowing that one's way of thinking is the way that will lead to the type of happiness that is not supported or built on superficial or materialistic factors, but rather from the merging of your oneness with God's, a marriage that will shine and last forever. One of the wonderful things about conflict within one's consciousness is that it sometimes dictates the level of earthy ties and experiences. It also delivers a powerful message that states that we need to reclaim our souls, and by reclaiming our souls I mean getting in touch with ourselves and measuring to what degree our earthly ties are controlling our lives, then reaffirming the seriousness to the unshackling of one's self to all these earthly experiences and ties.

My dear unborn, the goal is to mentally unbind these earthly links from our perception, pride, vanity, conceit, and arrogance, which at times are at the heart of the anxiety or the interpersonal conflict that creates or makes it somewhat difficult to experience transcendentalism. The shadow of the evil with respect to pride, vanity, conceit, and arrogance are the most powerful attributes that tend to affect man's soul, thus allowing or preventing us from experiencing transcendentalism. Unless we hope to surrender ourselves or are willing to forego pride, vanity, conceit, or arrogance, transcendentalism will be next to impossible. Without transcendentalism to shield the soul, it is only a matter of time before the cosmic portion of the soul is affected by all different types of earthly iniquities, thus making it more difficult for us to become one with the entities of the universe, clearing our path so that we may achieve even greater happiness in its highest form and with greater intensity. Once the human soul is conditioned to function in a manner in which it ought to function with respect to oneness, linking itself to God's, embracing the elements of the universe is as second nature as the air we breathe.

My dear unborn, once you condition your soul to behave in accordance with the holy circle of light, which is the embodiment of your Supreme Being, then even if you become the devil himself, you cannot gain any comfort unless you return to God, because your consciousness will cease to know any type of peace whatsoever.

However, when this happens to an individual, he or she is known to have a dead soul.

My dear unborn, a dead soul occurs when the energy between God and man is malnourished to the point where the individual may think they are beyond redemption in the eyes of God. Such an individual with a dead soul feels abandoned, frustrated, and empty inside. They may have all the earthly possessions and success, yet something is missing from their lives. They are conscious of their feelings of emptiness; they just do not know what is causing it or why they feel the way they do. Life has no meaning or purpose for them except for superficial attributes. Such an individual's spirit is stagnant and powerless, and cries out for an awakening, some type of meaning to existence. The most wonderful thing about the soul is that whatever negativity it experiences, possesses, or goes through, it is always redeemable. For this reason alone, mankind should never give up in spite of whatever adversity they face. A dead soul, in reality, is only a soul that hungers for the holy circle of light of the Supreme Being. It's a soul that spent too much time in darkness and bathes in self-doubt. It follows a journey that consists of no faith and is rooted in earthly ties. It's a dead soul from a human standpoint, but it's a living soul from God's.

THE FIRST MONTH

5

THE MANY FACES OF BEAUTY

My dear unborn, two friends and I were out drinking one night, a male bonding effort if you will, that has become as much a part of us as a necessity for food and air. As friends sometimes do, we often engage in idle chatting and gossiping about other friends, a thing that most males are reluctant to admit. But this night was to be a special night because it was to reveal something about my best friend of twelve years that for some reason had escaped me. As we conversed with each other, his distraction became apparent, which was later confirmed by an echo, "Goddamn, she is beautiful." His eyes followed a young woman's every step. "I agree, but I wonder to which face you refer," I commented. "Hell, the one I'm looking at," he replied. "But is it not important to examine the other as well before you reach a decision as to her degree of beauty?" I asked. "I guess so; you're right. Some girls may seem beautiful on the outside but nasty and ugly as hell on the inside. They make you even regret approaching them," he observed.

"Maybe so, but I was not talking about her two faces of beauty. Rather I was thinking about yours," I responded. "What the hell do you mean by that?" he asked annoyingly. "To the degree that you find someone beautiful or ugly is an exact measurement of your own inner reflection. You saw in her, whether it may be beauty or ugliness, what you yourself represent inside. As humans our assessment of beauty is based not on an external manifestation but rather a projection of our own internal attributes." My friend then asked, "Are you saying that if she was ugly to me, it is only because my inside, or other face as you put it, is also ugly?" "Yes!" I replied. "Most of us are just concerned with the face we see; we don't know or care about any other faces," he asserted. "Hence the problem, how can you judge the beauty of a woman without first judging the beauty of your own soul?"

My dear unborn, my friend's reaction to my comment was not an uncommon one. Frankly, some may even see it as a typical response concerning the beauty of a woman. However, how can we attribute beauty to a woman without first examining the other beauty within ourselves? When will men realize that an enlightened man is not drawn to a woman's beauty because of sexual gratification, but simply because a woman's body is the most majestic thing that God has ever created? It is the only living entity that possesses a soul that is so pure in God's light that he chooses to use it as a vessel from which a part of him may be placed on this earth—a gift and quite often a burden so great that only a woman or the Messiah could bear. When will men realize that whatever descriptive label they place on the mothers of our souls, it also deciphers the enigma of their own unprotected souls? A judgment of beauty is not in the eyes of the beholder, it is the beholder. As God's children, it was not intended that we see any aspects of his creation as unattractive or unworthy, but rather as shining examples of his magnificence. And women are his greatest achievement not because of what they have come to represent to us in our society, but because of their role in the total scheme of man's and God's existence.

My dear unborn, to say a woman is beautiful is one of the most unflattering comments a man could ever make to a woman, because in most cases he's addressing the shell of a woman and basing his comment from the social standpoint of beauty. Seldom does he see the woman through the eyes of our Creator. Like most virtues, most of us were blessed with an eye for beauty. However, unless a man walks in the path of the Creator and cloaks himself with a spiritual light, his concept of beauty will always be clouded by social context. I am always the first to say that we should be aware of concepts created by man not only to manipulate our existence but also to restrict our spiritual liberation. Words like unattractive, ugly, fat, etc., are not words that should ever be associated with our Creator in relationship to people, his children. Yet it never ceases to amaze me just how many of these words are used by men who claim to be men of God. A man's conscience is a reflection of his soul, and his thoughts are the roots from which his resurrection seeks to emerge. Therefore, if we are in a position where we are asked to assess beauty, any attempt to do this instigates the notion that not all things are beautiful, thus violating the spiritual essence of our metaphysical connection with God, leaving us once again with the social and shallow context of beauty.

My dear unborn, beauty has many faces, and we will see as much of them depending on the amount of beauty we have inside of us. Ask yourself: "How many faces of beauty do you have, and what exactly are they?" Unless you can identify them within yourself, you will never be able to identify them in someone or anything else. I would like to believe that mine are my conscience and my soul. Maybe yours are your compassion, humility, integrity, or convictions. Wherever they are found or whatever they may be, use them like a weapon to cut through the superficial and pretentiousness of life's daily mask. For if you allow the beauty in you to illuminate, it will deter you from any attempt to assess what is and what is not beautiful, making you so enmeshed in the person, place, or thing you wish to scrutinize that the reflection of your inner beauty overshadows all other flaws, allowing you to see only the beauty in them.

My dear unborn, a friend once asked me whether or not it was utopian to look for the beauty in everything, and whether or not I believed there was beauty in evil. He seemed somewhat astonished when I answered yes to both questions. "Utopia is the name given to a place that is ideal, the embodiment of perfection, a dream land, a repertoire of potentials. Can you think of any such place except for the one inside of you that meets this criteria? And if true beauty lies in you, then it will allow you to see and overshadow the source of evil, and it too will become beautiful. Because nothing shines brighter than the illumination of one's beauty." My friend replied, "It is naive to think evil is beautiful, but even more important, it is dangerous." "I did not say evil is beautiful, but rather the source, for even Lucifer was once proclaimed the most beautiful of all angels." "But what is evil?" my friend asked. "It is only the manifestation of man's imperfections. Hence if man is the source of evil, surely you can find beauty in your fellow man. And if you cannot, it is only because none is in you."

My dear unborn, there is beauty in all of us. Sometimes, however, it gets tarnished from life's tribulations and follies that are usually displayed by our fellow man. In the race of daily survival, we seldom have the time to focus on anything that would remind us of the beauty within, reinforcing the beauty in others. As a result, it gets suppressed deep within us to the point that we do not think there is any in us or in the world. Soon, we find ourselves becoming cynical and bitter with everyone and everything. Men like Hitler, Stalin, Mussolini, and even the practitioners of apartheid and slavery were not beyond redemption as far as beauty is concerned. They all had beauty within them, but somewhere along the line they became disillusioned and oblivious to the essence of that beauty, a disillusionment influenced by social changes, greed, power, impatience, fear, and ignorance. I like to think of people with tarnished beauty as young children being raised by their mothers and fathers. It helps me to see them not as they are but as they were, youthful souls filled with innocence until plagued by social, psychological, and spiritual toxicities. If you find it difficult to still see the beauty in these people, you must ask yourself to what degree the beauty in you is tarnished, for as Epictitus said centuries ago, "Men are not troubled by what they see but by their views of them." And our views are generated by mechanisms within. Surely, the expectation is not to forget their deeds and the impact they have had on our society, but rather to rise above them and penetrate our inability to forgive so the beauty within us will come shining through.

For if there are no enemies within, then the enemies outside cannot hurt you physically, psychologically, or spiritually.

My dear unborn, the ability to see beauty in everything can be misinterpreted as a sign of naiveté or even a sign of weakness because in some cases it gives the impression that you are ignorant of the evil and madness in which so many people engage. But if you are truly an individual of beauty, words and such perceptions will find your armor impregnable. For the power you have against these misguided souls is a by-product of the beauty within you. Sometimes the hardest thing for people to accept, including your loved ones and friends, is that in the midst of this chaotic world, you are not only able to keep your sanity, but you are also able to have some enjoyment in things that normally another person would not be able to enjoy under similar circumstances. Indeed, there is some truth to the notion that misery loves company. However, it then becomes your responsibility to teach them how to see in people, places, or things the beauty that usually escapes them— a task we should take on vigorously. It is selfish and meaningless to be in a position where we are the only ones who can see the beauty in others, for no man is an island and as such the interdependency we share as human beings dictates that we teach each other how to recognize the beauty that others are unable to see by first recognizing it within ourselves.

My dear unborn, the power of mental conditioning is imperative to the teaching process. It requires consistency, alerted consciousness, minor analysis of daily events, and a commitment to change. When we exercise mental conditioning with respect to teaching others to see the beauty in people, places, or things, we are telling ourselves at every given opportunity that we are going to do this until it becomes instinctive or second nature. It requires great strength and discipline. The conditioning process involves having the courage to find the beauty in some of the worst daily events that we face. Practice, however, in this case can make perfect. Start off by trying to find the beauty in any two occurrences as they relate to people, places, or things. No matter how dreadful the circumstances, find the courage to find the beauty. A fatal car accident, a person losing a job, a spouse cheating on a loved one, a beggar asking you for money on the street. Regardless of the situation, find the beauty in it. Then after a while, assess your own feelings, Then you will see that your whole demeanor toward life has changed for the better.

My dear unborn, we spend a great deal of energy finding the bad, the negative, and the not-so-pleasant in our day-to-day lives without even working up a sweat. Sometimes even before we are fully aware of what is going on, we automatically engage in behavior that is contrary to finding beauty. This goes for people, places, and things. The perception we develop turns us off, making it impossible to discover beauty. It was recently discovered that individuals spend more than 77 percent of their time engaging in self-talk, all of which was negative—meaning we spend 77 percent of the time talking negatively to ourselves. No wonder people find it difficult to see the beauty around them. It is important to know that before you can find the beauty in anything, you must first be able to find the beauty in yourself. I told a colleague that I can find the beauty in anything and he responded, "Say I just found out that my little twelve-year-old girl has leukemia. Where the hell is the beauty in that?" I went over and hugged him. "The beauty in that, my friend, is that you will never love and cherish her as much as you do this moment, and the passion that you are experiencing right now will be the route to a more energized life. For suddenly work and the rat race is not important to you anymore. Rather life, whether the gift of it or the absence of it, is now your focus, for anything, anyone, or any place that makes the true meaning of life our focus is beautiful. Sometimes we must become one with the brotherhood of death before we can truly come to know the joy of living. You see, finding the beauty in people, places, or things does not have to be directly related. Quite often it is indirectly related, meaning it emerges as a direct result of an association with people, places, or things. These variables may be just triggers for the essence of beauty."

My dear unborn, consistency is everything with respect to one's attempt to discover beauty. You cannot try to find the beauty in things for a couple of days, then stop and still expect to find the beauty in others or things instinctively. If you are not consistent in your quest to find beauty, then it is more than likely that you will miss the beauty in many things when they arise. The eyes must be trained diligently in this recognition. When you train your eyes to see the beauty in things, then your heart will begin to see the beauty in these things as well. Then your entire soul will be consumed by the imagery that has been taken in by your eyes and heart. Do not worry about the role your mind will play in the discovery of beauty. The role it plays is insignificant, and quite often it can be an impeding variable. Unless your mind dwells in the spiritual light, the message it gives you in terms of what is and what is not beautiful will always be based on a social or superficial criteria. Thus, if someone is fat, then he or she is not beautiful; an exhibition of arts put on in prison by a group of inmates is not worth seeing, etc. Therefore, open your eyes and your heart and resist the cues of the mind if you know they do not dwell in the light of your Creator.

My dear unborn, alerted consciousness focuses on the underlying premise that one has to be able to recognize the identity of a problem before one can do anything about it. Unless we are able to confront ourselves and rid ourselves of our own demons, the beauty within will not reflect on the world, and the world will not be a beautiful place to us. Hence, no matter how hard we try to find the beauty in people, places, or things without first finding it in ourselves, it will never happen. For we ourselves must possess so much beauty that when it is lacking in the outside world, the world can feed off us and get what it does not have so it too can become beautiful. One of the mistakes we make as individuals is that we look to others to validate the beauty in us. But the strength is in your own belief. If you do not believe that there is beauty in you, then no one else will, and the beauty in you will lay dormant forever, making the world a very unpleasant place. What you see in the world quite often is a reflection of what is inside of you. Remember, if you depend on others to validate your sense of beauty, then you also relinquish the power and control that goes with that aspect of your existence. Just as you give others the power and control to make you feel beautiful, you also give them the power to take away that sense of security from you. You must measure your beauty based on your own existence as it relates to your perception of self-worth. This way your beauty will be lasting in your eyes and in your heart as opposed to being based on the whims and moods of others.

My dear unborn, another major error in judgment that we usually make is that we allow others to convince us that we must let how we look on the outside dictate our sense of beauty on the inside. Social measuring rods are often used by getting a few models to be seen as having the ideal physique. This shallow image of beauty is then pursued, desperately attempted by women and men who are lacking true beauty within. If one has the need to go at great length to achieve pseudo-beautification in order to make one's outer appearance beautiful, then that's a cue that these individuals were once conditioned to believe that someone was needed to validate their sense of beauty on the inside. The sad thing is that no matter how much they change on the outside, they will always feel the need to keep trying to make their outside beautiful, because their inner beauty is the part that is lacking. Failing to understand this, they constantly search for new ways to alter the way they are seen by others instead of searching for the path that leads to inner beauty.

My dear unborn, unless we rid ourselves of these superficial ideations and plant our feet on the journey to true beauty, we will never really be able to understand and appreciate something that escapes us, something that if we are lacking in beauty ourselves we would not have known. Many of us have yet to discover the essence of beauty that is embedded in this universe, simply because we are not a part of these universal entities. To see the beauty around us, it is necessary to be a part of it, and unless you are one with our Creator's holy circle of light, then any attempt to see beauty will always be clouded by darkness. You will perceive beauty, but in a small and narrow spectrum as opposed to seeing true beauty in the huge magnificent scheme of the cosmos. If you are not a part of our Creator's holy circle of light, you will never be able to grasp the true essence of beauty in this world. Indeed, you may grasp some, thinking that you have seen all there is to see, but the true beauty will escape you. It is imperative, however, to look deep within ourselves because true beauty begins and ends with us.

My dear unborn, minor analysis of daily events is also at the heart of mental conditioning. The process requires dissecting one's daily life's experiences until beauty is discovered. The experiences do not have to be ones that you created but rather ones that are created by circumstances. The more difficult or tragic the situation, the more complex and challenging the quest to discover the beauty beneath. Finding the beauty wherever it may be is like anything else. It has a price, a price that if one is willing to pay can change one's life forever. The price one must pay in order to merge oneself in total beauty is the extinction of one's mental repertoire of life's worldliness and the knowledge of the social elements in which one lives.

My dear unborn, beauty is the offspring of innocence. Therefore, unless one is innocent in spirit and in heart, the true essence of beauty can be beyond one's reach. We must be childlike before we can be godlike. Many have asked, "How it is possible at my age to regain my innocence?" And I have always responded by asking, "What did you do to have lost your innocence?" Suddenly a list of life's experiences is read to me, most of which they felt were bad. Then they would turn to me and say, "See, I'm beyond saving." I responded in the same manner, "You can regain your innocence at one minute past midnight." Astonished by my answer, they grin. All have indicated that life's experiences are the culprit as to why they think they have lost their innocence. At one past midnight, start a new mental repertoire of life's experiences and a new day of innocence. "So what about the things I have done in the past? How can I just forget them?" "The past never goes away, it just hides behind the present and the future." But innocence has nothing to do with memory; it has to do with the views that are constantly seen by your eyes, heart, and soul. When you change your life's experiences, you open a new set of windows to your eyes, heart, and soul, thus regaining your innocence. You can never wipe away all that you have done, and why would anyone want that, especially since not all of life's experiences are bad or unpleasant? But with a new sunrise comes a new opportunity for a life filled with overwhelming beauty.

My dear unborn, the dissecting of one's daily experiences will lead to an axiom that true beauty is sometimes the absence of the appearance of beauty. When I speak of beauty, seldom do I think of heavenly picturesque or pretty designs nurtured by artistic patterns. Such is only a minute part of what I speak of, but rather the insight or realization that an act is innocent in purity and spirituality. A man went to rob a store, and after taking the money and about to shoot the cashier, he heard a song that was sung at his brother's funeral. He stopped what he was about to do, returned the money and ran away. This is an element of beauty: the realization that in the midst of madness our Creator's holy circle of light can still get through, if it's even for a moment in time.

My dear unborn, a commitment to change is the final aspect to mental conditioning with respect to one's search for beauty. Beauty is nothing unless it has found some way to change you in such a way that you have become more in sync with our Creator or his creations, whether they may be organic or inorganic elements. The roots of tangled beauty will not flourish in you unless they sense a commitment to change that will last not only for a day, a week, a month, or even a year, but for a lifetime and long after death. This commitment must involve the unleashing of raw emotions like hatred, anger, grief, and envy—the oppressors of true inner beauty. If you are consciously imprisoned by these raw emotions, your journey to inner beauty will be a very difficult one. Forgiveness is your only redemption. Regardless of the circumstances and no matter how wicked you may perceive an act or individual to be, forgiveness is your only salvation. However, when you do mention forgiveness, be sure and ask them to forgive you as opposed to you forgiving them. I did not say that the quest for spiritual enlightenment would be an easy one, but rather an achievable one. You see, it takes more courage to ask someone who has wronged you for their forgiveness than it does to say that you have forgiven them. A beautiful heart does not seek to assign blame; only you share that which is in it and to reveal the beauty that is in you.

THE FIRST MONTH

6

THE UNISON METAPHYSICAL THEORY

My dear unborn, there is nothing more challenging than our desire to unravel the mystery behind human nature. In a society such as this, one's very existence can rely on one's ability to decipher what another human being is capable or not capable of doing. Never violate the rules of social interaction by estimating what a person will or will not do. Therefore, always treat the best of friends as a potential enemy, and a potential enemy as the best of friends. There are many theories relevant to the human personality; some are better than most. All, directly or indirectly, try to invade the human psyche in attempts to better understand our fellow man. I would not be so bold as to presume to know which one of these will better assist you in gaining insight into the personality of man. But I would be derelict in my responsibility as a potential father who just happens to be a clinician if I did not prepare you for both the demonic and the angelic nature of mankind. I tell you that the notion of treating each person as a potential enemy will serve you well. Others, however, will question such paranoia, but a healthy dose of paranoia is a good thing. You do not have to be a clinician to understand the psyche of man.

Eventually, being a student of life will teach you well. But the foundation that I am about to give you will magnify the idiosyncrasies and behavioral patterns within the complexities of our souls.

My dear unborn, the unison metaphysical theory was created on principles unlike most Western therapeutic approaches with respect to the tenets of both spirituality and psychology. It is one of the few theories that embraces the notion that in order to understand and treat psychopathologies, one must embrace the principles of psychology in conjunction with the principles of the universe. A separation of the two will render any assessment of human nature inadequate. Therefore, to fully comprehend this theory, you must have an appreciation for the rules that govern both of these entities.

My dear unborn, the unison metaphysical theory, as stated earlier, is divided into two interrelated sections. The first part deals with the psychology in which the mind is divided into five major components: the autonomy, the creative, the explorer, the instinctive, and the emotional. Each of these components is an essential player in the way in which we behave and respond to various situations. This approach also maintains that each of these components is rooted in the biological etiology with respect to the brain, which means that for the five components mentioned, each is controlled by a particular portion of the brain. The unison metaphysical theory maintains that by learning to consciously trigger each component to behave in a certain manner, people can have much more control over their responses and reaction to certain circumstances. One of the fundamental principles of this theory is that when some aspect of an individual's mind becomes dysfunctional, so does the spirit of the individual, creating even more damage to the individual self as a whole.

My dear unborn, the second section of the unison metaphysical theory deals much more with the spirit of the individual. It maintains also that if the spirit is impaired, then it is only a matter of time before the individual becomes psychologically dysfunctional as well. Both the spirit and the mind coexist in the same sphere, thus making them more susceptible at times to the same type of extraneous intrusive particle.

My dear unborn, under the unison metaphysical theory, individuals are encouraged and taught how to develop cosmic consciousness, which is defined as having total awareness of how the laws of circumstances affect our lives by influencing the universal order of things. The individual's psychopathologies or idiosyncrasies are assessed and explored from a perspective that involves both the rules of psychology and the rules of the universe. Individuals are also taught how to strengthen and protect the self as a whole by embracing this theory. Only by healing the self and spirit can long-lasting mental health be achieved. The important thing to remember is that both the mind and the spirit are so intertwined with each other that it is impossible to promptly and properly treat one successfully without treating the other. When both the mind and the spirit are not treated simultaneously, then either the mind or the spirit will regress, thus creating chaos or disharmony in the entity that is not treated, Good mental health can only be achieved by an individual embracing the notion that both the mind and the spirit must be treated simultaneously.

My dear unborn, one of the purposes of the unison therapeutic approach is to help an individual learn how to use the five components of the mind effectively with respect to processing and responding to various internal and external stimuli. Once an individual is able to master this process, then the next step is to get the individual to fully embrace cosmic consciousness as well as to implement other metaphysical tenets that ultimately serve to strengthen the spirit.

My dear unborn, the autonomy is the leader or driving force behind the other four components. It is the part of the mind that possesses all the hidden capabilities and powers that quite often are hidden from the remaining components. The primary function of the autonomy is to regulate the other components, while at the same time checking its own functions. The autonomy has qualities and potentials that for several reasons have yet to be released to us. One of the essential reasons is that the other four components are probably not mature enough to deal with them. When the autonomy is not regulating the four components, they can find themselves carrying out functions that sometimes are not within their respective domains, resulting in disharmony or mental instability.

My dear unborn, the autonomy assesses both external and internal stimuli, then decides what components should be allowed to process the information and respond appropriately to the stimuli. Failure to carry out this function will compel one of the other four components to act as a leader. Being new to the role of leader, the respective component might then process and respond to the given external or internal stimuli. Sometimes the component that is taking over for the autonomy will appropriately assign tasks to the other three components and sometimes it may not. The autonomy ensures stability amongst itself and the other components. However, if it cannot, then disharmony or mental instability will set in, depending on how well the component that took over is doing in its place. Although the autonomy expedites information to the other four components, it has the capability to process and respond to information when information is not being dispersed to the other components. In short, response to stimuli can also be assessed and processed by the autonomy. The autonomy keeps unison amongst the other components but it is also responsible for the maintenance of its own equilibrium.

My dear unborn, the autonomy must also destroy impeding cues. These are variables that prevent the autonomy from maintaining its equilibrium. For example, certain concepts like hell, judgment day, torment, brimstone, and fire tend to conjure imagery that can interfere with the autonomy's state of equilibrium. Indeed, while a trained and mature autonomy is able to deal with impeding cues, many people allow them to disrupt this state of harmony. Most impeding cues create anxiety and some form of disruption within the soul, but the autonomy would much rather deal with these cues itself as opposed to allowing the creative component of the mind to do so.

My dear unborn, the autonomy can also, if it so chooses, put the other components on autopilot. It does this only when it feels that the other four components are functioning in total unison with each other. Still, they remain under the strict supervision and observation of the autonomy. Indeed, while the four components are able to assess, process, and respond to internal and external stimuli, they must all do so under the approval of the autonomy. If any one of the components is not able to assess and process the information appropriately, the autonomy will allow another component to process the information or do so itself.

My dear unborn, disharmony, unhappiness, anxiety, worrying, and slow response to the "calling," a concept which was discussed earlier, are all indications of a minor malfunction within an individual's autonomy. The second indication that the autonomy is not functioning to its optimum level is when information being assessed and processed are done inappropriately. The third is a distorted conditioning of the autonomy during the rearing process. For example, once a child's autonomy is conditioned inappropriately with respect to the assessing and processing of various stimuli, then the child becomes an adult whose autonomy will follow the same dysfunctional pattern. The fourth indicator that should alert an individual is conflicts between the five components in terms of which one should be allowed to process and respond to the various stimuli. When such conflicts arise between the components even after the autonomy has made a decision, it turns to the instinctive for assistance. Here the autonomy relies on the instinctive to bring some stability to the mind and the self as a whole by finding a common ground on which each component can operate. The fifth and obvious indication that something is wrong with the autonomy is when there is damage to the part of the brain that is primarily responsible for this function. In the event this should occur, the duties and functions of the autonomy would automatically be distributed amongst the four components until that part of the brain is healed.

My dear unborn, when one of the five components cannot carry out its duties or functions, then one of the other components will take over. If the autonomy is not impaired in any way but one of the other four that should be getting a specific amount of information to be processed and respond to it is impaired, then the autonomy will send the given information to one of the other components that it thinks is able to respond appropriately to the information. For example, if the emotional component should get the information from the autonomy but is unable to respond because of some type of impairment, then the autonomy, based on the nature of the information, would assign the task to another component. Indeed, while the component chosen might not handle the information as well as the intended component, more than likely it was chosen because—based on the nature of the information that was assessed and processed by the autonomy—it was better suited for the job.

My dear unborn, confusion, procrastination, and indecisiveness occur when the autonomy is trying to decide which component should be given the information to be processed. These defects can also stem from cross-processing on a chronic basis. Cross-processing occurs when each component with the exception of the autonomy starts to carry out the functions of one another without waiting for the autonomy to designate which one should handle the task. For example, the emotional begins to carry out the function of the explorer, or the explorer begins to respond to the information as if it is the creative.

My dear unborn, an individual can consciously train his or her autonomy to delegate the appropriate information to the other four components under any given circumstance. The training should also involve teaching the autonomy how to recognize when the wrong component of the mind is responding to the information. After severe conditioning by an individual, through principles of association, all the components will know when to act or react in a manner that will keep the mind, body, and spirit in total unison with one another.

My dear unborn, you may wonder why it is so vital to know these things as they relate to the self. A time will come when your existence cannot prevail without being in the presence of another. When this daily ritual takes place, it is paramount that you have a full comprehension of the human psyche. We live in an interdependent society. As such, more often than not our existence depends on one another. How you respond, negotiate, interact, and embrace another fellow man will quite often depend on your knowledge of the human psyche. Most people have problems with interpersonal relationships for the simple reason that they do not take the time to learn some of the basic fundamental principles that govern our associations. Day by day, they choose to wing it as they go along, then wonder why the essence of their interaction went awry. You do not need to be a psychologist in order to take a few minutes and learn about human nature. The unwillingness to do this, however, is like living in a society and not knowing the basic fundamental rules that govern the land. The degree of knowledge one has in both areas can sometimes be the deciding factor with respect to the outcome of a given situation. Many of us take the time to know a little bit about the rules of the country that we live in, yet seldom do we take the time to seek some knowledge about the human mind and what makes people tick.

My dear unborn, trial and error with regards to understanding the human mind is only worthwhile if one has insight into the basic foundation that governs the human psyche. Many of us depend on past experiences with others to assist us in making decisions regarding our present experiences. We do not embrace the dynamics or even the simple rules of social interaction when dealing with other human beings, much less the uniqueness of their respective personalities. We mentally manipulate the outcome of the past in order to acquire the present outcome we desire. For this reason, I am compelled to make you aware of the unison metaphysical theory.

My dear unborn, I now turn your attention to the creative component of the mind. The component is that part of the mind that allows us to think of new ideas and new ways of how to make our lives better. The primary purpose of the creative component is to find new ways to make us feel good or pleasant. It is also that part of the mind that develops ways to eliminate or escape that which is not enjoyable or fun to us. The creative component also reduces some of the problems of its fellow component, the explorer. It does this by making sure that the explorer does not come up with responses that involve overindulgence or overgratification. For example, the autonomy sends information to the explorer in order for it to be processed and responded to like, "Sit down and watch your favorite show." The explorer is gratified in doing this. However, sometimes it may allow the person to turn up the volume on the television too loudly without giving much consideration to the neighbors or roommates. Here, the creative component would step in and provide an opportunity for the person to watch the TV show with the same level of enjoyment while appeasing the neighbors and roommates by inventing new ways in which a compromise would satisfy both parties.

My dear unborn, anxiety that stems from fears and uncertainty is the causative factor in over 90 percent of all human inadequacies. While anxiety tends to manifest itself in overt symptoms, you must learn to embrace the underlying manifestations. This type of anxiety occurs within the creative component because of the lack of complete development. This underdevelopment starts in the rearing process. However, when the creative component is mature and fully developed, then any individual is able to cope with a given provoking stimuli. Being anxious is not strange to the creative component, but how we respond to the anxiety-provoking stimuli often is. When the creative component is unable to deal appropriately and effectively with our anxiety, then the creative component clearly needs work. Indeed, the rearing process mentioned before has provided us with the means to develop and strengthen our creative component and will only fail if the rearing process itself is dysfunctional. Life's experiences that embody trial and error also serve as a strengthening force for the creative component mainly because it allows development of innovative ways to deal with daily problems. This type of experience is inevitable, especially when the creative component is asked by the autonomy to process and respond to a brand-new dilemma, one that it has not before faced. Through life's practices we are able to deal with these new challenges—challenges, my dear unborn, that ultimately will mold the self into what it is destined to become. The creative component will take over the leadership role when the autonomy is impaired. If it remains impaired for an extended period of time, then it will send and designate the component besides itself that is better able to process and respond to the given information. Inadequacies will emerge depending on how effective the components are with respect to dealing with certain dilemmas. If and when the creative component cannot come up with innovative ways to resolve a person's problem, then feelings of inadequacies will set in. Like the autonomy, the creative component can ask for help from the instinctive or explorer in resolving issues. But regardless of the problem, if the components function in total unison, whatever the problem, it will be dealt with appropriately and effectively, resulting in an illuminated self.

My dear unborn, I would now like to turn your attention to another component, the explorer. The explorer is that aspect of the mind that gets in trouble a great deal of the time. It is the essence of curiosity that often creates extra work for the other components. Its primary function is to discover new avenues that will keep us challenged and do whatever it takes to make us feel alive. Unfortunately, the ways in which it has chosen to accomplish its task in most cases are detrimental to the other components if not kept in check by them. In fact, the explorer can literally jeopardize our sense of self by putting the self at risk under the delusion that its action will provide the self with needed thrills and excitement.

My dear unborn, the emotion is the name given to the other component. The emotion is that part of the mind that embraces all of one's sentiments, human frailties, and projection of the senses that often makes us warm and caring human beings. Quite often this component works in close relation with the explorer. Indeed, while all components work directly or indirectly with each other, some work closer together than others. The emotions sometimes tell the explorer when its actions are in the process of jeopardizing all the other components and eventually the self as a whole.

My dear unborn, the next component is called the instinctive. The instinctive is always neutral with respect to its dealings with the other four components. Frequently it is sought out by the other components when they are indecisive about the decision-making process, It operates on pure metaphysical energy. It is the only other component that taps into the hidden capabilities and powers of the autonomy. Here, the autonomy allows the instinctive to probe its domain only when it may be having difficulties with the decision-making process in terms of how to delegate information to be processed and responded to in a timely manner. The instinctive component is also responsible for channeling metaphysical information relevant to cosmic consciousness of the self and its relationship to God. It is the one aspect of the self that strives desperately toward spiritual enlightenment and homeostasis. The instinctive is the strongest link between God and one's self. This component possesses the pathway in which God can access the other components in order to assist the self as a whole. Components usually seek the aid of the instinctive component when uncertainties and unreliabilities cloud the decision-making process engaged in by other components.

My dear unborn, if ever the situation arises where you find it necessary to help another human being cope with their inadequacies, regardless of the forms that these inadequacies appear in, expose them to the unison metaphysical theory. Teach them about the five components; assess their knowledge of cosmic consciousness with respect to the role it plays on their self during their day-to-day lives. Ask them to word associate with a given list of metaphysical principles that have been discussed. Insist that the individual in question patiently practices the placement of stimuli into the components until it becomes second nature. You can accomplish this task by giving them a number of hypothetical scenarios geared around the components. When given these scenarios, the individuals should consciously decide where his or her autonomy should place the information to be responded to and processed. In short, he or she must decide whether the scenario given would best be handled by the creative, emotional, instinctive, etc. Dissect the placement of each scenario until the person fully comprehends the rationale as to why they have allowed their autonomy to assign the component to the scenario. If the scenario is misplaced, then challenge their autonomy until the appropriate component is given the scenario to be processed and responded to effectively. Here, there are no right or wrong answers—only a consideration of which components will provide the self with the best result. The best result is always contingent on which component is suitable to handle a particular circumstance effectively and appropriately. It is imperative that the individual be conditioned to be able to recognize when and where the information is being placed with regards to the five components, as opposed to putting and leaving their minds on autopilot. Unless the individual is conditioned to recognize the process, the autonomy and the autopilot will run rampant, sometimes even out of control, creating disharmony and misery for the self. The optimum result when played by the appropriate component will allow the self to be at peace with itself as well as find harmony in the decisions that have been made.

My dear unborn, the mind is never in control when it is left on autopilot or when the autonomy is randomly or arbitrarily left to assign scenarios or information to the other components on a whim. Unless the autonomy of each person is consciously controlling the components by relating to them in a manner that will complement their functions and responsibilities, the self as a whole will always be at a disadvantage. Ultimately, the desire is to make sure that the individual's cognition is operating in unison with respect to the five components. However, if any of the components is not in unison with the others, then that component can be retrained to fall in line.

My dear unborn, remember that all five components function consciously, always in a state of awareness. Only when we put and leave the mind on autopilot do we not consciously place the information in the appropriate components. As human beings, we sometimes become mentally unhealthy because we get lazy when it comes to exercising our minds, simply because we do not want to take the time to direct our minds on how they should behave. Hence we put the task on autopilot and leave it to chance. The autopilot has an essential function: It occasionally allows the autonomy to designate information to the other four components when the mind is not in a state of total awareness or is suffering from clouded consciousness because of trauma or altered states that stem from drug inducement. In these instances, the autopilot provides the autonomy with the time needed for it to slowly process the information or scenario and distribute it to the appropriate component. A person who is drunk or asleep tends to have their mind on autopilot, as does a person who daydreams. The reprocessing of information between the five components in order for it to become readily available to us at some later date occurs during sleep. As stated before, the reprocessing by the five components usually occurs in a state of autopilot or when people walk around not being conscious of exactly where the information is going. Indeed, when we allow the autonomy to place information into the other four components without being totally aware of their actions, then the autonomy on its own time can allow this very same information to be reassessed and rediscovered by any of the other four components at any time it so chooses. This process is sometimes referred to as the subconscious, when in reality it is not a specific location or level of the mind, but rather a mental network that involves reshuffling, reassessing, and processing data, very much like a computer. Information that lay dormant during this process will eventually emerge again. At this time the autonomy will then delegate the information to the component that is better suited to handle it. Needless to say, how the individual responds from this mental networking depends on which component the autonomy gave the task to in the first place.

My dear unborn, although the five components have the ability to function by themselves without consciously putting them in check with mental commands—the process we call "autopiloting"—this leaves little or no control with respect to one's mind and self or regulates how we behave as human beings. Leaving the mind on autopilot is not always to our disadvantage, mainly because this process provides the means by which the instinctive component can be activated. When the mind is on autopilot, it relies on the instinctive component for many of its cues before making decisions. In most cases, however, there are times when the instinctive component can become exhausted to the point where it can affect the autopiloting process in making the right or appropriate decision. When this happens, the mind is always reactive as opposed to responsive. Reactivity derives frequently from negative impulses, but responsiveness derives more from positive impulses. Mental commands given to the five components will eliminate drastically the factors that would permit the mind to be reactive as opposed to being responsive. While the autonomy is the regulator in most cases, thus taking the leadership role, all the other four components have the ability to engage in the decision-making process as well, and they do. The autonomy allows each of the other four components to assist the other when one is having difficulty assessing, processing, and responding to a given issue. Each component serves as a support system for the next, but the autonomy decides which component is better able to assist the component that is experiencing the difficulty.

My dear unborn, when the autonomy is impaired or undeveloped, the component that takes on the leadership role is inclined to take on all the duties of the autonomy in addition to its own primary function with respect to assessing, processing, and responding to information. The autonomy and other components that serve in this function quite often develop the tendency to attempt assessing, processing, and responding to all the information itself. When this tendency occurs, then the psychopathology known as obsessive-compulsive disorder can be triggered, mainly because the component serving as the regulator refuses to designate the necessary information to the appropriate component that would be next in line to handle the given situation or information. The tendency to do everything by itself often keeps the other components from trying to intervene. However, if it cannot successfully do this, then the autonomy or substitute leader will continue to do all the assessing, processing, and responding to information, regardless of the consequences to the self.

My dear unborn, the self is influenced by cosmic consciousness by embracing the dynamics pertaining to the universal energy and the five components. Cosmic consciousness is the means by which we possess total awareness of how the laws of circumstances influence our lives by affecting the universal order of things. Once the self is in sync with cosmic consciousness, then the probability of all events falls in line with the essence of one's spirit. Quite often the embodiment of this notion leads or is referred to as "luck," which is nothing more than when the laws of circumstances intersect with the universal order of things. Here, the five components functioning as a whole to produce a congruent self must learn how to handle the metaphysical principles of which it is a part, especially if it is to achieve long-lasting harmony. The self must pay reverence to its Higher Power at all times, thus realizing that this Higher Power lives in all things—for example, the flowers, the animals, the wind, and, of course, human beings. Another metaphysical principle that the self must embrace is the notion that the death of any variation of these things represents the death or destruction of a part of God's holy circle of light or energy. But the more the self is in tune or becomes one with these entities of the universe, the stronger the spiritual connection between God and man.

My dear unborn, although the self may have many goals over a period of years, its one true destiny is to make itself worthy to rejoin its Creator after its liberation from a sinful body. But until then, it must have a purpose to its existence, for a self without a purpose is like a rainbow without colors. Such a self will drift along the pathway of life until it is lost within its own mystery. Ironically, in order to unravel the mystery of life, we must first be willing to unravel the mystery of self because the essence of life lies within the consciousness of one's being and manifests itself through the dealings with one another. Life with all its simplicities and complexities can only become a mystery to us when we fail to comprehend that which we perceive from the environment or about each other. Therefore, cease the dissections of life's offerings; surrender your curiosity and false axiom that the unknown that bathes us daily will forever represent the true self. The self does not need a logical explanation to fully comprehend that which it perceives and resents any ideations that give rise to the notion that the question "why" must always be accompanied by a rational and meaningful response, a question that is usually made worse or exacerbated by an attempted answer. Indeed, the profound wisdom on which all faith is built is acceptance, and although a healthy curiosity is good, it is not a necessity to know the answers to the mystery of life; such time should be spent living it.

My dear unborn, the self must never be allowed to exist without the recognition of purpose; this is the third most important realization in the game of life. The delay in the identification of the self's purpose quite often is made unknown for reasons that lie in the mind of the

Supreme Being. Therefore, while we may struggle to define our sense of self, sometimes our effort will be futile because the revelation will not be revealed by the Creator until it is time. This can be a very frustrating experience for individuals. Being in a world where whatever we do we seem to lack direction in our lives can lead to a crippling sense of belonging, a force that can even cast doubt on our own identity. We do not create the purpose for our existence in life, and although it is a widely accepted belief, the things we do for a living, like our jobs, are not always synonymous to the purpose of our existence. The harsh reality is that in most cases when the purpose of our existence is revealed to us, we deny or rationalize that it is our true calling simply because it is not in keeping with the perception of ourselves or even others.

My dear unborn, the self is always one with its purpose; together they are inseparable. But they lack awareness of each other until Jehovah removes the spiritual blinders. The spiritual blinders are necessary to the growth of the self; they allow the self to compensate in such a manner that when its true purpose is revealed, it will possess the strength needed to conquer the dynamic entities that it will undoubtedly face. The purest of energy in one's self is still not enough to carry out its purpose if it does not learn how to become one as well as overcome the various entities of the universe. For example, in looking at the Messiah's life, we know that his self was pure with respect to its energy, for indeed he was divine. Yet, the true purpose of his existence was kept hidden from him until a certain period of his life. The question as to when Christ developed an awareness of self and the process of doing so tells us a great deal about our own awareness into ourselves. When did he know that he was divine and was also the son of the living God? Was it at birth, puberty, or during his adolescent years? Certainly, he went through the rearing process like most children, experienced the same dilemmas as most children, yet his divinity remained intact. Why then was this side of him not revealed during these phases of his life in a way that would magnify his divinity? Because to have done so would have meant depriving him of the opportunity and experience of conquering the necessary demonic entities that we all must overcome if the self is to develop with strength and character. Once the strength and character of the self have been established, then a commitment to the Creator is essential of the new developed self if ever it is to discover the true purpose for its existence. Christ's commitment to God, his endured faith, paved the way for the removal of the spiritual blinders, thus clearing the way for the purpose of his existence.

My dear unborn, like Christ we too will only discover the purpose of our existence once our commitment to the Creator has been made, for only then the spiritual blinders will be removed. Until the spiritual blinders are removed, the self will be molded by its environment and the climate of the era from which it came—a preparation, if you will, for its purpose, a purpose that it will be allowed to see once a commitment to the Creator has been made. This commitment does not have to be made directly to the Supreme Being. It can come in the form of us paying reverence to all things and holding them in the highest regard. But the self will cease to recognize its true purpose so long as we continue to deny, rationalize, and misconstrue the intent of the Supreme Being.

My dear unborn, the presentations offered by the five components of the mind collectively are referred to as the personality of the self. It is characterized as a group of behavioral traits often expressed by individuals. In reality, a definition of the personality is far more complex, yet is equally just as unimportant. The personality offers one significant contribution to the self: a face for the world to see. The personality represents the residual effect of the illumination of the mind, the unity of the five components. Frequently, however, the self and the personality are seen as an interchangeable unit when in reality the personality is only a reflection of self and is not synonymous with the self. Because the five components are complex in their networking, it is difficult to define its projections in terms of a collective body. The dynamic of the behavioral traits that stem from the components are constantly changing and as such the personality is seldom perceived as the same. But what it does offer is one of the greatest misconceptions and delusions known to us. While the five components engage in repetitious networking to the point where some of its projections can be observed as a usual pattern, thus giving the delusion that the personality of an individual is stable and steadfast, this is never the case. The assessing, processing, and responding of information by the five components are constantly reaching different resolutions.

Even if it wanted to do so, the personality could not become embedded long enough for it to be characterized or named as it often is by our fellow men. This, of course, is because of the continuous variations that come from the network of the five components. This is why people are so astonished by the actions of someone they thought they knew so well and are willing to bet their lives that the given individual would not have participated in the said actions. To be a part of this delusion, they would have needed to have seen the predominant behavioral traits displayed by the person's five components as the personality, as opposed to it being a flexible, fluid element of the self, easily changed depending on the nature of the information it has been conditioned to network. The essence of the personality is the embodiment of all the information that the five components have been conditioned to network over the years—similar to the adage, "you are what you eat," except in this case you are what you mentally process. Remember, the personality is the face of the self; therefore, any assumptions of knowing a person based on his or her personality is almost a guarantee to be wrong. This decision should be based on knowing the self because the personality, the face, of the self is subjected to change based on certain stimuli. However, the self is much more fixed or established within its own domain, making it not as susceptible to change as a result of the stimuli received. Hence, as stated earlier, never violate the rule of social interaction by underestimating what a person will or will not do based on their personality; rather, if you must judge another, then judge based on the root or nature of the self. Only by knowing the nature of oneself can we adequately decipher what a person is capable or not capable of doing; the personality changes based on the demands that society and other entities place on it, but the self usually remains intact.

My dear unborn, in dealing with your fellow man, you must transcend your thoughts and perceptions; you must embrace the notion that "men are troubled not by what they see, but rather by their views of them." You must see the personality, the face of the self, not as a true representation of the person but rather as a transparent image geared to address your concerns, whether through the seduction of your karma or through the enticement of your desires. You must at all times make conscious decisions regarding your mind, embracing the process of consequential thinking. You must discover for yourself that events or situations are propelled by the three entities—the laws of circumstances, God, and by the will of human beings—and that nothing in this world is left to chance. The secret is to comprehend which one of these three entities is governing a specific episode in your life and become one with it. You must never think of yourself or anyone as being beyond redemption, for in all cases God has forgiven us for all our follies long before we even ask him. The problem is never getting forgiveness from God, but for us to learn how to forgive ourselves. When someone says to you on your deathbed, "Ask God to forgive you," tell him that he has already done so, but that it is up to you to uncloak your sinful armor by forgiving yourself. In times of tribulations when you wish you were never born, you must find the strength to realize that being born in this world is part of the price we pay for salvation. Never let anyone tell you that salvation is free. Mankind started paying the price for salvation on the day the Messiah was crucified. It was not by chance that Christ stumbled and fell while carrying the cross and was helped by a fellow human being. Allowing us to carry the cross was Christ's way of binding us to his destiny, making us inseparable. This "act" is a partial payment that was completed by our birth and has created a path of forgiveness that cleanse us all with every drip of blood that Christ shed. Christ's last wish before he died was for God to forgive us for the things we do, not just for crucifying him but everything thereafter. The problem has never been seeking and getting forgiveness for our sins, yet our guilt lets it appear to be so.

My dear unborn, you must be humble, yet firm; most important, you must fear no one or anything. The strength of your fears is a measurement of your faith. If your life is truly in the hands of God, then your trust in him will sustain you, thus diminishing all your fears. You must never waver from your own philosophy of life merely because it fails you at times, but rather celebrate perfection in an imperfect world and the inevitability that as life changes so must your philosophy with it. You must deprive yourself of having expectations of your fellow man because with them come an uncontrollable urge to judge, a luxury that only a perfect soul can afford to possess. You must give your life meaning, not by achieving but by serving. Do not attempt to serve while time is your friend and comes in abundance, but rather let the world know that you are here to serve when a moment of your life can deprive you of a day of joy and a week of conveniences, for it is easy to give when one has enough.

My dear unborn, you must never see love as the opposite of hate, but rather as a reflection of itself, for the word "love" is holy and casts no shadow of iniquity, and as death claims you in your final hour, think back not on regrets and failures, but of what price, if any, you have paid that another may find happiness and discover for themselves the true meaning for their existence.

My dear unborn, under the unison metaphysical theory, we must successfully demonstrate our ability to utilize not only the five components of our minds, but must also demonstrate cosmic consciousness with respect to how it can be used to offset negative predicaments, thus embracing the solicitation of positive energy. Character defects are washed away by rigorous strides toward self-growth. Indeed, the effectiveness of psychology will never reach its peak or define its purpose until clinicians come to the realization that in addition to the mind, body, and spirit functioning in total unison with one another, the self as a whole must also be reassessed in terms of how the laws of circumstances and the universal order of things with respect to cosmic energy interface with the physiological and environmental variables in order to produce the manifestation of a functional and harmonious self. There can be no greater error than to associate all psychopathologies as a direct result of some physiological and environmental etiology. While the tendencies are to view cosmic and universal variables as environmental triggers of psychopathologies, it is paramount not to embrace this myopic delusion. Indeed, what clinicians tend to call environmental triggers in some cases are a group of universal entities collectively referred to as metaphysical spiritualism because of their direct linkage to the two opposing forces, the Supreme Being and Lucifer. The difference in these concepts lies in one's ability to bear testimony to the truth versus one's frequent attempt to unravel the mystery behind the deluded psyche. Metaphysical spiritualism possesses tenets that allow the clinician to be able to detect what aspect of an individual's psyche is affected by various influences, whether physiological environment or the laws of circumstances/the universal order of things. It is a powerful indicator as to what psychopathology ails the person because each individual's presenting problem is associated directly or indirectly with some metaphysical cause. Knowledge in the art of universal entities narrows the scope of the individual's problem, which appears not to be rooted in traditional etiology, thus serving as a pointer with respect to where a clinician should start the search.

My dear unborn, the philosophy behind metaphysical spiritualism is one of self-discovery and introspection with the underlying premise that we spend most of our lives concealing the neglected truth: As human beings we spend most of our lives trying to fool ourselves. One of the many goals of metaphysical spiritualism is to help others find harmony in the chaotic world in which we live. To accomplish this goal, we must conquer the greatest enemy within the world, our inner selves, by understanding our true nature. By identifying and embracing each emotion from within, we are compelled to challenge ourselves to avoid expressing them or to choose to engage in a state of denial regarding their existence and impact on the manner in which we live. "If there are no enemies within, then the enemies outside cannot hurt you." For where there are enemies there is anger, a toxic element of the self. When a man gets angry, he places himself outside the harmony of nature, and once outside the harmony of nature, he is no longer in sync with the laws of circumstances. As human beings, when we fail to become in sync with the laws of circumstances, we will inevitably become their victim. Metaphysical spiritualism teaches individuals how to become one with the laws of circumstances so as not to be a victim of them but rather a conqueror.

My dear unborn, in order to become one with the laws of circumstances, metaphysical spiritualism embraces anticipation and prevention as a daily practice. Although the mind, body, and spirit must be in line with one another, in some cases they are not, making harmony beyond our reach. Our inner ability to cope and deal with life's tribulations often tests the limits of our body and suppresses the strength of our spirit. But in every negative there is some element of positive, for when the fragility of the body gives out, then we must summon the energy from the spirit and the mind to pave the way for the body until it is able to once again cope on its own. The management of turbulent events in our lives brings us closer to a state of harmony. Simply by not letting a daily mishap start a negative chain reaction, thus setting the agenda for the entire day, we are able to better deal with the self and preserve its inner tranquility. Remember, a fraction of a positive force within an element of madness can also be used to restart a positive chain reaction of its own, thus changing the course of an entire day.

My dear unborn, under the umbrella of metaphysical spiritualism, death is seen as a transitory process that will either be feared or embraced based on our own spiritual attributes as a person. This is the one ultimate saving grace for which all avenues within our lives reach the same crossroad. Everything stops! Those who fear death do so not because of death itself but because of the uncertainty that lies within their souls as to whether or not they have earned redemption, the gateway to salvation. The realization of this uncertainty is like a thorn in their sides, constantly reminding them and curbing their appetites for some of the things that make their existence worthwhile. He who is at peace with death is truly at peace within himself. The enlightened acknowledges that death, as we know it, is an illusion that can only become real by becoming one with the experience. Everything that has happened to humanity since the beginning of time has happened before. Our birth, our entire lives, are like a rerun being played back for our sake, for although God is omniscient, even he likes to have an edge. The joy, the mistakes, the pain, are all part of a heavenly "recall," one that we are experiencing for a second time, though it appears to be our first. The past is really our present, and déjà vu is just a residual effect of a time when all life forms graced the earth. This is not reincarnation or a revolving of the soul that happens during another phase of our existence, but rather a pilot study of the idiosyncrasies of human nature and their ability to care for the promised land, earth.

My dear unborn, it is not by God's standard that we will be judged but by the standard that we use to judge others. It is not in the heart of man that God will look for answers but in the heart of their souls. It is not the "Book of Life" that will bear testimony to our lives but rather the imprints that can be found on each line of the heart of the soul. Do not concern yourself with the prospect of dying, for the womb is the birthplace for both life and death, though we celebrate one and dread the other. I tell you that unless you celebrate both, the flame of your passion will be dimmed. Live for today and only for today, yet conserve some of your blessings for tomorrow. When you dance, dance in the rain in remembrance of those who cannot, both the living and the dead.

My dear unborn, while the principles of metaphysical spiritualism probe into the afterlife, in essence, the philosophy is primarily recognizing the seen and unseen forces that make us wonder what else there is to our existence, and is it enough? And if it is not? How can I embrace or prevent the factors that serve as obstacles to my self-growth, and what price am I willing to pay?

My dear unborn, our love for the Supreme Being is not enough under the guidance of metaphysical spiritualism; the reasons behind our love are what define its purity in the eyes of God. When you cross the threshold that brings you face to face with God, it is not fear or hope of gains that he wishes to see in your eyes, but love and reverence. Although these attributes are often mixed, they must be clear and distinct when you gaze in the eyes of the Messiah. On too many occasions the love of God seems for the most part to be contingent on the promise of eternal life instead of the already existing conditions that entail being alive, being here, in our present domain, and enjoying the blessings he has already given to us. True love for our Creator is not pure in essence if it is guided by mere potential heavenly rewards or glory. The epitome of giving is one that is done with little or no expectation of any kind of return. The emergence of soul from nothingness into an entity that can feel, touch, hear, taste, and see should be enough for anyone to show the Supreme Being the love that is desired by him for the rest of one's life. Images conjured up by words defined by men, deeds that plague our past but are presently regrettable in our eyes, impulse driven by a conflicted spirit . . . God knows man's intent and the source of man's fears long before man has entertained them. Still, his love remains steadfast, and when he punishes us it is for being evil, not for being human; there is a difference.

My dear unborn, it has been said by many that man cannot judge God by human qualities, for he is divinity and we are not. I tell you that the "state of grace" from which man has fallen has left God with a feeling of emptiness in all ways humanly possible. As you weep for the unfortunate, weep for the Almighty as well, for the depth of his soul is deeper than ours and his feelings are much more overwhelming. The abundance of his love makes him more tolerant to the follies of man, for his goal to return man to a state of grace is yet to be reached. The more he gives, the further they seem to drift away. Hence, his goal is an impossible one, even for a God. Although he has the power to change this course on which man has embarked, he will not do so, for to do this would mean violating the covenant he has made with man regarding free will. Ironically, the same attributes that make it possible for him to love so unconditionally are the same attributes that produce his feeling of emptiness that derives from man's absence from grace. He is caught between the proverbial rock and a hard place, for any attempt to drastically alter the direction of man's destiny would give birth to the violation of his own basic spiritual tenets. Blinded often by our wickedness and transgressions, he tolerates the fallacies of the human condition while observing the demarcation between tolerance and acceptance, a demarcation he wishes human beings to pay close attention to when faced with differences. The lesson is simple: To tolerate that which is different or strange to us is not synonymous to acceptance. As human beings we get angry and afraid, which generates reluctance to tolerate for subconsciously we have told ourselves that to tolerate is to accept. We have an inherent right as human beings not to accept that which is different or strange if we so choose. But we do not have an inherent right not to tolerate that which is strange or different, simply because lack of tolerance feeds the urge to judge, a right that is reserved only for the Supreme Being. Unless you can define the color of a man's spirit, you will never know to what tribe he belongs.

My dear unborn, brace yourself, for within the next decade more people will die from sickness and unknown causes than ever in the history of humanity. Spiritually, socially, and physically, humanity will be tested beyond its limits. It will be an era of evil where the steps of Lucifer will sound like thunder in an attempt to stamp out the voice of the righteous, an era when loving your enemy will not only be an impossible task, but to do so would be to bathe one's self in hypocrisy, for the manifestation of the dark force will be too prevalent and grotesque. Confronted by such evil, do not search yourself for love, for it will be replaced with empathy, and the perpetrator of these deeds will create a temporary blindness of God. Still, empathize even when chaos and confusion reign. Frustration will be at its peak for our attention, and focus will be directed toward science and those who will convince you that the answers to your tribulations are within their grasp. Pseudo-omniscient will be the embodiment of daily forecasts by those who are under the influence of the negative opposing force as social paradox dominates the era. The poor will be spiritually rich, and the rich will be spiritually poor. The old will possess the heart of the young, and the young will possess the heart of the old. Evil will sleep in the dark of night and awake in the light of day. The living will cry out for death, and the dead will wander aimlessly in search of life. I tell you this that whichever of these dilemmas graces your path, cloak yourself in the holy circle of light and use its beam as a guide to the Messiah. When the frailties of your body can no longer sustain the will of your spirit, then commend it back to the Creator. There are those who will shun this idea, but reject them for they would have you believe that when the gift of life becomes a burden where it is no longer considered a gift, it is still not within your right to return it from whom it came. If the Son of Man were allowed to verbally surrender his life force in the hands of the Supreme Being during his moment of agony, why would God not extend this empathy to his other children? It baffles the mind to think that some people believe that the U.S. Supreme Court can take extenuating circumstances into account before passing judgment, yet would think that God would do any less.

My dear unborn, I have outlined the dialogue between Ellineas and the Holy Ghost as a response to your question:

>Ellineas: *"Wow!"*
>The Holy Ghost: *"Welcome, Ellineas."*
>Ellineas: *"Wow!"*
>The Holy Ghost: *"Yes! We often get this reaction from other souls."*
>Ellineas: *"What a place you got here!"*
>The Holy Ghost: *"No, Ellineas, not my place. This is your place."*
>Ellineas: *"My place? Are you joshing me? Who are you anyway?"*
>The Holy Ghost: *"Oh, I'm sorry. They call me the Holy Ghost. You're in heaven now."*
>Ellineas: *"Heaven? This is heaven? So I'm dead? I'm dead, aren't I?"*
>The Holy Ghost: *"You're alive, Ellineas; nothing dies here."*
>Ellineas: *"Come, come, you know what I mean. Did my heart finally get me?"*
>The Holy Ghost: *"No, Ellineas. God finally got you. Yes! The world as you knew is replaced by what you see before you."*
>Ellineas: *"Not a bad tradeoff. That's funny, I've never noticed it before."*
>The Holy Ghost: *"Noticed what before, Ellineas?"*

Ellineas: *"Your race."*

The Holy Ghost: *"Is that important?"*

Ellineas: *"I see you don't get to earth very often."*

The Holy Ghost: *"Here in heaven there is only one race."*

Ellineas (sarcastically): *"And what is that?"*

The Holy Ghost: *"The color you are right now."*

Ellineas (looking himself over): *"But I am colorless."*

The Holy Ghost: *"Here in heaven, there is only one race, the colorless race."*

Ellineas: *"This sounds like the place to be, but what am I supposed to do here for eternity?"*

The Holy Ghost: *"Enjoy your senses!"*

Ellineas: *"My senses? You mean I came all this way to heaven to lose my marbles?"*

The Holy Ghost chuckled briefly: *"No, Ellineas, heaven is more than what you see. It is the epitome of a heightened satisfaction of all six senses combined."*

Ellineas: *"You mean five senses, don't you?"*

The Holy Ghost: *"No, Ellineas, I mean six. The sixth sense is a combination of the pleasures that derive from all the five senses together and sanctified by God himself, making you susceptible to pleasure as never before, thus allowing you to experience this kingdom like no other. It is also the channel that serves as a spiritual link between God and man."*

Ellineas: *"Where is he?"*

The Holy Ghost: *"Where is who?"*

Ellineas: *"God! I made it here; the least he can do is to show his face."*

The Holy Ghost: *"No one sees God's face, Ellineas. But trouble not yourself for when you see me, you see him, for We are one and the same."*

Ellineas: *"I must see him! I have already seen you."*

The Holy Ghost: *"We are one and the same, Ellineas."*

Ellineas grew frustrated from what he thought was the Holy

Ghost's attempt to block him from gazing in the eyes of his Creator. *"Fine, then you won't mind if I see him instead of You."*

The Holy Ghost: *"I'm afraid that is not possible."*

Ellineas: *"I have suffered and humbled myself in the presence of my fellow men. I have loved my neighbors and gave all that I had. I have obeyed all his commandments. I have earned the right to see his face. I must see him."*

The Holy Ghost: *"Ellineas, God has kept his word. Look around, all this belongs to you."*

Ellineas: *"It is not enough. I must see him. I have earned the right to see him."*

The Holy Ghost: *"Ellineas, seeing God's face has never been a right but a privilege which only he alone can grant."*

Ellineas: *"I must see him!"*

The Holy Ghost suddenly disappeared only to return a couple of minutes later. *"I am sorry, Ellineas. I have asked and the answer is no."*

Ellineas: *"I must see his face!"*

The Holy Ghost: *"No!"*

Ellineas resorted to rage: *"I will turn heaven into hell unless I see his face!"*

The Holy Ghost grabbed his ears as if he were in excruciating pain. *"We do not use that word or tone here, Ellineas."*

Ellineas: *"All this means nothing to me if cannot see his face. I must see him."*

Once again the Holy Ghost departed and returned with an indescribable look on his face. *"Your wish has been granted, Ellineas."*

Ellineas was quiet for a moment before he responded. It was as if asking to see God was a matter of defiance and this resolution defeated his purpose. *"Good, let's go!"*

The Holy Ghost: *"There is one more thing."*

Ellineas: *"What now?"*

The Holy Ghost: *"You can gaze on the face of God for thirty seconds and lose your soul forever, returning to a state of nothing-*

ness, or you can forego your request and enjoy this, your heaven, for eternity."

Ellineas stooped and put his head in the palm of his hands. *"Wow! I never thought. . . ."*

The Holy Ghost interjected: *"There are consequences for the path we choose, Ellineas, even in here."*

Sweat dripped from Ellineas's eyebrow as he pondered what path to take. He looked around at his heavenly kingdom and began to perspire even harder. *"I must see his face."*

The Holy Ghost warned: *"Once you gaze in the eyes of God, there is no turning back."*

Ellineas: *"I must see his face."*

The Holy Ghost rested his hands on Ellineas's shoulders and said, *"Eternity is yours, so why is it so important to see God's face?"*

Ellineas: *"Because I have earned the right. Yes! Tell him if that's the choice, I must see his face, for heaven is just another place if men are forbidden to see the face of their God."*

My dear unborn, are there things worth losing one's soul? Only if the circumstances possess a predisposition of a scenario that falls beyond the reach of God. For like Ellineas, there are some for whom heaven is not enough. You ask whether sex has any place in the quest for one's spiritual enlightenment. Sex is a variation of love, which is synonymous to the art of living; both concepts transcend just the need to quench one's thirst for sex and other desires. The art of loving and living, when nurtured spiritually, functions on a higher plain where the energy of all sexual acts and desires are channeled through the Almighty in order to purify the process. To live is to love and to love is to live; sex in both processes only serves to consummate the bond between the two. One cannot exist without the other if the essence for which they both stand is to prevail. I feel your pain, but I tell you, yield not to the spiritual conflict that stems from desires or passions for the opposite sex, for the art of loving and living was created not by man but by God. Yet, we're constantly plagued by guilt when we choose to devote our lives to God and find it impossible not to entertain thoughts of erotica. Embrace these feelings because they serve as reminders for all the essence of life that makes it worth living. This is not to say that a vow to God should be placed secondary to man's desire, but rather that each should be secondary to none, for one cannot separate the creation from the Creator. Practitioners of metaphysical spiritualism must bring themselves to see love as an unrehearsed linguistic symphony between souls, a feeling resulting from an eternal embryonic reunification, and the purification of an existential attachment that has been sanctified by the ecstasy of the living God. Indeed, the art of loving takes on many forms, and the feelings we receive depend from where the form originates. Recognizing the origins of the forms is paramount to the sanctity of loving because each form is either a projection from God or his adversary. Unless you function in the spiritual realm, it is impossible to tell who the driving force is behind your perception and your ability to love and live. You will not be able to see what facets of both processes are distorted, perverted, or lacking because the demarcation between the holy and the unholy spiritual arenas is as slender as a spider's web. When love lacks fulfillment, it creates an emptiness that can never be filled and a black hole within one's soul that pulls one down in the pit of turmoil. Any attempt to express this type of love will cloak the partner in a cloud of darkness with no hope of light piercing through. But a love that is whole and pure can become life's focal point, serving as a bed on a tireless journey, an armor that protects in a pasture of evil and a trigger of repressed emotions. I tell you that the greatest loving you can bestow on another has nothing to do with reaching an orgasm, but rather an engagement in a spiritual seduction that involves making the object of your heart the zenith of all five senses where pleasures reach their peak in all their respective domains. Imagine a level of pleasure that is based on a spiritual foundation from where the height of sensations regarding seeing, tasting, hearing, smelling, and touching spring forward and come together creating an exotica that far outweighs the reaching of any orgasm. Once again, unless you function in the spiritual realm, the awareness of the type of pleasure will escape you for the quest for spiritual enlightenment seldom focuses on the pleasures of the flesh, but rather the pleasures of the spirit.

My dear unborn, it is never an orgasm that makes sex pleasurable, rather the perceived interpretations of the five senses under the direction of the heart. The heart realizes that sex plays a little part in the art of loving, therefore under compelling situations it tends to deliberately sabotage the initiation of the sensations needed by the five senses to be interpreted by our loved ones or admirers. In short, the heart provides an atmosphere where the achievement of an orgasm will be short-lived and becomes merely physical while lacking long-term fulfillment. An individual's physique is geared toward short-lived ecstasy, but the spirit engages itself in passions that are everlasting. The art of loving is not measured by one's ability to give or reach an orgasm. It does not involve a repertoire of foreplay tactics set out to arouse and to excite. It is not a variation of positions created by contortionist lovers. The art of loving is the exchanging of spiritual appetites at a moment in time when both souls have been chosen to share the same stage in the theater of life. Conflicted and consumed by the pleasure we seek from the flesh, we convince ourselves that by replacing them with vows to God, the urges that torment our souls will cease, thus keeping us on the path to enlightenment. The overwhelming accusation of members of the priesthood molesting young men of their congregation has taught us that spiritual ritualism and vows to the Creator can never replace human insatiable desires for the flesh. The suppression of such desires is an open invitation to the Prince of Darkness, for he lurks in the shadow of our unwanted emotions as a reminder of how vulnerable we are to his temptations. Therefore, any quest for spiritual enlightenment that negates a climaxing experience with the flesh—sexual or otherwise with regards to the human desires—is one that is based on falsehood. The energy spent avoiding these feelings could best be used serving the Creator and enjoying the fruits of his labor, regardless of what shape they come in. This is not to say that sexual freedom, an aspect of the art of loving, should not be blessed by God; instead, only to highlight the notion that if one's love for another is pure in nature, then vows and promises to the

Messiah are not a necessity. Indeed, the love you share for one another would have already been placed in the bosom of God. A time will come when man will realize that nothing that emerges from the Creator's holy circle of light is in need of blessings, for one does not bless or anoint that which is already holy. The blood of Christ, the holy circle of light, and the teardrops of God contain building blocks that are made only of love. Hence, our vows and promises serve not his purpose but ours in many cases—a feeble attempt to convince ourselves and others that the testimony of our love is real and true, only later to have the hypocrisy unveiled by the true essence of love.

My dear unborn, I am troubled, for although the love of God is great, the distance between him and man has grown wider, giving the illusion of closeness, yet so far, far away. Even with the sacrifice of the Messiah, the gap between God and man is miles apart. The common ground that was created by the death of the Messiah seems to have gone invisible. The difference between man and God has driven them further apart, as both desperately seek to capture an illusion of similarities in hope that the gap that separates them will bring them closer. But if either man or God is to reach this task, one must become more Godlike while the other becomes more humanlike. God must relinquish a part of his divinity and equate himself more with human attributes, or man must continue to struggle with his delusion of becoming Godlike through whatever means necessary. Man has chosen science as an avenue to become more Godlike, and God has chosen the Messiah as an avenue to become more humanlike. Without a common ground, both still lack the necessary means needed to transcend their differences, differences that cripple the salvation that they both seek from a state of grace that now lacks harmony. Indeed, faith is the only common ground in which both the similarities and differences of man and God intersect at the same crossroad. It is the one essential axiom needed to bring them closer together. God must have faith in man that with all his bungling mistakes, he will find his way to the truth, and man must have faith in God that when the price for salvation has been paid in full, then God will allow man to return to his sacred place of grace. Unless an alliance between man and God is built on faith, the distance between both will never decrease.

My dear unborn, prayers, like meditation, are an essential tool in order to access God's holy circle of light, a step sometimes necessary to initiate a level of communication needed to be one with the spirit of the Messiah himself. But there will be times when your prayer will appear to fall on deaf ears, an empty voice crying out in the wilderness longing and hoping for someone to feel your pain and suffering; a time when you will no longer humble yourself before the Messiah, but instead rebuke him for having taught you his prayer that seems to lack substance and comfort in your hour of desperation and distress; a time when you will ask why your prayer is still unanswered and the hole within your heart grows larger. Genuflect and pray again, for prayer when done right is always answered and does not fail. Remember always that prayer takes on the appearance of failure only when we choose to deny the answer for which we seek the question; when we choose to accept and implement only a part of God's response to the questions asked in our prayers, and when we deliberately choose to alter the chemistry of God's prayer simply by the truthfulness or lack thereof on which our tongues deliver his words. Indeed, the equation of prayer is like the compound of a chemical mixture: remove an element, and the entire equation can result in a different outcome.

When we take medicine, we are trusting that the pharmaceutical company made the medication that will help us heal without any contraindications. But if for some reason the medication prescribed for us was not balanced according to the right chemical equation, then the outcome can be effectively useless or devastating. Such is the case with prayer, only its equations contain elements of truthfulness, sincerity, love, forgiveness, self-sacrifice, faith, and total surrender. If the equation to your prayer is not balanced with some of these elements, then like the medicine it will be effectively useless and can be devastating depending on the situation. While many use prayer as a way to praise God and to thank him for his many blessings, I urge you to use it as a way to explore the feelings of the Almighty, for by doing this you would have offered him the greatest praise ever.

Let your prayer be a series of questions geared around him, not you. For example, "Father, how are You feeling today? Is there anything I can do to restore and strengthen Your faith in me and my brothers? What can I do to ease Your disappointment in those who have yet to embrace Your teachings? Are You angry with me or the way in which I live my life?" I tell you this that before the sun goes down or rises the next day, he would have answered your questions, for when we consciously explore the feelings of another, we open up our own heart, thus revealing the core of our soul. "This is My Son, of whom I am well pleased." The Baptist's spirit needed confirmation of the Messiah, but his question allows God to see the extent of his love for him and the entire process of baptism. Frequently we take for granted that our selfish desires and wants are not the only thing that matter on this earth. We find it incredible to think for a moment that God who loves us would want us to take time out and inquire about his feelings, his pain, and his desires. We neglect to realize that the variation of human attributes that makes us who and what we are is the same type of variation that runs parallel in the spiritual realm as well. This myopic view makes us blind to the idea of exploring God's feelings as well as his mind-set. We sometimes forget that what we have as human beings, we get from him not by chance but by his will. We become just a little too complacent with the Bible, relying on it only as a source in which we can know how God thinks and feels regarding a number of issues. We are almost afraid to deviate and engage in independent thinking based on our times and era. We have the will to change our mind based on circumstances, yet we constantly hold God steadfast to his words, decisions, and actions, regardless of the nature of the situation that we face. Because he is the same yesterday, today, and tomorrow does not mean that this precludes him from holding and changing his views. We do not think less of anyone for doing so, so why should we think any less of God for acknowledging that what might have worked a thousand years ago will definitely not work now? People say the Bible has too many inconsistencies, but the truth of the matter is that the inconsistencies are within us. We want to have the flexibility to readapt and readjust depending on a given situation, but we are unwilling to afford God the same luxury and tend to get bent out of shape when he does what he has to do. Disappointments flood our hearts, and we blame the Bible for not living up to the expectation we possess. God is constantly supporting changes and growth, not only by giving us new technology but by reinventing himself to be able to adapt and adjust to the world around us.

My dear unborn, I tell you that when you pray to God, pray for him as well. Remember, my dear unborn, that within any lifetime, each man will have one uncontrollable passion that eventually will manifest itself in the form of a talent or a flaw. Any man who is fortunate enough to have prayer as his passion is destined to be a great man or will become a simple man destined to do great things. Indeed, prayer is the golden key that unlocks all doors, leading to the staircase to God's ears regardless of the hour. Prayer is the saving grace that avails itself even to the demons in hell at all times. It is a circle of positive energy strong enough to brace itself against all evil. If your prayer serves only to fulfill your spiritual obligations or to ask something from the Heavenly Father, then search your soul and question the selfishness of your action. Although these acts are noble, going to a place of worship and praising him, then turning about in the same breath and asking something of him diminishes the experience. In one glorious moment, save your breath and release it only in powerful and tearful prayer for him. For while he is always there for us whether we deserve it or not, show him in that one instance that you are there for him, not because of what you seek.

My dear unborn, the unison metaphysical theory stresses the importance of the mind, body, and spirit functioning as one, in total unison, before the self can fully experience the dynamics between God and the various entities within the universe, dynamics that are the propelling influence behind the seen and unseen forces that shape our lives. Some of the principles and tenets that teach us about these influences and that are discussed in this book are the embodiment of this theory, which is sometimes referred to as metaphysical spiritualism. The theory emphasizes the essential factors that should be focused on as it relates to the mind, body, and spirit as well as the other mechanisms of the universe, factors that are vital to the knowing of one's Creator and the world in which an individual lives, factors that when fully understood can assist one in avoiding the pitfalls of one's day-to-day existence. Metaphysical spiritualism shows the beauty and advantages to being spiritually enlightened. Its primary focus is to challenge an individual to question his or her life, principles, religious doctrine, and that which makes up the very core of that individual's existence. It is not imposing nor is it judgmental in its quest to introduce you to the Creator. Instead, with great humility, the doctrine simply asks that you search your soul today by reexamining your way of life, the philosophy that governs your entire existence. Its contention is that by removing the blindness from one's eyes, mind, and spirit, only then can the self see clearly the dynamics and the various entities within the universe, both the seen and unseen forces that shape our lives, thus making us more susceptible to the voice of God.

The Second Month

7

Christ's Suicide

My dear unborn, when the gift of life becomes a burden to the point where it is no longer considered a gift, return it to the one who gave it to you. Do not wait patiently in hopes that you will go gently through the night, for as the Messiah came to us and willfully gave up his life that we may obtain salvation, it is indeed within our rights to engage in similar action. Do not allow your dignity or self-respect to be stripped away by diseases or other ailments simply because the naive have told you that an act of suicide will seal condemnation. There is always a reason to die, and if the reason is good enough, God's mercy shall greet you at the door to his kingdom. Is it not so that Christ could have prevented his death by defending himself? Did he not know the precise manner and time of his demise, yet he still allowed it to take place? Did he not prevent the prolonging of his suffering on the cross by placing his spirit briefly in the hands of his Father until his resurrection? Why then do you think the Heavenly Father would show you less consideration for returning your spirit to him when, like Christ, your body can no longer sustain you? People suffer needlessly because they lack conviction and trust in the full extent of God's mercy. They pay lip service to the power of his forgiveness and understanding but fall short when they must wager the strength of his love against their souls.

My dear unborn, when the timing of your death is apparent and inevitable, when your nights and days are filled only with unbearable pain and modern science watches helplessly, when your prayers appear to be unanswered and you have no more tears, rejoice and pray again, but not for relief but rather for the courage to send your spirit home to the Creator, while maintaining your dignity and self-respect that death would otherwise claim. Do not listen to the rationalizations driven by fear and lack of faith; instead trust in the mercy and love of God. The pain that plagues your failing body was once endured by Christ, and he has already reminded the Heavenly Father of the limitations on human endurance. Life is precious and should be guarded at all costs, but there will come a time when nothing is left to be protected; a time when the invincibility of our youth and vitality is replaced by dependency and youthful decline; a time when the smell of spring is accompanied by the season of lifelessness in the fall, and when the distance between each step can no longer be measured; a deterioration process that is relative to each individual with one noticeable similarity, the drums of doom beat on. Do whatever you must, but do it quickly, for the certainty with which you carry out your decision is indicative of the trust you have in the mercy of God which awaits you.

My dear unborn, the idea that there is no redemption for those who commit suicide is one of the biggest religious myths that has plagued our time, thus scaring people into suffering needlessly. Some religious doctrines would have you believe that a single act can wipe out an entire life commitment to God. They would have you believe that this is the only time God considers you unworthy of salvation. They would have you believe that such an act is an affront to God and all that he stands for. Some religious doctrines maintain that since a person who commits suicide is no longer in a position to ask for forgiveness, then condemnation is sure to follow. Yet, countless biblical teachings indicate that asking for forgiveness for an act regarding an issue is not an uncommon practice before the act is actually committed, and that forgiveness under such conditions has been granted, depending on whether or not God thinks the circumstances warrant the action taken. Why then would God turn his back on those who choose to end their lives for rational reasons? When your system of beliefs concerning the self is in direct contradiction with the laws of man, allow your decision to be affirmed by your spirituality. Only then will you know whether your view or the laws of man are correct in governing the situation. One who lacks an abundance of spiritual elements within one's life will constantly struggle with under what circumstances they should allow their soul to return to God's holy circle of light.

My dear unborn, the death of Christ paved the way for the answers you seek regarding your own existence, both in life and in death. The mystery to unravel your existence and the purpose behind it were created not by God but by man, who finds it extremely difficult to accept most things on faith. Life is a cycle comprising miseries and pleasures with death at the end; therefore, one must live on faith until it's time to die. You exist only to serve God by way of serving your fellow man. The time that has not been consumed by this effort can be extended into maximizing pleasure and minimizing pain on your behalf. Each man must devise his own purpose for his existence, for without a purpose his life will become like a compass that is not able to yield to a specific direction. Christ was a sacrificial lamb who deliberately removed all obstacles that would aid in his survival.

His reasons were clear, and so will yours be if ever your life becomes burdensome by the presence of your body. When you call on the angel of death to assist in preparation of returning to the living God, remember that reluctance rides on the backside of fear, and where there is fear, faith is rooted in a foundation of uncertainty. Sitting idly by while others attempt to persuade you in making a decision that is contradictory to your own beliefs or needs will only serve to intensify the uncertainties that are already in your heart, uncertainty that stems from not knowing what lies ahead after you have surrendered your life over to the Creator. But as Christ trusted the

Heavenly Father to deliver him from the arms of death, so must you, for it is only then that your faith will make clear the righteousness behind the act that you have committed. Do not attach your concerns or decisions to the cloak of those whose lives have yet to mimic your pathway. The advice they will give will be empty in essence, for there is wisdom in the old adage that unless a man walks in your shoes, he can have no idea of the things that irk you. Friends will inform you of the glorification of life and the necessity to preserve it at all cost, a noble gesture from one who undoubtedly has not been forsaken by good health or whose world remains untouched by the prospect of engaging in an eternal sleep.

My dear unborn, the returning of one's life is a responsibility that rests on the shoulders of one for whom life has been unbearable. Only this individual and this individual alone has the right to seek departure from his or her earthly existence. No man may choose to make this decision for another or should take it upon himself to carry out this act of deliverance for another regardless of the circumstances or ties that bind them together. This decision is an intimate covenant between the Creator and the individual, and only these two entities can salvage the necessary elements needed to ensure the appropriate platform for the returned soul. Third-party interference in this ritual will only serve to jeopardize the integrity of the process as well as place this third party at risk of losing his or her own soul. Christ could have had enormous help from angels and even his followers, but this third-party interference would have tainted the entire process, thus breaking the potential covenant between him and man. Indeed, the responsibility must be solely the individual's for whom life is best served by returning it to God. Therefore, unless one possesses the courage to embark on this journey alone without the assistance of others, one should prepare oneself to adhere to dying at nature's will while succumbing to its sometimes harsh inconvenience. It is ironic, but as a society we have the right to take life for the betterment of civilization, but as individuals we do not have the right to assist in the taking of a life regardless of the circumstances. This holds true because society must be protected from deviants in order to maintain law and order.

However, no single individual may execute these decisions in order to protect society from these same social deviants. The point is that with God, the opposite holds true when an individual chooses to end his life. Individuals have the right but friends or significant others of the individual do not have the right to assist. The majority is not in the right in this case but serves only to confound the issue. The commitment of this one soul with all its suffering will capture God's ears. Like Christ, this individual must bear his cross alone.

My dear unborn, a life that is filled with your experiences, regardless of what they are, will be the measuring rod for how fate will attempt to shape your destiny. Whether you live or die in accordance with the principles of your Creator will ultimately depend on how high of an esteem you have held your life. Many will place emphasis on the preservation of life, but I tell you this: your energy will best serve you if you embrace each morning in search of a purpose or a reason to lay your life down for another. Death should not always be at the focal point; instead, the relinquishing of a part of you that will change you forever can also be an attainable goal. By giving another a piece of you, for which it is impossible to reclaim, you would have shaped your fate in concert with your destiny. Remember always that one's destiny is not always experiences groomed by fate, but rather experiences designed to restructure fate. In short, destiny controls no one except for those who are not one with their fate. There is no need for one to be preoccupied with death or the rendering of one's life to another, but when the preservation of our existence takes precedence or governs our degree of involvement for fear of threat to our own life, then we allow ourselves to coexist in a vacuum of emptiness; the life we once held dear and cherished so much suddenly becomes meaningless. Christ's suicide is a lesson for us all, for in his last moment on the cross he taught us more about grace, forgiveness, and love than the entire time he walked the earth. Had Christ not died in the manner in which he did, many would see him only as another prophet. The seduction toward salvation for man did not occur because of the way Christ lived but by the way he died. This epiphany escapes so many. Unlike Christ, your destiny may not be preordained; therefore, the greatness you will encounter must be of your own making. The deed you leave behind must be a tribute to the life you have led, and each word that echoes from your lips must soften the hardening of man's heart or raise another's consciousness, or bring comfort and hope to the less fortunate.

My dear unborn, the stigmatization of suicide will be a powerful influence over any spiritual decision you may take if ever you find yourself in need of taking this path. While it is taboo in many Western cultures, suicide is embraced by other cultures as a form of discipline that symbolizes honor and noble sacrifice. In Asia, for example, many soldiers during World War II flew their planes into Allied ships after they made their peace with Buddha or their Higher Power. In certain circumstances, many committed *hari kiri* as an act to regain honor. Further extrapolation shows us that the Bible makes several assertions relevant to the giving up of one's life for another as one of the greatest acts of love. The Bible goes on to state that those who love their lives too much would lose it, etc. These rationales serve not as justification for suicide, but rather an attempt to alert your awareness to the fact that the views of those who engage in dogmatic thinking are not the only ones that should be taken into account. Regardless of the ideation concerning suicide, ultimately your beliefs and your reasons are the only ones that count. This decision is a personal one, and no one has the right to dictate whether you should or should not follow through. I must stress most vehemently that your reason for acting on this gesture must be perfectly clear to your Creator. He must be able to see within your heart the sincerity and genuineness behind your decision. It matters little if anyone else can comprehend why you have done what you have done. Only you and your Creator must fully understand the nature of your act.

My dear unborn, from a social context, people will attempt to convince you that the mere fact that you are contemplating suicide is an indication that you have become mentally unstable. They will claim that no rational human being would think about taking one's own life. Next, they will attempt to explore your soul in order to see what part of it is filled with the sickness that led you to believe it is okay to return your life back to the Creator. Think for a moment about the presumptuousness and audacity on their part to feel as if they have the right to tell you what you can and cannot do with your own life, much less to accuse you of being sick simply because you do not subscribe to their beliefs about lying helplessly in pain while disease slowly eats away at your flesh and dignity. It takes a very selfish person to watch and accept another human being going through agony of this nature, while all the time crying out their convictions in opposition in the name of God. More treachery and outrageous acts have been committed in the name of God than in the name of the devil himself. My dear unborn, many have accused God of not being there during their hour of need and suffering, but he has always been there. We are the ones who have turned away or turn a deaf ear because we lack the courage to acknowledge what we must do in order to save ourselves. Realizing that God will not greet us face to face with instructions on what to do, we close off the channels or process that is used as a means of communication with him, thus justifying our own cowardly behavior, which ultimately continues to make the situation a graver one. God has always embraced the limitations of our endurance and refuses to push us beyond that limit. Still, some people who would have you believe that the road to salvation is paved with pain and suffering and that without it we deem ourselves unworthy. Indeed, while pain and suffering are a natural part of life, God does not want us to experience these unnecessarily. Christ has already paid and endured the pain and suffering for us all. He did this primarily so that we would not have to endure that aspect of life too frequently, especially if it goes beyond what we are capable of bearing. God gives us life so we would not be preoccupied with death. Yet when death is near he wants us to have the courage to manipulate it in our favor, just as we have with life, which means using to our advantage all options that are available to us. Granted, this is not to say that one should take one's life every time the going gets rough or even refuse to fight when faced with certain adversity that is considered hopeless by many. Indeed, quite the contrary: one must fight to sustain life with one's last breath. However, when all cards have been played and death still holds the winning hand, then have the dignity to lose with style and grace. Christ taught us how to live in grace, but even more so he taught us how to die with dignity. In my eyes, there is no finer person to emulate at any level. The greatest victory one can obtain over death is to choose the manner in which one dies, as opposed to letting death make that choice.

My dear unborn, if you surrender your life to God because of what you were told by doctors, false prophets, or even friends, then you are a fool. It is not prudent to allow anyone to influence your decision-making process in this private matter, except yourself. As mentioned before, this decision is between you and your Creator. When others encourage you to terminate your existence but there is doubt within your mind, then listen to the voice of your inner self and fight. Fight for the gift that God has given you, for each individual is bonded to both the forces of death and the forces of life.

As such, one will know deep within one's soul when it is time to relinquish the life force and embrace the death force. It is of great importance that returning your life to God is your decision and yours alone—not your doctor, some specialist, or even a situation that may appear hopeless at the moment. If a doctor tells you that you have three months to live, or a priest tells you that because of your sins you cannot receive absolution and will go to hell, smile and relieve the burden from your heart, because God, not man, resides over both the forces of life and the forces of death. I tell you this, my dear unborn: when the angel of death knocks at your door, greet him with respect, then decide your own fate, remembering that although there is always a reason to die, there is nothing more pleasing to the eyes of God than someone who fights and struggles daily to remain a winner in the battle of life.

THE SECOND MONTH

8

REALISM VS. SPIRITUALISM

My dear unborn, in my assessment of realism and spiritualism, I have always adhered to something Christ said centuries ago, "Render what is to Caesar unto Caesar and what is to God unto God. Paraphrasing him, quite often you will find yourself conflicted between the practical aspects of your life and those things that are needed to fulfill your spiritual need and growth. Some of these things will go far beyond conflicting with your spiritualism; they will violate the very essence of your morals and value system. You will find yourself using all types of rationalizations in order to abstain from doing what is clearly against your spiritual growth. You will engage in a cost-benefit analysis and more times than ever attempt to violate your spiritualism simply because the cost to you in practical terms is just too great. You will struggle with guilt and frustration, ultimately getting angry at yourself for not being able to choose that which you know will nurture your spiritualism. Soon, you will displace the resentment you have for yourself onto the world; then you will feel unworthy to place yourself in the presence of God, leaving the door wide open for procrastination and temptation. Shortly thereafter, you will question the legitimacy of your own beliefs, pondering whether or not you are truly a disciple of your Higher Power. As time goes by, you will attempt to make small compensations for the wrong choices you have made against your spiritual growth, questioning yourself as to whether or not you are serving two masters, and if so, what has to be done to separate yourself in order to walk more closely to God. It is true that it has been said that man cannot serve two masters at once, for he will love one and hate the other. But in a world that is embraced by pragmatic means, a world where your very survival often relies on your ability to play host to the system, it can often be impossible not to be indebted to two masters at once. Regardless of how hard you try, you must choose for the sake of your existence in this world and the next.

My dear unborn, we are living in a world where the rules for both realism and spiritualism in many cases run directly opposite to each other. The things we do for one often mean violating the rules to meet the other. This being the case, it is illogical for anyone to think that under such circumstances we would not be compelled to serve two distinct masters. In another era when things were much simpler, a time when choices were much easier, the idea of serving only one master was not an issue. But now the world is as complex as it will get; therefore, we are blessed if two masters are the only ones we are beholden to with respect to our loyalty. The secret is never to lose sight of the One that matters most of all: the living God. The others may leave us no choices with regards to making them a part of our lives, but it is still within our power to choose the one to whom we will have eternal allegiance, spiritualism over realism.

My dear unborn, spiritualism entails accepting the tenets from certain religious principles that give rise to the notion that a Higher Power has stipulated certain rules in which all followers' lives should be governed. It transcends all superficial existence and links us to a higher purpose than ourselves. Realism is the idea that we live in a world where pragmatic issues must be faced and dealt with in order to prevent the clashing of various realities. Here, both concepts create the dispositions that unless certain rules are adhered to, the desired goals will not only be lacking, but the self as a whole will not be able to keep the benefits that come from understanding the power that each concept has or conveyed when embraced in their respective domains.

My dear unborn, you must embrace both spiritualism and realism if your life as well as the world you live in will ever be complete. Grant you, they will polarize your heart as well as your spirit. Still, this is unavoidable, for one cannot exist without the other, and you cannot exist without them. Realism will occasionally interfere with spiritualism by producing and defining the opposing forces that may or may not be suitable for spiritualism. Spiritualism, on the other hand, will infrequently interfere with realism by creating moral dilemmas and causing one to question the righteousness behind certain actions. Unlike realism, spiritualism is a sacrificial element that is constantly trying to get others to see that no one is beyond redemption, sometime at a great cost to itself. Spiritualism often clashes with realism because realism is a self-serving component that does not embrace the notion that there are things we cannot see that are greater than ourselves. It believes only in the equations of the five senses and reluctantly acknowledges even the probability of a sixth sense. Hence, when confrontation between these two concepts occur, intrapersonal conflict will result.

My dear unborn, each individual is equipped with both spiritualism and realism; one is usually more dormant than the other. The ability to reach and maintain a balance between spiritualism and realism will allow the self to make decisions that will decrease the struggle between both. Yet, by possessing a strong spirituality and a weak realism, one is still able to keep harmony within the self as a whole. Only when spiritualism becomes secondary to realism does the self become out of balance with harmony. When realism is much more powerful than spiritualism, the self will put on cognitive blinders in order to prevent it from seeing what it has become. It will indulge in a wide range of delusions in order to convince itself that spiritualism is still being held in the highest esteem and as such should have very little say in how the self conducts itself as a whole. Unless the self has never activated its spiritualism, this undoubtedly will be the case.

My dear unborn, both spiritualism and realism are very much a part of the self. However, in some cases one will successfully overpower the other unless homeostasis is maintained. In many cases, tension between the two is at a minimum mainly because the spiritual aspect of the self has learned how to tolerate the impracticalities of the realistic aspect. As noted earlier, to tolerate does not necessarily mean to accept. But the ability to be able to do this keeps the self humble and non-judgmental. One of the major fallacies that realism has contributed to our society is the idea that the nature of human beings has changed drastically over the eras, that the primitive forces and elements that we possess are replaced by sophisticated ones. Indeed, realism will occasionally experience a degree of transformation, but not to the degree where the essence of one's self is altered to the point where behavior stemming from the inner nature will also be severely metamorphosed. One can no more escape the nature of one's being as one can escape reflection of one's shadow. The repression or suppression of one's true nature is not tantamount to an alteration within nature itself but rather a predisposition for the emergence of forces geared toward strengths or weaknesses that will either be productive or counterproductive to the self as a whole. The manifestation of these forces will actualize in a manner that meets the need of the individual's psyche. The link between the self and psyche will determine the nature of the predisposition. In short, the repression or suppression of one's true nature will result in an intense collaboration between the self and psyche, thus producing a transparent and illusive image that ultimately will prove problematic not only for the individual but for others as well.

My dear unborn, spiritualism possesses the qualities essential to the transformation of one's true nature that will and often does create a variation in the presentation of the manifestation of the self. In fact, unless one's spirituality is constantly transforming, thus allowing the self to develop a heightened sense of purpose with respect to being one with the spirit of the Messiah or enhancing the closeness to one's Higher Power, something is seriously lacking within one's soul. Spirituality is a growing entity that if stagnated for a long period of time will quickly reach its demise. The stagnation of spiritualism comes in many forms. One of these is the inability to be able to breathe life and love into others by sharing in their passions in hopes that when realism and spiritualism interface, harmony will result.

My dear unborn, some aspects of realism can only be seen by the depth of one's spirituality. The unmasking of these realisms becomes obvious only when one has chosen to make conscious decisions regarding the growth and enhancement of one's spirituality. Only then will the essence of what is considered real reveal itself for what it is: an illusion supported by human delusions. The self must extricate its spiritual side from darkness if both realism and spiritualism are to fulfill their quest for harmony. Indeed, the true essence of realism can only become clear to the self when it allows its spiritual side to be developed to the point where its visions become that of God's. Only when the self is rooted in spirituality will what is truly real become evident, especially to those who struggle and strive for spiritual enlightenment.

My dear unborn, the true essence of realism allows itself to be unmasked by spiritualism, for without this process, realism is seen merely as that which is based on one's perception of the five senses. This perception pulls the self toward the things of the world. Seldom does it create channels that are pathways to the Higher Power, channels that are essential in allowing our Higher Power to reveal unto us the things that are truly important and real, and not just the illusion of life's definition of what is. The revelation of all that matters to the self in order for it to reach a state of nirvana can only come from the Higher Power.

My dear unborn, the fundamental principles on which all channels to and from God are based are on spiritualism. Therefore, the self can only discover what is real and what is not by means of spiritualism. In order for one to decipher what is real in the world we live in, one must be guided by spiritualism; otherwise the perception of realism will camouflage itself in illusions and delusions. Many have rejected their spiritual side and embraced only realisms simply because they are not willing to take the time to embark on the journey that will tap into their spiritual energy. For many, it is much easier to base their lives on realism, where the focus is simply what the five senses are able to look into, thus making it possible for these individuals to regulate what will or will not have an impact on their lives with respect to only the forces that they can see.

My dear unborn, each of us has a spiritual side to our being, whether we choose to embrace it or not. It plays such a powerful force in our lives that subconsciously it assists us in governing our existence, even when we reject the notion of its existence on a conscious level. Spiritualism influences our conscious mechanism, even when we deny the role it plays. There is no escaping that side of us even when it is suppressed. Our refusal to acknowledge its presence in our lives serves one purpose. It provides an avenue for realism to become the predominant regulator in our lives, thus blinding and preventing us from experiencing what is truly real, leaving behind only a stream of illusions and delusions that has become so embedded in our day-to-day rituals that the doors to the mystery of the self are either closed or negated.

My dear unborn, one cannot help another on the journey to spiritualism unless he or she has already been enlightened or has a willingness to allow God to come into one's life. You cannot bring someone out of darkness unless you are a member of the holy circle of light. When spiritualism has become the bed upon which you lay your head, it is not you who will speak to another lost soul; rather a representative of the Higher Power will speak through you, in order to deliver that soul from darkness.

My dear unborn, spiritualism is about the human being's ability to transcend earthly bounds and ties in order to embrace the expectations and principles laid down by the Higher Power. It is a constant cleansing process geared toward bringing the consciousness in line with the essence of one's soul. It is the link between divinity and the temporal. But more important, it is the core of all salvation and redemption, for without it there can be no communication between God and man.

My dear unborn, do not strive for perfection in your quest for spiritual enlightenment, for if perfection was a criteria to enter the kingdom of God, all mankind would dwell in hell forever. I am now certain that there is a hell, a place intended to deal with the consequences of man's transgressions. A place existed as a form of accommodation for Lucifer and his fallen angels, but unfortunately, when some of us drink from the same cup as Lucifer, we must also digest the consequences of what was swallowed together. But man already has his own private hell; it comes from within himself. It is the embodiment of all that keeps him away from God, thus creating a web of illusions that are not in concert with the harmony of life.

My dear unborn, forgiving without forgetting is not forgiveness, but rather a hypocritical gesture to prolong hatred and discontent. Yet, very few of us have what it takes to embrace this philosophy. How do we rid our minds of the pain and suffering inflicted on us, especially by those we cherish? How do we forget in order that we may comply with the essence of forgiveness? Should forgiveness be followed by consequences? If so, is it truly forgiveness?

My dear unborn, in the world of cosmic consciousness and spiritualism, to forgive does not preclude consequences. Rather, forgiveness binds us to the inherent responsibility to one another with respect to dispensing consequences with mercy. Our humanity dictates that ultimately we will still be bombarded by the memories of the things or persons that we choose to forgive; however, the hypocrisy comes when we allow those memories to govern and influence how we treat others who we claim to have forgiven. Indeed, it is human not to be able to forget, but it is counterproductive to our spiritualism and our self-growth to allow memories to regulate how we would otherwise behave.

My dear unborn, forgiveness obtained from God involves purging completely that which you seek forgiveness for, especially the memory. While we do not have the power to do this, it is within our reach to determine how we have decided to allow the memories and feelings to affect us. Self-analysis and introspection have often shown that anger plays an essential role when negative memories constantly compel how we treat individuals whom we are desperately trying to forgive. In order to find the courage to forgive and the strength to eradicate the negative impact of the memories, you must first be willing to embrace the anger and give acknowledgment to the fact that, like you, the individuals whom you are trying to forgive are also human, a humans, filled with fears, insecurities, needs, uncertainties, and foolishness. Therefore, seeing and knowing the frailties that we possess somehow make it easier to forgive.

My dear unborn, your Higher Power can assist you with the strength and courage to forgive, but only if he is asked. God will not interfere in your life unless you ask him, and even when he does, it is to a limited degree. Still, the will to forgive others is a wish he will always grant. God does not expect us to master the skill of forgiving without forgetting. He only asks that the memory we hold does not make it impossible for us to treat the person we claim to have forgiven in a manner in concert with his principles. God is not against punishment or consequences. He only asks that both be tempered with mercy and leniency. When the punishment and consequences are tempered with mercy but become repetitious, especially when forgiveness was offered, then you should seek forgiveness from God. You cannot forgive someone and still sit in judgment of that person time and time again.

My dear unborn, all acts are forgivable, and all men are redeemable. People can corrupt themselves with their minds and their bodies, but they can never corrupt their spirits. The spirit, as mentioned before, is the direct link between God and man. Ultimately, the spirit is what defines us in the eyes of God. It determines our ability and drive with respect to the testing of how we deal with life's demands. When our sins seem unforgivable and our transgression unredeemable, spirit paves the way for our salvation. Indeed, when the consequences and punishment appear to be more than what we can bear, it is sometimes prudent to question the Higher Power. Question not his wisdom, but rather seek the revelation for what transgressions you are being disciplined. Approach this question with humility, and the answers will be revealed unto you, for his arms and memory are long, his words are always true. Vengeance belongs to him, and it frequently manifests itself in punishment and consequences at a time when you least expect it. No one knows in what form consequences or punishment will visit them, only that the trip will be made. But seldom do the consequences for our unrighteous deeds derive directly from God or his heavenly assemblies. Usually by our own hands will retribution befall us.

My dear unborn, remember that which comes directly from God can never be evil or corrupt, hence there will always be zero correlation between consequences and the spirit that we all possess. Unlike our spirit, our minds and bodies are the two main entities that frequently engage themselves in unfavorable acts. The negative residual effect of the mind and body tries to influence the spirit over a long period of time, but the light of God makes it impossible for it to be tainted by unholy elements. Punishment and consequences are geared toward affecting the body and mind in the eyes of God and not the spirit. People are the only creatures that fail to realize that they cannot mold the spirit, for it does not belong to them and as such cannot be shaped in the form of their likeness at will.

My dear unborn, God does not relish the idea of punishing us. The consequences he has chosen for us are seldom a reflection of his love. Yet, it becomes a necessary evil, for there are those who will constantly abuse his love and mercy in the absence of such disciplinary measures. The consequences he gives are always centered around a learning experience; it is never only about causing discomfort. Consequences teach us what we should and should not do. Remember always that God seldom punishes us for our transgression against him, but only does so when the transgressions are against his children. He is especially quick to react when the children we choose to harm are meek in nature and appear matchless against the tyranny of which men are capable, because unless God has charged you with the responsibility to judge his children, you are not at liberty to punish them.

Lucifer's transgressions against God had gone without consequences for a while, but only when he started to commit transgression against God's children by corrupting them did God respond with fury. But even today, if Lucifer would redeem himself by seeking God's forgiveness, even his transgression would be forgiven. The link between

God and man, the spirit, is very much a part of Lucifer as it is with any of us, and that which is a part of God can never truly be evil. Therefore, even Lucifer is not beyond redemption. People can corrupt their minds and their bodies, but the spirit within all of us is untouchable for there is no such thing as an evil spirit. While arrogance stands in the path of Lucifer with respect to why he would not seek salvation from God, it does not make his spirit evil, only his mind.

My dear unborn, we sometimes find it extremely difficult to forgive others but even more difficult to forgive ourselves. The grace of God makes it possible to always receive forgiveness when asked. Yet for many this forgiveness still leaves a void within their souls, the type of void that no rationalizations are able to fill. Still, whenever possible, atonement can be an avenue that leads to the forgiveness of self, for when one makes atonement for one's sins, the sins of that person are automatically forgiven by the mere gesture of humility.

My dear unborn, if you cannot get forgiveness by making atonement to the one you have wronged, then you must make atonement to God by making an offering involving a commitment to do or engage in some deed in which God will find favor. But remember always that if those whom you have wronged will not accept your forgiveness, you must still forgive them before you will be able to feel and embrace your own humility, thus clearing your path in order for you to be able to forgive yourself. The achievement of forgiveness by the self will become clear when it begins to feel compassion or when the acknowledgment of your own empathy far exceeds the anger and pain of those who have refused your atonement and forgiveness. Do not allow yourself to be stressed or saddened by this refusal, because ultimately once the gesture has been made, the only two other persons from whom forgiveness must be sought are God and yourself. Indeed you and your Higher Power have guaranteed the purification of all transgressions once the refusal of atonement and forgiveness are rejected, simply because the power to forgive one's self rests with God and you alone.

My dear unborn, always seek forgiveness with realistic expectations and with the courage to transcend all manner of ill feelings that will be directed toward you from those you have wronged. You must momentarily allow yourself to be the receptacle for those feelings of wrath, but only to a degree. Harshness must be met with understanding, and the pain of others must not outweigh your willingness to forgive. Remember, those who do not accept your forgiveness are also prisoners of disharmony held in a state of confusion. When you meet them, free them, for by freeing them you would have also freed yourself. Many will refuse to forgive you, for they thrive on the void and bitterness that come with unforgiveness. They have nothing to replace or fill the space that now occupies their poisonous feelings and must depend on these feelings to feel alive, for without them, the reason to exist is an empty one. Hence, they are willing to go to their graves with this bitterness before offering you an olive branch, which is why it is important not to allow yourself to be powerless as a result of one's unforgiving nature. Indeed, seek forgiveness from those whom you have wronged, but never allow them to turn this desire in an act of desperation or guilt on your behalf. Forgiveness can be earned at the price of one's humility, but never at the price of one's dignity.

My dear unborn, in the world you are about to become a part of, it tends to be much easier to live outside the realm of harmony than it is to live within; as such, we behave the way we do, simply because most of us are not at peace with ourselves in addition to not being in harmony with nature and the entities of the universe. Here, the entities of the universe are defined as circumstances that affect our spirits directly or indirectly with respect to keeping it in harmony or disharmony. When the spirit is not at harmony with the self, nature, and the entities of the universe, the mind and body will always be at a disadvantage.

My dear unborn, people live outside the realm of harmony as a habit because they tend to close themselves off to the spiritual cues that operate on the instinctive portion of the mind. They march to the drums of their minds and bodies much more than their spirits. They fail to see that all these entities must function in harmony with one another or that one's protection against the laws of circumstances will not be at an optimum level, and the self as a whole will be left unprotected. In order for the mind, body, and spirit to function as one, they must adjust themselves in order to receive their cues from that part of the mind that seldom operates on the temporal level but serves as a direct channel to and from the spiritual realm. Harmony is seldom reached by taking cues from the elements of this world alone. The roots of this world frequently do not plant themselves in spiritual principles and as such seldom open the doors for anyone who wishes to live their lives under the guidance of divinity. When people live outside the realm of harmony, they are governed by needs and desires. However, when they live within the realm of harmony, they are governed primarily by the sixth sense and the spirit of the Messiah. The key to maintaining harmony in one's life is to do whatever it takes to ensure that the self finds comfort in the direction that the mind, body, and spirit has taken once they are able to function as one.

My dear unborn, people are conditioned day by day to live outside the realm of harmony. No one lives within the realm of harmony without making an effort to do so, a gesture that very few people are willing to make unless some metamorphosis occurs within their lives that compels them to adhere to the "calling." The calling is the avenue that God uses to encourage his disciples to spend time in his presence. It is a driving force that pulls us closer to his holy circle of light in times when we allow ourselves to become too consumed by other worldly distractions.

My dear unborn, living inside the realm of harmony goes well beyond embarking on a spiritual journey. It is an existence perpetuated by righteous and conscious decisions in the presence of adversities and marked by a confrontation of goodness that serves as a shield against evil and self-serving motives. It is a philosophy comprising sacrifice, humility, and a will to travel the path of the Messiah. It embraces the forgiveness of Lucifer and constantly prays for his redemption. But more important, it places emphasis on the reunification of man's soul and God's on a temporal foundation before total harmony can be achieved. This reunification can only be placed on a temporal level when an individual's mind, body, and spirit function in total unison with one another, thus making it possible for God to tap into the energy exerted from all three entities. The energy that is then channeled through the instinctive pathways provides the necessary communicative links between God and man.

My dear unborn, unless a reunification of this nature takes place, an individual's sense of happiness will not only be short-lived but in essence, it will be a pretext—a pretentiousness if you will—for true happiness cannot exist outside the realm of harmony. Therefore, the individual would have been doing a good job with respect to the deception of oneself.

My dear unborn, it is not enough for an individual to exist within the realm of harmony, for if by the grace of God he or she is able to live a life of happiness, deep faith, and contentment—one that has become the embodiment of harmony—it is only the beginning of the journey. The other half of the journey entails the development of spiritual and moral responsibility with respect to helping others. Remember, when we assist others on their journey of life, we inadvertently shape their destinies for a lesser or greater purpose, one that they can only finalize. Helping others live within a realm of harmony is a spiritual and moral responsibility. The first step in leading others on the path to harmony is to take them down a road of self-discovery and introspection in hopes that they too will achieve their goal of spiritual enlightenment. Your words should neither serve to persuade or convince but only to enlighten by allowing them to question and seek answers to that which is confusing and strange to them. Indeed, it is not your duty during this role to give them the answers to philosophical interrogatories, but rather to demonstrate the true art of mindfulness by letting them see the fallacy within their own interpretation of cosmic consciousness, hence challenging their own level of insight with respect to what is already embedded into their psyche through the power of reasoning.

My dear unborn, the power of reasoning that I speak of should not be yours but theirs. Their reasoning will take them to the crossroad of harmony and spiritual enlightenment. Your job is to guide them into seeing that an existence within the realm of harmony is far more meaningful and purposeful than one without. Guide them that they may discover for themselves that spiritual enlightenment not only leads to harmony, but that in order to find happiness and become one with the spirit of the Messiah, both spiritual enlightenment and harmony must coexist and be mutually shared by the self.

My dear unborn, one of the essential ingredients for spiritual enlightenment as well as the development of harmony is self-liberation. The liberation of the self from our own idiosyncrasies frequently makes the road to our spiritual destination less strained. Self-liberation is a major part in seeking harmony. It starts from within and later progresses to a point where it involves dealing with the eradication of external forces that would only serve to stifle the illumination of the self. The liberation of the self involves a protective mechanism designed to render other mechanisms harmless by diffusing its ability or willingness to create harm to others. Self-liberation is the pinnacle of spiritual passive assertiveness. Its protective mechanism, as stated earlier, possesses the ability to disarm without harm, to submit without surrender, and to provide genuine comfort in the absence of compassion or empathy. It is self-growth rooted in paradoxes, yet striving on life's realities while maintaining spiritual homeostasis.

My dear unborn, self-liberation is a constant metamorphosis of the mind, body, and spirit, collectively and independently of one another. Each entity can and does subscribe to its own unique purpose and function but exerts the necessary energy needed to assist the self in achieving its freedom from unwanted forces. For example, an individual may have a relatively great body, mind, and spirit, but barely utilize them on a daily basis. But when placed in a traumatic situation, the individual summons these entities to come together in order to deal or cope with extraordinary circumstances.

My dear unborn, a man who has to convince himself as well as others that he is better or stronger is the weakest of all men, a defect that can be attributed to an inadequate self-liberation, a failure to embrace the qualities necessary to disarm without harm by diffusing one's willingness or ability to create harm. Man's destruction against himself and others always centers around the demons he is unable to repress and the inner visions that force him to see them within the world. He will not extricate himself from this path of destruction unless he is convinced not only that you can see his demons, but the struggle to repress them will become your struggle as well. Therefore, to disarm without harm, you must submit while having no intent to surrender.

My dear unborn, the greatest aspect of self-liberation is knowing that you have the ability to assist another soul escape the demons from within, if only for awhile. The accumulation of life's experiences can weigh heavily on our shoulders, often consisting of a repertoire of wanted and unwanted memories geared to either strengthen or weaken our spirits. The purpose of a liberated self is to teach others how to live a life of contentment by demonstrating through example and without making anyone feel badly for things that they have done in the past. The focal point of this gesture encompasses the art of providing comfort in the absence of compassion or empathy by the liberated self. Pride and arrogance cannot be a part of the equation when the purpose is to assist another on the journey to self-liberation.

My dear unborn, defiance, rejection, and cynicism are characteristics of individuals whom you will attempt to enlighten with respect to self-liberation. Such individuals might test the very limits of your confrontational skills. Indeed, you will encounter provocation that will make you question your very own humility. Still, you must continue boldly in your effort, always keeping in the forefront to render this individual harmless, and by "harming," I mean saying or doing anything verbally or nonverbally that might decrease the chance of this individual's spirit becoming enlightened and liberated. Heighten their awareness about the burden they have placed on themselves. Teach them the fundamental principles of self-liberation in hopes that they will take the necessary steps needed to free themselves. Let them see through your eyes the enormous amount of stress and energy that is spent racing against themselves, a race that ironically enough is also partially responsible for the significant probability of early death that arises from discontent. This race consciously and subconsciously tells them that something is missing from their lives, that they are not doing enough with their lives, ultimately causing them to question their self-worth. This very same race convinces them that their existence must be embodied by an eclectic group of experiences before they get to an age where they can no longer afford to do these things or before death claims them first. Show them the futility of such a race. Remind them that nothing happens before its time. Such is not only the law of God, it is the law of nature. Pleasure from life does not derive from quickness but from awareness.

My dear unborn, the race against one's self can only be terminated when one reaches the realization that the measurement of one's destiny does not fall within the materialistic realm but within the spiritual one. He who has no relationship with the living God has no measuring rod for himself or his destiny. Indeed, a world of experience without God at the center is matchless against one singular spiritual experience with him at the heart of your life. Self-liberation is more than just the liberation of the self from idiosyncrasies that make us inhibited, depressed, and afraid to love. It is a necessary process, for without it the spirit is not able to flow as freely as it should. A liberated self impacts the spirit positively, but an imprisoned one leaves negative residual effects.

THE SECOND MONTH

9

THE SPIRITUAL DEMON

My dear unborn, the spiritual demon is an artist in all manner of evil, sins, and seduction, an entity that feeds off the human spirit only to devour the flesh when it can no longer endure. It is conscious of our weaknesses and as such places great strain on the human spirit that causes the body to surrender in an atmosphere that is the embodiment of social, economical, and geopolitical climate. The spiritual demons strive in these three areas in search of ways to use them against the human spirit. Armed with these three variables and with fear as its counterpart, the demons create desperate situations, making it possible to break the human spirit, unaware that the spirit is untouchable. Still, with illusions and fear, the demons get people to embark on a destructive journey, exhaust them with failures along the way until the spirit is covered with darkness to the point where it is imprisoned. Once imprisoned by darkness the flesh then surrenders, not knowing that there can be deliverance.

My dear unborn, because the human spirit comes directly from God, it is untouchable even to the spiritual demon. Still it is vulnerable to an entity that functions in the spiritual realm, and as such, the spiritual demon is able to imprison it with darkness, the only avenue that avails itself to the spiritual demon, because it lacks the power to destroy or create harm to it directly in any way. Indeed, the spiritual demon serves two main purposes: first, to cloud the human spirit with darkness, thus rendering it useless, and second, to inform Lucifer of the best possible approach to utilize in order to convince an individual that his way is the only reason that makes life worth living.

My dear unborn, the spiritual demon brings darkness to the human spirit by excess or extreme limitations of that which we think we hold dearest to us. That which is in abundance soon loses its significance, and that which is deficient in nature dreads not being able to sustain itself. The spiritual demon will create abundance, often worldly possessions that manifest in many forms, abundance grounded in an emptiness that leaves a void within one's soul, confusion of the mind, and a profound sense of disassociation from any spiritual connections. This abundance may be so overwhelming that it gives one a false sense of security, the type of security that creates the illusion that the world is within the palm of one's hand, an illusion provided by the spiritual demon for a period of time before the emptiness takes over and pulls the individual into the darkness. The darkness usually rides on the shirttail of perversions, the type of perversions that are relative to each individual's primitive forces and further driven and fed by the spiritual demon.

My dear unborn, extreme limitations when plagued by the spiritual demon will illustrate misery and poverty at its worst. When shaped by the spiritual demon, the human eyes behold these things as famine, war, earthquakes, hurricanes, and indifference to human suffering. In the attempt to escape such agony, such darkness, individuals often do things that further cloud their world with darkness. The spiritual demon in these cases does things in order to ensure that the road one has chosen in times of desperation will be the one that leads them further into darkness.

My dear unborn, the spiritual demon has one major advantage over the human spirit. Like the human spirit, it too comes from the spiritual realm and is familiar with all the human spirit's intricacies. The human spirit, however, is untouchable in that it comes directly from God while the spiritual demon sits on the right hand of Lucifer. The spirit cannot be harmed directly and must therefore be rendered helpless indirectly through manipulations and illusions, but the only weapon the human spirit has against the spiritual demon is faith, the type of faith that tests the spiritual demon's patience, one that will outlast its efforts. You see, regardless of what reign of terror befalls an individual from the spiritual demon, no matter how painful or agonizing, the spiritual demon respects and fears faith. Remember, when all else falls, the spiritual demon out of frustration will attempt to extricate your last breath from your body. But even on your deathbed, you must not lose faith, for only then will you obtain the needed victory over the spiritual demon. Your body will be weaker, and like Christ, you will think God has forsaken you, another one of the spiritual demon's illusions. But you must hold steadfast in your faith and confess to the spiritual demon that even in death your love for God will only be strengthened Never, never lose faith regardless of the methods tried by the spiritual demon. Soon, Lucifer will command his right hand of hell to retreat.

My dear unborn, it is paramount to understand the nature of this retreat. The spiritual demons retreat to allow an individual to relax and become complacent both in faith and love for God. With complacency and relaxation of the human spirit comes lack of awareness. During this period of unawareness the spiritual demon will resurface and claim what Lucifer seeks to possess, the human spirit. The sad commentary is that many have turned over their spirit to the spiritual demon unintentionally.

My dear unborn, the spiritual demon, if nothing else, is a master of manipulation. This entity strives on turning free will into his will. Ignorance is the enemy, but I have removed this enemy. Still, if you choose to live your life in a vacuum and question the existence and purpose of the spiritual demon, then you would have already won half the battle for the spiritual demon. Life is a constant struggle, Christ fighting on the side of the living God, and the spiritual demon fighting on the side of Lucifer. As men sit and wait for the antichrist, they inadvertently overlook the spiritual demon who not only is paving the way for Lucifer, but will soon self-actualize into the anti-christ himself, a reward for all the human spirits that he has made amenable to the ways and wishes of Lucifer. When you think of the spiritual demon, think of the antichrist as an unborn spirit being molded in his father's image.

My dear unborn, as you still belong to the spiritual realm, undoubtedly you will encounter the spiritual demon, for his work knows no boundaries and timeless is the measurement by which he has chosen to start his work. Remember, the confrontation is only fire embracing fire, with the one exception that the heat of his flame is matchless against yours. Your flame comes from the holy circle of God and is dim in comparison to that derived from Lucifer. Even in your world, faith is still the best weapon against the spiritual demon. But on the temporal plane he will dazzle individuals with whatever rooms are left unattended in the human spirit. If the rooms of the mind, the body, and the spirit are not filled with love, mercy, forgiveness, compassion, and all the other fruits of God's table, then the spiritual demon will move right in and take up residency, making your very own address his address as well. Indeed, this entity is called the spiritual demon essentially because it is fully aware of how the human spirit functions, including its weaknesses.

My dear unborn, the human spirit is only a small part of this spiritual demon's role. The larger part can be found in the spiritual arena itself where it constantly tries to corrupt those spirits that are on various tasks for the Messiah. This entity camouflages its appearance in order to be seen only as the right hand of Lucifer, not knowing that the heavenly assembly has seen it already for what it is, the antichrist. Do not look for the spiritual demon in the form of a man or any other physical appearance. As the spirit of God conveys its intent through the instinctive channels, the same channel that serves as a link between God and man, the instinctive component also absorbs the messages of the spiritual demon, messages that are designed to impact the spirit of the individual in a way that is contrary to the principles of the living God. These messages then severely alter and distort the perception, reasoning, and consciousness of the individual. Through these means the human spirit is corrupted and eventually imprisoned by darkness.

My dear unborn, the human spirit has another advantage over the spiritual demon—one, however, that cannot be exercised unless the individual lives a lifestyle that involves being a part of the holy circle of light. This advantage is an individual's ability to distinguish incoming messages from the spiritual realm, the ability to be able to decipher the messages that are from God or the heavenly assembly versus messages from the spiritual demon and his legions. In order to be able to hear the voices of the heavenly assembly or the Messiah, one's spirit must be cleansed by the holy circle of light on a regular basis, a task that can be achieved through worship, fellowship, or meditation.

My dear unborn, an individual who clearly notices the channeling of the spiritual demon can choose to disrupt this communication, thus preventing the spirit from being affected. Disruptive methods for this channeling can be prayer, altered state, or covert assertion, a method Christ used quite frequently. One example is "Get behind thee, Satan." Only by disrupting the messages of the spiritual demon can one render him powerless, causing him to retreat. But remember, retreat does not mean giving up, only postponement for a time when you will one day become more vulnerable. This all depends on the choices that one makes regarding the spiritual demon, because there are those who have willingly chosen to listen and welcome the voice. They do this because they have already consciously made up their minds to live a life where Lucifer is at the heart.

My dear unborn, the spiritual demon is particularly attracted to people who are negative in nature. A negative person is defined as one who intentionally or inadvertently blocks positive energy, then attempts to provide amoral or psychological justification for one's conduct. The spiritual demon, while fixated on God's disciples, finds it easier to influence people who already have a dark soul and frequently uses them to assist with his bidding. They serve as a magnet for the spiritual demon, simply because of the essence of their souls. Still, this is not to say that such individuals are doomed forever, but rather more susceptible. Indeed, only by the grace of God can these individuals prevent being used by Lucifer's right-hand demon. There must be a willingness on their part to totally emerge from the darkness both within and outside their soul, yet seldom are these individuals willing to make this small sacrifice, for two reasons: first, sometimes they are not aware of the spiritual demon's presence in their lives, and second, they lack the spiritual foundation that would give them insight with respect to the various circumstances that are usually manipulated by the spiritual demon. Hence, they are unnecessary casualties in the spiritual war.

THE THIRD MONTH

10

FORGIVENESS AND CONSEQUENCES

My dear unborn, one of the greatest myths about God is the idea that where there is forgiveness, there are no consequences. As much as his love knows no bounds, his mercy endless, and his blessings infinite, man will be held accountable for his actions. But the heart of man will dictate the essence of God's forgiveness and consequences. Those who have chosen to use forgiveness as a means to an end with respect to engaging in shabby deeds, then conveniently expecting God's gentleness, will not be disappointed. You will indeed be forgiven, but the measurement of your forgiveness will not dare exceed the embodiment of your consequences. Therefore, remember always the sin you have committed against man or God, for the nature of that sin will set the tone and criteria on which God will be judge you. The consequences you bear will be rooted in the nature of that sin as well. Watch not for the time or the hour of these consequences, for while forgiveness by God is rendered immediately, consequences undoubtedly will be delayed. Forgiveness is God's way of introducing man to redemption and consequences, both built on the foundation of love yet serving to teach man about the error of his ways. God gets angry but never to the point of vindictiveness; his actions only serve to teach and enlighten.

My dear unborn, obtaining forgiveness from God is never an issue, as incredible as it may seem. He has forgiven us for all our sins, no matter how wicked, long before we ask him. Yet, if we are troubled it is only because we have not forgiven ourselves, for getting forgiveness from God is easier than forgiving ourselves. When a void remains in our soul for some deeds that we have done, we must atone for our actions. We must decipher for ourselves how to right the wrongs that we have done, for through atonement the burden will slowly be lifted from our shoulders. Our atonement must not only be genuine, but with it must come the reflection of empathy and great humility, the empathy to embrace the reactions of those we have wronged, many of whom will be quick to anger and slow to forgive. Humility must be the foundation of our strength, a strength that we will need to constantly fight in the struggle to obtain forgiveness or positive acknowledgment from those whose anger flow in our direction. Unless we atone for our deeds, we will be prisoners of our action, but even more importantly, we would not have provided the opportunity for those we have wronged to escape the prison they are in. Remember that atonement may bring us peace of mind, but it will set free as well those we have wronged. For this reason we must be bathed in humility so we will remain strong in the face of anger and defiance.

My dear unborn, when anger and suffering leave no room for forgiveness from those whom we have wronged, we must not have a heavy heart. The ability to forgive is not within all men. Therefore, choose not to wallow in self-pity or guilt when your effort is proven futile in the attempts to right your wrongs. As long as you have tried, seek comfort in knowing that God loves you and demands that you forgive yourself. Man's reluctance to forgive the transgressions of others stems from his existence being empty and meaningless without them. He would much rather be a prisoner of these transgressions than to free himself or his enemy. Hence, free yourself and let him remain in the prison of his own making. Indeed, while God engages in handing out consequences, his justice is not without limits and neither will he allow you to be punished forever.

My dear unborn, the unwillingness to forgive another is indicative of toxic elements embedded deep within one's soul. Like a cancer, it will grow unless it is rooted out by faith and spiritualism. Remember that the judgment you have cast on someone will be the exact criteria used by Jehovah to judge you. Each man controls the extent of his own judgment, simply by demonstrating to God the judgment he has cast on others. As the Messiah said, "Forgive and you will be forgiven. Judge and you will be judged." Human frailties and idiosyncrasies are no excuse for behaving in an inhumane manner toward one another. Such rationalizations will not be a factor in God's judgment against man. The spirit should not be a follower of the body; quite the contrary, and as such, man will be judged accordingly. The mind, body, and spirit must function as one, or they must be aligned in a fashion that allows the self to express its true representation.

My dear unborn, the closer man gets to God, the less he will need forgiveness or consequences. Man's relationship with God is frequently strained not only by his propensities to sin but also by the high esteem in which he holds God. Indeed, God above all should be held in the highest regard, yet by all accounts not to the extent that it strains the effort to be close to him. The more unique and dissimilar man's view is of God, the more unlikely man will be able to establish a relationship based on trust and love. Trust and love come more easily and naturally when the parties involved are perceived to have more in common or a clear pattern of characteristics on which mutual respect can be based. To reiterate a point once made, love without respect is like a flower without water; soon it will fade away and die. Therefore, we need to earn God's respect before attempting to become worthy of his love. Man already has God's love and respect; the question is whether or not man has what it takes to become worthy. A nurturing bond between man and God can further be strengthened by coming to the realization that some of the essential elements that make us human are the very same elements that came from God. The more man's perception of God is one of similarity, the greater the chance of developing a bond where closeness is not an issue. When God is placed too high on a pedestal, it is more difficult for man psychologically and spiritually to even fathom the idea of any real closeness. Indeed, it is to our advantage that we focus on the attributes and qualities that we have in common with God versus the ones that are obviously not even within the realm of possibility. Building a relationship with God is like building a relationship with any other. First, one looks for the attributes of similarities, then makes a commitment to use the opposite or different characteristics in a manner that will produce the same effect as those attributes that are similar. Some individuals might think that they have little or nothing in common with God. He is up there and we are down here, so what could they possibly have in common with him, they ask. This type of negative thinking only suggests that such an individual must first have faith in one's self before attempting to have faith in God or anyone else. So, the degree of closeness one acquires with God totally depends on that individual.

My dear unborn, one's relationship with God still does not absolve one from being held accountable for his/her actions. The extent of one's forgiveness or consequences are not contingent on how much we are loved and respected by God. God's justice does not discriminate; he renders it equally and unconditionally. Although God's distribution of justice is fair, having a relationship with God as opposed to one who does not signifies the degree of disappointment that God feels when that person transgresses against him. The hurt of God is not without pain when his children fail to live up to their given potentials. Consequences are not handed out by God in a cheerful manner, but rather in sadness and hope that the justice he renders will be the only one given. Yet, he knows that as long as man continues to stay away from the holy circle of light, man will undoubtedly remain vulnerable to the manipulation of his opponent, Lucifer. Remember always that God does not relish handing out forgiveness or consequences. When man seeks forgiveness, it is usually an indication that some transgression has been committed, and while God knows that man is far from being perfect, he would much rather not deal with these transgressions. Man's faith is the empowering fuel that can evoke the Almighty at all times. Once he has been called on for assistance, rest assured that it is only a matter of time before an answer is given. However, sometimes the answer is no. God's assistance of others is based on the "infinity syndrome."

My dear unborn, the infinity syndrome states that your needs, prayers, or that which is asked of God will be answered depending on the urgency of the problem in relation to the entire population in the world in which one lives. Further, because God is infinite in wisdom and existence, the assistance given to any individual is done in an orderly fashion with respect to one's suffering and how long he or she will remain alive. Therefore, in addition to your problem, the length of your life is compared to your fellow men before responding to your request. The infinity syndrome also entails bringing man to a level of awareness where he is able to ask, "Is there someone's problem that deserves priority over mine; am I truly the worst of the worst at this moment?" Individuals who are still struggling to fulfill God's criteria for his kingdom are given more priority in terms of their issues versus those who have already met the criteria. According to the infinity syndrome, the issues of these individuals who have met the criteria for his kingdom can wait. Even if death should claim them, then they are still at a greater advantage over those who have yet to meet the criteria. Indeed one may ask why God does not help each individual all at once, but everything about God does not involve a miracle, although many would like to believe this.

My dear unborn, God is here for you!

THE THIRD MONTH

11

THE DARK SOULS

My dear unborn, be aware of those who claim your soul in the name of God on the one hand and your worldly possessions with the next. If salvation could be bought, no man would be able to afford it, for how could one possibly put a price on the sacrifice of God's only son? Yet, there are those who will attempt to associate salvation with the amount of money you have contributed to the church, soon to equate your worth and value in the eyes of God based on your tithing or offerings. When the measurement of your faith is seen in terms of what you can and cannot give by those who bring you the words of God, your duty becomes rejecting these individuals with such dark souls.

My dear unborn, people with dark souls are those who have already made a conscious decision to disconnect themselves from God and all that is righteous in order to do what they feel is necessary, or what they think will ensure the reaching of their given misguided goals. It should be noted that these people do believe in the existence of a living God as well as embrace the notion of a hell and a heaven. The darkness of their souls are so cloaked in unrighteousness, however, that their fears and reverence for God is at the bottom of their list of priorities. Instead the breaking and manipulations of both God and man's rules are at the top of their list. These individuals have little or no conscience and seldom engage in reflection or introspection simply because they need to maintain their sense of stoicism as opposed to constantly being reminded of who and what they are. Ironically, they are frequently seen by their friends and relatives as warm and kind individuals who appear to have strong religious principles and convictions. They are perceived as people who can do no wrong and further feed the pretext by openly making contributions to charitable events and being strong proponents for moral and social issues, a believable disguise that fools many. In most cases, they are well versed in the scriptures, but you must remember always that even Lucifer can speak the words of God but he can never walk in the footsteps of the Messiah. When a caterpillar refuses to change into a butterfly, it is usually for a good reason, and those with dark souls cannot hide their true nature forever.

My dear unborn, when you are confronted by an individual with a dark soul, one who seeks to take advantage of you in spite of your kindness, one whose manipulation is crystal clear even before his feeble attempts begin, embrace him with compassion and remember that such an individual is not beyond redemption. But if he is, it is only because he has chosen that path. By this I mean he has consciously made the decision to forsake all avenues that might at least introduce him to the love and grace of God. Yet with commitment and love, a truly enlightened individual may be able to show this dark soul one of the many doors that will lead him to redemption. Even a traumatic experience can play a role in bringing a dark soul to the realization that the path he or she is on is indeed the wrong one. Also, an experience relevant to some great epiphany about life, human nature, or God can remove the darkness from their souls—a darkness that clouded their souls not by chance but by intentional steps taken by them over a period of time by systematically engaging in certain actions that drove them further away from God. Once a dark soul is converted to the path of light, he or she seldom reverts to the old ways. However, the journey to this destination can be long and hard, and the experience itself is usually so dramatic that the conversion has a long-lasting impact.

My dear unborn, there is another type of dark soul who is truly lost. These individuals do not believe in God or anything beyond this world. Such individuals simply believe that man's existence is limited to the time they spend in this world, hence life stops forever, thus returning to nothingness. Indeed, they do not believe that man has a soul that will one day be judged by a Supreme Being. This type of dark soul, realizing that there are no consequences for his or her action with respect to hell or heaven, except that which is provided by man in this world, lives a life with no purpose except to dominate through destruction and self-serving interests. He or she has a tendency to engage in self-destructive behavior, even though he or she seldom realizes this flaw within their nature. Survival of the fittest, or only the strong should survive, is a code by which such people live. This dark soul is a danger to self as well as others—frequently a menace to society as a whole—because he or she lacks happiness and must fill the void with the misery of others.

My dear unborn, unlike some of the other dark souls, this type cannot be changed through some great epiphany because the defense mechanisms that are used to keep their cognitions from a path of reason are too embedded within their psyche. Rationalizations and intellectualizations create a level of toxicity that keeps their cognitions rooted in darkness. Anything that happens to change the individual's life, no matter how traumatic, is simply explained away using his or her own distorted and irrational views. This type of dark soul is not beyond redemption because the idea of salvation is foreign to him or her, but rather because he or she has chosen not to accept it because he or she does not believe in anything but themselves. Indeed, one would think that through some form of association, a dark soul of this nature might somehow gain some knowledge that in turn would give him or her the necessary insight needed to resurrect his or her soul from darkness. The problem is, however, that such an individual associates with other individuals whose souls are as dark or even darker, and therefore has a tendency to view as a threat individuals who could possibly create a change in him or her. Once the threat is perceived, steps are taken to disassociate himself or herself immediately, sometimes to the extreme with respect to the initiation of some harmful impact on the person's life.

My dear unborn, when confronted by a dark soul of this kind, one has two choices. First, attempt to change the dark soul by appealing to reason and sense of humanity, an effort that will turn out to be an exercise in futility. The effort is futile because of the strength of defense mechanisms that serve as a protector or shield against unwanted knowledge contrary to what he or she uses to feed the darkness within the soul. Second, one can create an illumination of self through a metamorphosis that is built on faith and illusions. When I speak of the illumination of the self through a metamorphosis that is built on a foundation of faith and illusions, I mean one has to make a conscious commitment to ignite cues that will arouse repressed emotions within the dark soul of which the dark soul is not aware. A bold and dangerous gesture may even lead to your death if certain precautions are not taken, yet is a necessity in order to bring about the desired response from the dark soul. The steps taken on your path must involve faith, because without the strength of your faith you can easily be convinced or swayed into taking on the characteristics of the dark soul. In short, the dark soul may convert you as opposed to you converting him or her. The second variable is illusion. To get close to such a dark soul, you must appear to be something that you are not, because if the dark soul perceives you as someone who is enlightened, your association with the individual will be short-lived. Hence, you will not be able to create the desired change as planned, for he or she will avoid you at all costs, even if it means your own death. Your own life will become an issue if the dark soul developed an attachment to you and is now feeling betrayed because he thinks you have led him to believe that you are something that you are not. However, if he or she thinks that the betrayal is caused largely in part because he has gone out of his way to perceive you in a certain manner, then the dark soul will begin to doubt the extent of your role in the misrepresentation. In short, if there are questions in his own mind as to whether or not emphasis was placed on you deliberately betraying him, then the relationship will end in only anger as opposed to the need on the dark soul's behalf to take some drastic punitive measure.

My dear unborn, the dark soul must see the illumination of self, yourself, from his perspective. Your behavior must complement or exceed his. Therefore he must perceive your soul to be just as dark or even darker. The dark soul's cognitive distortion will quickly embrace your misrepresentation. However, as stated earlier, a strong faith is needed because the illusion you created for his purpose can easily become real to you as well. Then he would have won, for both souls would now be sharing the same path, the wrong path. The dark soul must be allowed to see a part of himself in you, a part of the illusion he must be convinced exists. Indeed, this is essential to the potential transformation that might occur within the dark soul. As he continues to see himself in you and you are convinced that this is the case, then slowly the illusion of what he sees begins to disintegrate while at the same time nurturing your bond with this individual.

My dear unborn, this process must be slow so as not to alert the individual to the pretext of the metamorphosis. Remember, the more this individual identifies with you, which is a central piece of the illusion, the more he is inclined to be dramatically impacted by the transformation. The goal is to initiate subtle changes within the individual so they may one day question the logic of their own existence. Once this chain of thinking begins, self-doubt will follow and part of the individual's psyche will embrace the transformation. Indeed, with transformation, the path to redemption is more likely. The dark soul will soon find himself making noticeable changes with respect to taking on the characteristic with the enlightened person. Soon, one hopes, that the dark soul will emerge from darkness and join in the quest for spiritual enlightenment.

The Third Month

12

The Beast Within—Is God Responsible?

My dear unborn, sadly to say it is true that the birth of anger sometimes comes with having been born. There are those whose entire life is devoted to being angry with God for allowing them to have been born in this world. Indeed, God did create man but the hardship and the unfairness of this world are by-products of man and not God, and to nurture such anger will only serve to create a sickness of the soul. When the mind or body is sick, then man's action can clearly be attributed to a category of behavior that can be termed as maladaptive or imperfect. But when the soul is sick, the manifestation of behavior comes out as pure evil, man's imperfections to an extreme.

My dear unborn, the disharmony of life is also caused by those who occasionally are discontented with their places in the universal order of things. For some individuals, the world will never be a place where they can become one with the entities of the universe. In short, no matter how hard they try they will never be able to fit in, thus developing a place of belonging. Once an individual realizes that no matter how hard he tries he will never be able to fit in or be able to establish a suitable niche, then the cues of the subconscious displacement reaction begin to transform themselves into overt resentment toward man and society. When man's effort to establish a state of belonging within himself and within society has failed, learned helplessness soon sets in and the strength to continue the struggle of being one with self and the entities of the universe ceases. Not long thereafter, such an individual's association with others will become toxic, passing on to others the negative energy he possesses. During this interaction with others, discontentment is passed from one individual to the next, and the openness that is needed to accept God is suddenly closed, filled up with the beast within: anger. The anger derives from the sad truth that for some people this world will never be the right place for them.

My dear unborn, for these individuals, the anger toward God is further compounded by the realizations that they did not have a choice with respect to being born. They feel betrayed by God and argue that the notion of free will is tainted by the very premise on which it is founded, the idea that each individual can choose for himself/herself the state of existence and the path of destiny. Free will and the choice of whether or not to be born should have the same birthplace in common, but they do not. Man obtains free will only after he is born, and as such this further perpetuates the anger that stems from the feelings of inadequacy because of the perceived lack of control he has over his existence.

My dear unborn, the concept of free will was conceived on a false foundation, if indeed it involves the omission of the right to be born at the time it was presented to man. If God denied man the opportunity to choose whether or not he would like to come into existence, then I submit to all those who believe in free will that the very premise on which it was formed is false. Hence, like fruit from the poisonous tree, its entire foundational principle then become an illusion. But did God deceive man by refusing to extend free will by giving man the opportunity to choose for himself whether or not he would like to be born?

My dear unborn, one of the greatest errors man has made is the fact that he thinks that God has robbed him of the opportunity to decide for himself whether or not he would like to be born. By holding on to this false premise, man has the necessary fuel to feed his anger, no matter how misguided it might be. Indeed, free will was not born after man came into existence but before. The fact that man has no recollection of his conversation with God before he was born does permit allowances for his unfounded rationale about the conception of free will. If anything, our anger should be geared toward God for not allowing us to remember our experiences with him prior to our birth—for example, his majestic presence, his face, and the indescribable part of his kingdom where all souls are allowed to play and share in the joy of having been created by him.

My dear unborn, most men wonder if they will ever be able to see God, failing to realize that they have already seen him. The question, however, should be whether they will be worthy to see him again. Having been born into a sinful world and having the soul tainted through our deeds by engaging in all types of questionable behaviors legitimize man's concern about seeing God again. God did not create the soul of man with a mask over his head or with a blindfold on man's eyes during the process. God did not obtain the love he has for us simply by willing it to be so. No! He learned to nurture the love through interactions and admiration long before we came into this world, so when we arrived it was easy to continue loving us. Although it was extremely difficult, God's love nurtured by the memory he has of man prior to man's birth gave him the strength to ask his only son to die for us so we may live.

My dear unborn, the transformation from the soul of God to the soul of man, the transition from God's realm to the realm of man, could not have been accomplished without the free will that is still being embraced by humanity today. Indeed, man was an active participant with respect to the choice or decision to be born into this world. The truth be told, the only two people who did not have a choice and were arbitrarily created were Adam and Eve. Man might not have known what lay ahead, and thus the decision to exist was not based on informed consent. Nevertheless, no man can blame God or his parents legitimately for having been born.

My dear unborn, our lives are sometimes governed by the philosophy that what does not exist in the mind does not exist at all. Another fictional finalism that has often led to dogmatic gestures by man is that unless it can be verified by the five senses, the reality of it is questionable. No wonder the Supreme Being pauses before releasing some memories from man's recollections. The anger toward God for having been born is therefore misplaced because the choice of whether or not to be born also rested on man's shoulders. God is not responsible for this perceived transgression regardless of the aftermath of man's birth; indeed, man must take some responsibility for the molding of his destiny. The aftermath of man's birth, no matter how difficult, cannot be attributed to God. Once a man develops self-awareness, he must set in motion the variables that will clear the path to his destiny, the first being reestablishing a relationship with God and the Messiah.

My dear unborn man is confused about the nature of his anger toward God. Being born is not the primary source of his anger, but rather the aftermath of his birth: the experiences that he must confront as part of the human race on a day-to-day basis, the people he is sometimes forced to associate with, and the sacrifices and compromises he must sometimes make in spite of his principles and virtues. These are really the driving forces behind his anger—not life, the gift from God, or the idea of being born, but the world itself.

My dear unborn, man gets angry with God for the simple reason that he has the power to change the suffering that they endure and frequently cannot comprehend why a God with all his power and love can still stand by and allow man's anger to continue. In man's suffering, he is not able to philosophize, for one who is starving does not ask where the bread is coming from that is about to stop his hunger. But when his belly is full, he can then see clearly all the rules that were violated in an attempt to quench his hunger. Indeed, for those whose lives are filled with promise and success, yet fail to remain conscious of the plight of humanity, the question may never be asked. But for those whose lives are less fortunate, the question must be answered, and when it is not, the suffering they feel is compounded by rage.

My dear unborn, you can live twice in a lifetime and still not receive the answer from God concerning life's issues and concerns. The unraveling of the mystery of life must begin with the belief that the Creator of life itself is worthy of reverence, the type of reverence where trust and love are at the very heart of its foundation. Once this is established, then the question one has to ask is more important than the answer one needs to receive. The premise of true faith is not accepting only that which can be confirmed by one or more of the five senses, but rather the strength of one's willingness to believe in the absence of confirmation.

My dear unborn, the frequent lack of response by God to man's many questions does not stem from lack of respect for man or from the notion that man is undeserving of an answer, but from the notion that God is deserving of our respect, love, and faith. Once these things are given to God from our hearts, then on our faith alone it becomes unnecessary to offer an explanation as to why certain things are permitted to happen in the world in which we live. In most cases, as children we trust our parents to provide the type of environment which will ensure that we are given the opportunity to grow up strong, safe, and to our full potential. Seldom do we as children question the method in which it is accomplished, and in the event we should, it is seen as a sign of disrespect. Why then should our Heavenly Father feel the need to justify his methods for the universal order of things? When questions are based on a more personal level with respect to one's own life, the determination for a response from God is based on one's personal relationship with him as well as the strength of one's faith and the essence of it.

My dear unborn, if your faith is like a handkerchief and God fails to reply to your question, then the problem is yours not his. By this I mean, for example, that the only time you hear from some relatives or friends is when they need something from you. Usually it is money, yet when these same individuals are having a period of "good harvesting," they become invisible until when the time of "bad harvesting" sets in again. This type of behavior can lead to resentment. If and when you use God in this manner, then your faith is indeed like a handkerchief. God is at your disposal only when it suits you, and for this reason alone the answers you seek from God makes you unworthy to receive them.

My dear unborn, as human beings we must participate in each stage of our lives, one stage at a time. Our lives are seen by us one fragment at a time. We lack knowledge of the entire scale on which our lives are measured; we do not know how one stage in our lives will affect the next. But since God, on the other hand, can see the entire global picture with regards to our lives, he knows how each stage will affect the other. When we seek help from God based on our knowledge or limited experience of the one fragmented piece of our lives that we are presently experiencing at the time, totally unaware of how it is about to impact the future stages, then it is not prudent on God's part to grant us our wish when indeed he knows how the consequences of that wish will affect the rest of the other stages. A good father protects us even if it means protecting us from ourselves. So, in the event your prayer is not answered, do not question why, but rather give thanks to God who can see the larger scale on which your life is being measured, and thank him for his wisdom. This is the embodiment of a strong faith.

My dear unborn, I cannot afford the luxury of being angry with God when the very air that I breathe comes from him. My love for God is greater than my capacity for anger. Yet with all the suffering I have seen, I mourn for the weak and endure sleepless nights contemplating on the difference my existence can or cannot make, and when the burden becomes too heavy my faith sustains me. When I am at the end of my rope, thinking my load is too heavy, the death of the Messiah revives me, for I will not allow his death to be for nothing. When you cast your faith aside because your burden is unbearable, you have allowed the death of the Messiah to be in vain, and for me this is not an option.

My dear unborn, fear and lack of faith are the primary factors that are at the heart of man's inability to harness spiritual fulfillment from himself and from God. Man fails to realize that lack of happiness is frequently a result of the spiritual and psychological voids within himself, voids that can only be filled by coming to terms with the internal forces that are barriers to the psychological foundation of the self as well as being able to nurture a relationship between himself and God. Both tenets, fear and lack of faith, serve as a premise for this inability to obtain fulfillment for the self. Indeed, unless these voids are filled, the beast within will always be the dominant influence that governs one's life. Man is not as angry with God for being born as much as he is terrified of not being able to satisfactorily develop a sense of belonging in the world in which he lives. He often finds himself being drowned in a pool of insecurities and uncertainties relevant to his very existence while putting forth a persona for the world to embrace, a persona that can quickly be shattered by an introspection that ultimately will reveal the nature of the defense mechanisms that are used to reduce his fears. But such an introspection will seldom take place because these defense mechanisms are relied on so strongly by the individual in order to be able to live a continuous, shallow, and superficial existence, one where self-truth or discovery is not an option, for his rebirth has yet to take place.

My dear unborn, each man experiences two births before his physical death, a spiritual birth and a physical birth. The spiritual birth came about when man was allowed by God to be separated from the holy circle of light. The holy circle of light is the realm from which each soul at one point or another belonged. It is holy because the light itself illuminates directly from God. The very same energy that can be founded within all man is the essence of the soul. This energy from God is then transitioned into the woman's womb where man is allowed to experience a second birth, the physical birth. Here, this energy from God, now in the form of a man, is allowed to take on a body. Upon self-awareness, man must once again re-pledge his commitment to this spiritual birth and be born again, a commitment that is carried out through baptism, confirmation, or another method. Regardless of what ritual is used, the commitment to this spiritual birth must be validated by self-awareness. This validation is a by-product of free will. Here, man must consciously decide for himself if he will, indeed, embrace the concept of faith and the principles on which each respective one is based, but the opportunity dictates that each individual makes this decision for himself or herself. After all, no one can secure salvation for another no matter how noble the effort.

My dear unborn, it is important to do what is necessary to safeguard all aspects of the mind and body, but it is even more essential to do what is necessary to protect your spirit. Remember always that whatever the mind and body are exposed to eventually leaves a residual effect on the spirit. For this reason it is paramount that each of these respective entities be allowed to transform themselves through spiritual, psychological, and physical hibernation occasionally. Each entity will have the chance to metamorphose and ultimately transcend their superficial attributes, which are usually earthbound. Unlike the Messiah, we all cannot take off forty days and forty nights into the wilderness, but nevertheless it is paramount that we find some time to remove ourselves from the everyday pitfalls of life, hence securing a time to retreat and regroup spiritually, psychologically, and physically. Indeed, happiness is the absence of any spiritual or psychological voids within one's soul and the inability to feel complete because of these voids. The psychological void stems from some form of deficiency of the mind and body, and the spiritual void stems from a deficiency in one's relationship with God. The deficiencies are relative in each person, but unless one finds out what they are and embraces them, they will influence the rest of that person's life forever and serve as a feeding frenzy for the beast within.

The Fourth Month

13

Beyond Redemption

My dear unborn, it has been said that the greatest trick the devil has ever played on the world is to convince the world that he does not exist. But now that we know that he does, he would have you believe that if you are a child of Lucifer, then you are beyond redemption and as such you should ascribe only to his philosophy of life, one that embraces darkness and denounces the holy circle of light. But as the Messiah has demonstrated, contrary to what Lucifer has said, mankind is not beyond redemption. The irony is that neither is Lucifer himself beyond redemption, even though he spent a great deal of effort trying to persuade some of God's children that salvation and redemption are not within their reach. God forgives all, such is his love, and even Lucifer does not fall outside the boundaries of this love. The first step to redemption is always openness, and those who find it difficult to walk through have yet to experience the love of God. All the guilt, inadequacies, and emotional turmoil that are keeping your soul captive will magnify tenfold if the distance between you and the love of God cannot be measured. But if the closeness leaves no space between you and his love, your burden becomes his burden and soon your entire load will become lighter.

My dear unborn, seeking freedom for your soul is not as impossible as one may think. All it takes is a commitment, not even to love God but rather to allow him to love you. Once you have opened yourself up to God's love, then he will allow you to see through his eyes that the redemption you seek is only an arm's length away. The only thing he asks is for you to reach out that he may pull you within his bosom. Do not blame Lucifer for the distance between you and God's love, for he only supplies the partition or the wedge and can do no more unless you give him the power to do so. The decision to use that wedge to create a distance between you and God's love is a matter of choice. Lucifer supplies the tools for man's transgressions only because he is confident that man will use them. But God's love bears testimony to the truth that constantly serves as an obstacle for what Lucifer would like to see you do with the life that God has given you. God's love bears testimony to the truth that he allowed his son to die that you may live, and if you choose to live in him, you too will never die. Indeed, he's speaking not of the flesh but of the spirit.

My dear unborn, do not allow anyone, including yourself, to be convinced that you are beyond redemption, no matter how atrocious the sins you have committed. For to reiterate a simple truth, no man is beyond redemption. Man's inability to forgive himself should not be displaced unto God. Even in hell the path to salvation is still clear and obtainable. My eyes behold an angel of fire, her body gives off no heat, yet possesses a burning flame that can barely be tolerated by the naked eyes. Her hair is red like a stream of blood producing a picturesque against the fiery sky that troubles the mind, yet comforts the spirit. Filled with the power of the Holy Ghost, her eyes soothe the confused hearts as she directs the lost souls to the path of salvation from hell. Breathing a sigh of relief, the spirits hurry toward the Messiah whose bosom welcomes these once-lost entities back to a state of grace.

My dear unborn, her beauty is beyond compare, yet pray that she does not consume you with her hugs, for the quest for redemption will cease to exist even in hell. But embrace her smile, and the directions of her eyes will send you in the arms of the Messiah. Behold, my beloved, for the keeper of the gates of hell is not a member of Lucifer's flock, but an angel of fire sent by God.

My dear unborn, she will facilitate the ultimate and final test designed to tap into the darkest region of man's consciousness, a test that will decide where your soul is spent forever. The passing of this test will send you straight to the kingdom of God, while its failure will leave you only two choices. The first is to relinquish your soul forever into a permanent sense of nothingness, a dying tree with no roots. The second choice is to reemerge in this world once again in hopes that you become worthy to rejoin the heavenly family of the living God. Oblivion or redemption through reincarnation—indeed, free will grants man a safe passage to these choices. Either way, the choices that have been made will not be questioned and will be respected by the heavenly assemblies. In the end, our destiny is in our own hands. Yet a man who fails to seek redemption in this world will be given a second chance in the next. The angel of fire lives in hell for this reason: to provide a final opportunity for man to save himself and prove once and for all that he is not beyond redemption.

My dear unborn, my vision tells of a second chance at redemption, one that was given in a lonely place called hell. Though this notion goes against all religious doctrines, it tells of the greatness of God's love, a love so great that the death of his Son was not enough, and provisions were made that a deserving soul might redeem itself even in that lonely place called hell.

My dear unborn, bad things happen to people for several reasons. One, because some of these people are not in sync with the laws of circumstances as mentioned in earlier chapters. Two, because it is often a fulfillment of a promise made by God—divine retaliation or retribution, if you will—that stems from pouring vengeance on those who have severely transgressed against his children and have somehow forgotten their deeds. This also holds true for some people who are considered to be good people, for even good people sometimes break the laws of God and inadvertently do things for which consequences are necessary. Vengeance by God is not based on vindictiveness or spite, or geared toward disrupting and uprooting one's life for negative deeds. Rather, vengeance is based on delayed consequences embodied by forgiveness and love. Indeed, the hurt one feels from God's consequences always possesses a learning experience from which one can develop wisdom and strength.

My dear unborn, there is also another harsh reality as to why bad things happen to people. It usually has nothing to do with God, but rather one's lack of awareness and ignorance that is frequently rooted in the heart of one's own stupidity. This reasoning may seem aloof, yet nevertheless it is a fact that many are afraid to embrace because of the compassion and emotions that usually follows the misfortunes of others, regardless of the causative factors. In some cases when these misfortunes occur, it is hypocrisy not to call the scenario that triggers the entire circumstance what it really is, in order to spare the feelings of others. It is plain stupidity. The cloaking of the truth by civility and rationalizations only serves to feed one's own hypocrisy, the type of hypocrisy that will avail itself when others who have seen the very same type of behaviors are compelled to inform the individual in question of his or her flaws.

My dear unborn, self-liberation must first be accompanied by the recognition of all that is wrong with the self. Without this recognition, purging, which is a necessary process, will not occur to the degree that is needed to rid oneself of all the human toxicity and inadequacies that have to be extricated before the self can be truly free. The key principle behind this type of recognition is pure, raw honesty, the type of honesty that comes not only with oneself but also with others, for self-liberation cannot exist within a vacuum. Many people spend half their lives trying to fool themselves and the other half trying to fool others. By fooling I mean lacking the courage and honesty to tell oneself and others of the truthfulness that is called for at a given time. People have become so wrapped up in trying to spare themselves and others' feelings that the truth is seldom ever a part of the equation anymore. Indeed, they are conditioned to place pure, raw honesty secondary to all things. The modification of the truth has made it possible for them to live with themselves, so instead of pure, raw honesty, one gets a slightly tainted version that makes it more amenable for human acceptance. What is not seen is that the modified version of one's pure, raw honesty ultimately gives birth to the type of self-liberation that, in essence, lacks certain realities. Unless self-liberation embraces the truth with respect to complete honesty, the harmony achieved by the self will be short-lived.

The Fourth Month

14

Religious Arrogance

My dear unborn, as I have told you before, if perfection were a criteria to enter the kingdom of God, then all men would dwell in hell forever. Therefore, trouble not yourself about the lack of righteousness on your part. The sins of your father combined with that of your mother are not enough to cast a stain on your chances to enter God's kingdom. Man's sins pale in comparison to the weight of his arrogance. Hence it is not sin that will keep man from God's resting place, but arrogance.

My dear unborn, religious arrogance is one of the essential disobediences that is responsible for man's fall from grace. This type of arrogance attempts to create a division between the Son of Man and his Father, a philosophical ideology that recognizes the living God with no tribute or reference to the Son. What logic is there for a man to live his entire life in an unselfish manner, always practicing deeds that serve only to epitomize the love for his fellow men, then gladly lay down his life in a horrific manner so that man may continue to find a passage to the Creator, if indeed his claim to be the Son of the living God was not the truth? It has been said that a man will die for what he believes to be true, but seldom, if ever, will he die for something he thought to be false or untrue.

My dear unborn, there can be no profound thinking behind the thought process that embraces the notion that one can offer a reasonable explanation for the existence of Christ, except for the one that was given by Christ himself. Yet, we are living in a world where there are those who accept the reality that Christ did exist and even go as far in their thinking that it is quite possible that he did some of those amazing miracles that were documented, but still refuse to entertain the fact that he was the Son of God. But where does this refusal stem from? It stems from religious arrogance and religious conditioning. Long before the coming of Christ, the Jewish people's main focus was God. Their faith and worship were centered only around God, the one and only true God. Those who were committed were devoted to God and he alone. The teachings, commandments, and principles that governed their lives came from God and no one else. Prophets and messengers of God have always made it clear that all that was relayed to them had come from this one God to whom all is responsible and should be obeyed. This was, indeed, the wish of God. So, for centuries the Jewish people were conditioned to believe and had faith based on their relationship with the almighty God himself. He was all they knew and had. Their entire existence was centered around him, as it should have been.

My dear unborn, soon the prophets started to forecast the coming of the Christ, the living, breathing Son of the almighty God. The prophets and messengers of God started to recondition the Jewish people to the idea that soon they would have to adapt and adjust to a new manner in which they have been worshiping God. In short, a new change of command was being implemented in their spiritual rituals, the ritual being accepting and going through this coming Christ in order to obtain salvation through God's wonderful grace.

My dear unborn, the analogy can be made that it is like working for a big company, where at one time you could, as an employee, walk in and talk directly to the CEO, but after a change in the policy, you would now have to go through perhaps a vice president or a specific person designated to serve as a liaison. Things are still the same in the company. It is just that the new policy now requires that you go through another person before actually seeing the CEO. Well, if you are an employee who refuses to comply by adapting and adjusting to the new changes in the policy that require you to go through this designated person before getting to the CEO, then your complaints or concerns will never be addressed and ultimately you may even lose your position in the company.

My dear unborn, I mention this analogy because the Jewish people are like this employee who refuses to adhere to the changes in the policy, by refusing to accept Christ. Not only will their concerns not be heard, but they run the risk of losing their salvation all together. Christ said, "He that denieth me before men, him shall I deny before my Father." He later said, "I am the way, the truth and the life. No man cometh unto the Father but by me." Making it clear that like that designated person in the company, you must see him before you can see God, I do not know whether this lack of willingness to accept Christ is because of arrogance or a misguided faith; no one can or should fudge. Sometimes, however, I wonder if the Jewish people do not realize that God has the right to alter any spiritual ritual, principle, or belief that has to do with getting into his kingdom. People sometimes forget that just as we can decide who lives in our own house as relatives or guests, that it is also within God's discretion, a discretion that was turned over to Jesus, to decide who should or should not live within his house forever. Many great men, Gandhi, Buddha, and even Christ, have had to change their minds on certain issues after realizing that they had inadvertently taken a crooked path. It takes more courage to go against the majority than it does to conform with them.

My dear unborn, regardless of your status in life and what others may think, your innate right as a human being is to decide for yourself what does or does not make sense with respect to your spiritual edification. Indeed, it is unwise to jeopardize an eternal resting place for your soul because traditions dictate that you remain on the same path even when that path is questionable. God gave man free will not that it may be manipulated by guilt or blind faith triggered by those who are locked in the past. While it is noble to follow the footsteps of mothers and fathers and a generation who have practiced the same faith, remember that the only footsteps that matter on the journey to the truth, the truth being Christ, are yours.

My dear unborn, man will be judged by God as an individual entity and not collectively with significant others. Therefore no individuals should allow relatives or friends to influence them to the point where their soul becomes endangered for failing to accept a religious or spiritual truth or premise. Although most of us were conditioned as children to believe in a specific religious ideology, it becomes our duty and responsibility to reassess and reexamine the philosophy of this religious ideology in adulthood. The conclusions of this evaluation must involve a commitment to change the belief system one has if it does not offer truth or spiritual fulfillment. This change will take great courage on an individual's part because it may involve going against a generation of beliefs in addition to losing the approval of significant others. Yet, this result pales in comparison when one thinks of what is at stake with respect to not adhering to the criteria set forth by God in order to be a part of his kingdom. Indeed, if ever there is a time and circumstance that warrants an individual exercising free will, it's this one concerning salvation. Man's defiance relevant to the acceptance of Christ is not rooted in arrogance, but rather in the unwillingness to come to terms with a change in "the policy." This unwillingness, however, does fall on the border of arrogance, man's biggest demon. This demon more than any other will be the primary factor behind man's downfall with regards to his desire to enter the kingdom of God. To reiterate a point, there is nothing wrong with arrogance, as long as it does not exceed one's humility. When it does, it can blind an individual to the truth, often using self-importance and other overinflated personality traits. The choice one makes about Christ now will not only affect a person's life in the next world, the spiritual realm, but ultimately will set the tone and the direction of that individual's existence today. When a conscious decision has been made by an individual to cast Christ by the wayside and be arrogant enough to seek a relationship only with God, then you will be ignored in the same manner that you have ignored God's Son. Men who are familiar with Christ and choose to pray, worship, and pay tribute only to God will not be heard by God. The prayers will not be answered, and the same stubbornness that has been shown in accepting Christ will befall such individuals. The acceptance of Christ is not up for a vote; it is not a democracy or a popularity contest. Man has free will to accept or not accept Christ, but many seem to have forgotten that attempting to access God without Christ through prayer is like mailing a letter with no stamp; it's not going anywhere.

The Fourth Month

15

Spiritual Aggression versus Passivity

My dear unborn, in this world it is quite difficult to exist without some type of label being placed on you. People find the need to label others because labeling makes it possible for people to mentally define the individual in images that decrease the fears or inadequacies that are aroused by the person whom they feel compelled to label. People have a tendency to believe that those who label others do so to mock or tease, which stems from insecurities. Indeed, there is some truth to this observation, but more times than most the person who labels does so simply because they are afraid, holding the type of fear that blinds the person from facing the existing realities of the person whom they feel the need to label. A man who is truly enlightened must never criticize, judge, or label others, and when he himself is judged, labeled, or criticized, he must respond only with the windows of the soul. The message that must be sent by your eyes is one of firmness and compassion. Show no fear or be timid, but allow them to see from the reflection in your eyes a full understanding of the fear that lies within their hearts. You must know, however, that when their fears become unbearable and their words ineffective, they will attempt to speak with their hands what their tongues have failed to say. We are taught by the

Messiah that when a man strikes you on one side of the cheek, you must turn the other, a gesture that many perceive as a sign of humility and weakness.

My dear unborn, when you commit yourself to righteousness and God, you must transcend your sense of self as well. You must not perceive yourself as anything less than a general in God's army, one who stands firm in the presence of the Supreme Being, anointed as a soldier against anything or anyone who is against the Messiah and his Father. The sound of your steps must roar like God's own thunder, leaving no doubts in the heart of man concerning your faith or courage. When you are slapped on one side of your cheek, you must be bold in your response, whether or not it comes through words or deeds, for your response is not for you alone; it represents a response from God as well. When you serve in God's army, you are a representative of the heavenly assembly, and your response should signify as such. There are those who are convinced that a man of God is weak, because it has been said that when slapped he turned the other cheek out of fear and the type of humility that comes from being timid. But it takes a strong man to be responsive and a weak one to be reactive, for ego is frequently the driving force behind one's reactions. But one's response runs on the wheel of the thinking process. Therefore, be careful not to react; however, let your response, verbal or nonverbal, be one that will not soon be forgotten. Remember always that you live and exist to please God and not man, regardless of the consequences.

My dear unborn, sometimes when my heart is filled from the sadness that comes from man's transgressions, I am convinced that in my last days the one regret I will have is to have been a part of the human race. Yet I must be spiritually strong and aggressive, and as such I cannot afford any man to weaken my soul. Therefore, do not let any man label you as passive, nor should you take any shame in being spiritually aggressive. When you are struck on the cheek with your back up against the wall, retaliate. Somewhere along the line, man seems to have picked up on the belief that by "turning the other cheek," it gives him a license to mock and mistreat the children of God. When the Messiah speaks of turning the other cheek, he did not mean it to be a format on which Christians would be used as floormats. It was not a gesture designed to show the world that a child of God wears his humility on his shoulders. Rather, by turning the other cheek his disciples should look for alternative ways to resolve the present problematic situation that they might find themselves in at the time. Indeed, the cheek that is slapped represents an initiation of battle, the throwing down of the gauntlet. But by giving your enemy the other side of your cheek, you are offering him a second chance for peace, an opportunity to see things as if a gauntlet had never been thrown down, an alternative way to resolve the issue without conflict, and the drawing of a line in the sand. The representation of the line in the sand is the most serious of all the interpretations because the unslapped cheek is also an invitation to do battle in the event it is given the same treatment as the other. The Son of God is a man who believes in second chances, even if man fails to use them wisely.

My dear unborn, while humility is one of the essential ingredients to the practicing of one's faith, spiritual aggression is even more important. The time of timidity is over, for as the time for Christ's return grows nearer and nearer, Lucifer is becoming bolder and bolder. The true believers in the Messiah can no longer afford the luxury of serving God in the closets or only when it is convenient for them. The time to be aggressive spiritually with respect to the openness of our faith and the love we possess for the Supreme Being is now. Let any man whose faith deals with his struggle to embrace the divine, one who recognizes Jehovah as the one true God and Jesus as the Messiah, be your brother. Let any man who searches for the quest for spiritual enlightenment regardless of his faith be your friend, and he who has denied the Supreme Being and all his wonders be only an associate. Trust no man except in God for he knows that we are hypocrites in each other's eyes, all pretending to be something that we are not.

My dear unborn, do not be afraid to bear witness to the glory of God, regardless of its consequences, and make no mistake: at times there will be consequences. Be wise in your knowledge of both the laws of circumstances and those that are of the actions of Lucifer, so in the time of turmoil you may be able to decipher the true nature of its origin. Never delude yourself in the belief in the goodness of man; see him for what he is, for only then will you tolerate the manifestation of his imperfections. Let your deeds represent the shadow of God's love and your compassion the guiding light to his arms. Be gracious with your kindness, yet be swift to remove it from those who see it as a weakness and would attempt to use it against you. Allow your thoughts to be consumed constantly with God by not allowing any day to pass by without having him enter your mind. Let the course of your day be directed by the hands of God and your every decision be guided by his commandments. Do not place any man above you or yourself above any man. Remember that the purpose for any social hierarchy is to elevate man's sense of importance and not the importance of God. Identify yourself only with the Messiah, yet allow yourself to be nurtured intellectually and spiritually by anyone who offers to do so regardless of their position or status in life.

My dear unborn, passivity is sometimes seen as a by-product of humility, and to a degree it is. But one can be just as aggressive in the exercising of passivity without feeling the need to be humble at all times. Passive-aggressiveness when used for the cause of righteousness can be a powerful tool. In fact, many great men of peace used it in a manner where it has defeated the mighty tyranny of their enemy's great forces. If used correctly, passive-aggressiveness can compel others to look deep within themselves and question their own sense of mercy and compassion. For example, when Gandhi was fighting for independence against the powerful British soldiers, his passive-aggressive attitude allowed him to defeat the British without stooping to their level of hatred. Gandhi simply refused to surrender, but rather aggressively placed himself and his followers in circumstances constantly that were seen as acts of defiance by the British, while remaining non-violent and openly passive regardless of the abuse that they sustained In order for this approach to be successful. Love, understanding, and a willingness to trust in God had to be at the heart of the gesture. Now is the time to be spiritually aggressive in all aspects of your life, and if you must be passive, then let it be a stance of passive-aggressiveness and not passivity as it relates to a timid type of humility. The time is now when the children of God must be the strong arms of God. There is no more room for turning the other cheek for the devil, as his spiritual demon will only slap the other as well. So, when you speak of God and the Messiah, let your words breathe fire into the air and your footprints leave traces that will not soon be removed. Let those who would dare to mock you tremble at the mere sight of your presence. Be passionate and spiritually aggressive in your proclamation of God's love even in the face of ridicule and hatred. Wear your faith like a shield against false prophets, hypocrites, and the modern Pharisees of our time. Be true to yourself and your faith, and God will be true to you.

THE FIFTH MONTH

16

TRANSFIGURATION: A HIDDEN MYSTERY

My dear unborn, a young poet once wrote: "I may possess my father's eyes and even a part of his soul, but my ability to reason will always keep us separate." Here, the poet clearly believes that regardless of how much he has in common with his father, the one thing that makes the father distinct from his son is the son's own ability to think for himself. God's ability to reason is the primary thing that makes him one with his Son, the Messiah. They think as one, hear as one, speak as one, and more importantly feel as one. Man has yet to understand that the crucifixion of the Messiah meant the crucifixion of God himself. He suffered as Christ did on Calvary, was tormented as Christ was leading up to his crucifixion, and will forever carry the scars on his soul as Christ will, scars that will attest to the greatness of God's love. The one thing God could not do is to allow himself to physically die as Christ did for humanity, for eternity and humanity would have died with him. Hence, he sustained himself so he may not only resurrect his Son on the third day but also fulfill his promise of eternal life to all those who have proven themselves worthy. Although God has shared his ability and powers with his Son and followers, the one ability he reserved for himself alone is the ability to breathe life where there was none. Therefore, it was only logical that the entity who created all things sustained himself for the good of mankind, for without him all things would have ceased to exist.

My dear unborn, many will disagree with what I am about to tell you. Remember always that God himself possessed the body of Christ and remained with him up to the point where Christ was about to relinquish his very last breath. What man has embraced as the transfiguration was more than just a heavenly visit; instead it was the enmeshing of two eternal souls. It was a time when the living God was escorted down on earth to possess the body of Christ in support of the ordeal that Christ was about to face. In preparation for the crucifixion, the living God merged himself with the spirit of Christ in order to strengthen him and prepare him for the task that was at hand. Christ went to that mountain as a son and a single spiritual entity, but he left as the Father and the Son, two entities possessed by a single body. Although Christ's disciples could not see or comprehend the true nature of the transfiguration, it was not meant for them to be privy to this knowledge. Indeed, it was not until both Father and Son were nailed to the cross, blood drained from their bodies, that God departed from his Son's body in preparation of receiving his Son's soul. The departure from Christ's body was made apparent when upon feeling the void he asked, "Father, why hast thou forsaken me?" Christ then was speaking not only of a spiritual departure but also of a physical one as well. Indeed, the loneliness he felt was both physical and spiritual. He had expected his disciples to physically abandon him momentarily because of their fears, but he did not know or understand that God would leave him as well during that precise moment of his crucifixion. Yet, as stated earlier, God's brief physical departure was a necessity. God had to leave the body of Christ before Christ's actual death in order to secure Christ's resurrection. Had both entities physically died on the cross, who would have been the keeper of the souls in order to ensure their resurrection? Once you are dead, it becomes somewhat difficult to raise yourself, even for God. Therefore, because Christ could not raise himself from the dead, God resurrected him. Just as Lazarus could not raise himself from the dead and Jesus had to resurrect him, God knew that if he had died no one would be there to resurrect him, for the power of his spirit could not be entrusted with anyone else because of its purity and fiery nature. Hence, God's departure was essential to the existence of all living things in addition to the entire world.

My dear unborn, suffering on the cross with Jesus was also God's way of bearing the burden of man's sins. For God, it was necessary to risk ceasing to exist by leaving the holy circle of light, the source of his life energy, in order to help open the doors of salvation and redemption for man forever. Yes, Christ alone wanted to bear the burden, but the Father and the Son had always done everything together; hence, this was a journey that both entities wanted to embrace as well. Seldom has God ever allowed total separation from his Son or his life energy, for they exist as one and frequently share the same pain, joy, and love for all things.

My dear unborn, I realize that many see the transfiguration as a heavenly visit by Moses and Elias to give Jesus support and even a message from God. But remember that Jesus has always been in constant communication with God, at all times, as demonstrated by all his miracles. He knew the heart of God just as well as he knew his own heart, for they were one. He did not need a heavenly visit to tell him what he already knew. Seeing members of the heavenly assembly was not on his list of priorities then, for he was preparing himself for the job he came to do. Plus Christ was not in the habit of calling down angels just to prove his existence. However, after being on earth for a while, it was necessary to transform Christ's body to the height of purity in order to welcome the purest of all beings (God's spirit) into the merging process of Christ's spirit, allowing both Father and Son to literally share the same body on earth. Indeed, this was the true essence of the transfiguration. This act also demonstrated the greatness of God's love, for not only did he send his only Son to die for man's sins, but he himself suffered the most excruciating pain and humility so he too might share in the payment of man's sins.

My dear unborn, although God himself knew of the transfiguration, Christ himself was not privy to this information until later.

Christ had no idea that this transformation was about to take place until the very moment of the transfiguration itself. All the torment and mental anguish he endured prior to that meeting was his alone to be endured. The conviction and commitment to see this task through never wavered. His faith and diligence to fulfill his Father's wishes as well as his own remained undaunted, always constantly affixed to the fulfillment of the prophesy. Not once did Christ question the certainty or the legitimacy of what had to be done. Each decision he made was carefully orchestrated to ensure that each aspect of his life would come together, producing a global projection that in time would cement his destiny in man's memory for all time.

My dear unborn, Jesus had become the seed of life from which man could embrace the second genesis of his existence. It was all that he could do in order to save us from the inevitability, the wrath of God. He knew that with all his sacrifice, with all his suffering, with all his love, still he could not save us from ourselves, and that only a handful of us would one day be worthy to be a part of his Father's kingdom. Yet no sacrifice was too great in an effort to save us from ourselves, and although for many this effort bears the fruit of futility, for the Messiah even his own existence would be empty without it, for as he said on numerous occasions, it is for this reason and this reason alone that he came into the world. Man will forever be fortunate that God's ability to forgive and show mercy far exceeds his eagerness to show anger, an anger that is usually tempered with understanding and patience, an anger that is controlled but nevertheless focused when it has to be, an anger that the world would have no choice but to embrace had Christ not sacrificed himself for us.

My dear unborn, if the question has to be asked why was God so angry, then such an interrogatory would have been entertained by someone who obviously has not been living on this planet. Indeed, that which angers God stems from the world being as it is today, yesterday, but definitely not forever. People fail to comprehend that the crucifixion of the Messiah not only meant our spiritual survival through grace and salvation, but our physical survival as well. The day Christ died was the day man received his reprieve from God—a stay of execution, if you will—and a covenant between God and all living things to live and endure to the end was born. Christ's physical death meant the spiritual rebirth of man as well as the sustaining of man's existence through a compromise between the Messiah and his Father.

My dear unborn, there is harmony between heaven and earth because of this great compromise. Since it was Christ who pleaded our case to his Father like a prosecuting lawyer setting a new precedent in front of the U.S. Supreme Court, he has more than earned the right to decide who should or should not be allowed to enter the kingdom of God. There are those who see him as a prophet who will be allowed to recommend to God who is worthy on that great day to gain access to the heavenly kingdom. Sadly to say, they have drastically and grossly undermined the extent of his role on the day of judgment. Indeed, we all must choose for ourselves the direction of our destiny, but I urge you, my dear unborn, to let your faith cling to the words and prophesy of the Messiah. Open your heart and welcome all those whose faith deals with the commandments and love of God. Let he who denies the Messiah as the Son of God also deny you if he or she so chooses. But be at peace with all regardless of their faith or whether they have chosen to accept the Messiah or not. He alone has earned the right to judge us, whether we are for him or against him with respect to being the Son of God.

The Fifth Month

17

Born to Die

My dear unborn, the laws of circumstances in conjunction with the laws of nature at times collaborate in order to achieve a consequence that is essential to the homeostasis of the universe or the destruction of man. In an effort to balance the existence of all living things, some people are born to die, just as are many of the things around us. All things, as mentioned before, have a place in the universal sequence; this sequence entails man and the universal elements. They are placed in exact order and must maintain a perfect balance if all living things are to continue in existence. Therefore, mother nature demands that some things continue to live while some die. In essence, that which exists through any means of birth do so only to die, thus ensuring the births of others. In order to accomplish this task, mother nature uses her elements to indicate to man when things are drastically out of balance with each other, hence the projections of earthquakes, tornadoes, storms, and other uncontrollable forces. All these phenomena are nature's way of fighting back in retaliation for all the unnatural ways that man has treated nature's precious elements. Each time man mistreats some entity of the universe, it drastically alters some equation of the universal order of things, throwing the sequencing off balance and creating disharmony or chaos amongst us.

My dear unborn, mother nature does more than just use her own elements against us. In an effort to ensure that the universal scale is balanced, she uses the laws of circumstances by allowing them to place people or things in perilous situations where she can then use her elements to eliminate the necessary life-form needed to keep the universal scale in perfect balance. For example, the laws of circumstances on a given day may place two hundred people, people who are not in sync with the laws of circumstances or who lack cosmic consciousness, at a precise location where mother nature can then ignite the necessary forces needed to create a powerful earthquake or some other elements that will kill those two hundred people on that specific day. Furthermore, while these two hundred people are being eliminated on that same day and time, using the same type of collaboration, mother nature is causing another hundred to be accidentally killed in a plane crash because of bad weather, thus adding to the amount of individuals necessary to keep the universal scale balanced and in harmony through this avenue of eradication. While these deaths are taking place, somewhere, someplace, the exact amount of births have occurred.

My dear unborn, one should remember that the universal scale can also be tilted, where, for example, there are not enough life forms in existence and something has to be done. This, however, is rarely ever the case because people and other life forms are constantly being born more so than dying. Frequently the focus is on the elimination process. It is important to note that although God has nothing to do with this elimination process, both mother nature and the laws of circumstances make each birth of a child a matter of question, the question being, "Is this child being born to die?" The answer to this question depends largely on how that child will be taught with respect to the openness of his or her mind as it relates to cosmic consciousness. Sadly to say, in most cases people die simply because they are not aware, whether it may be lack of awareness of their immediate surroundings, lack of awareness of certain warning signs being put forth by their body, lack of awareness of their spiritual deficiency, lack of awareness of the true nature of a significant other, or lack of awareness of their own limitations and capabilities. Whatever form the lacking of cosmic consciousness may manifest itself in, be sure that both mother nature and the laws of circumstances will only be too happy to seize the moment with respect to taking advantage of this deficiency. In many cases bad things happen to good people simply because they have some preconceived notion that the world is a wonderful place filled with elements of happiness and joy, while being totally oblivious to the wickedness and the evil that lurks in the heart of man until they come face to face with what would be their worst nightmare, the inevitable. Only by then it is too late for them because in most cases it has cost them to pay the ultimate price—the taking of their lives. My dear unborn, we are living in a society where very few people learn from the mistakes of others. Their inflated ego has somehow managed to convince them that they must experience all aspects of the human experience for themselves regardless of the consequences that their predecessors have suffered. Remember, my dear unborn, that a man who enters into a lion's den to prove to himself and others that he is not afraid of lions is guilty not of courage but of stupidity. Therefore, learn from the follies of others and learn well, for there is no shame in embracing a lesson that will not only protect your life but will also provide the opportunity where you can pass on that wisdom to others in hopes that you may one day prevent the tragedy of another person. A man who is truly brave and whose heart is filled with courage has little to prove to himself or to others.

My dear unborn, there are men who were born to die, and there are men who are born to live, but each man must decide for himself what path he will follow in order to meet his destiny. No one can make that decision for you. A true friend may assist you on your journey, but the fulfillment of your destiny is solely in the hands of the man who must walk the path. The man who applies himself and truly studies the dynamics of the laws of circumstances in conjunction with mother nature has increased the probability of his survival rate more than 90 percent in comparison to the man who lives day by day with no faith and leaves everything to chance and the dynamics of the universal order of things. Remember always, my dear unborn, that the universal ordering of things operates by the random assignment of individuals in order to fill the slack for various shortcomings within its systems. But the laws of circumstances and mother nature systematically place individuals in predicaments through premeditated calculations. This heightens its probability with a greater emphasis on precision on a given target than the procedure illustrated by the universal order, which has a tendency to focus on random assignment and not systematic sequencing to frequently ensure accuracy. In short, one leaves things to chance, the universal order, and the laws of circumstances and mother nature do not.

My dear unborn, make no mistake, we were all born to die. Yet before dying each individual is destined to fulfill a dream that was meant to impact the world in which he lives. Mighty and powerful forces are constantly trying to impede each person from impacting the world in a manner that was meant to be. Indeed, very few people live long enough to do what they were meant to do, simply because of their lack of insight about the forces and dynamics that are blocking their progress. As stated earlier, when one acquires knowledge about these forces, one increases drastically the opportunity to fulfill his/her destiny and can successfully accomplish what God had intended for that person to do in the first place. Even an aiding soul serves a purpose, if it is only to assist another to find out the true purpose behind his/her existence before passing on. But each man was born in to this world for a purpose and must devote a certain amount of energy trying to find this purpose. While some individuals may find the purpose for their existence easier than some, with a deep faith in God sometimes your purpose will find you. Man must master the art of finding this purpose while juggling the laws of circumstances and their collaboration with mother nature. Being reluctant to master the skill of doing so only restricts the extent of one's self-preservation. My dear unborn, once an individual realizes that he or she was primarily born to die, the burden of everyday life should become as light as a feather. But the notion of being born to die must leave an indelible mark on one's mind for the person to truly appreciate the senseless act of worrying about life as a whole, when it is so fluid, and can be so easily taken away. I have seen people who literally worry themselves to death, driven by the fear of losing materialistic things to which they have grown attached. Indeed, this demonstrates a serious flaw within these individuals' sense of spirituality. No individual should love anything or anyone to the point where they become afraid of losing them by dying. This indicates a weakness in one's love for God, for to love God is to love the things of the world as little as possible. Death should energize people to live life with passion and with all their fiber, not cripple them with fear or kill their zest for living. Unless an individual finds a way to conquer death and live forever, except through Christ, death must be embraced if one's existence is ever going to have any true meaning.

The Fifth Month

18

Death and Pain

My dear unborn, although death is inevitable, it remains one of the most feared and misunderstood obstacles. Many who fear death do so mainly because they are uncertain of what lies beyond as well as the potential for pain that sometimes comes with death and dying. In addition, they are not prepared to meet God. A man who has unshakeable faith in God and all that he stands for will see death for what it really is, a transition from one realm to the next. The fear of dying is indicative of lack of faith and insight into an individual's lack of readiness or preparation to meet the heavenly assembly. Preparation as well as faith will drastically diminish the feelings of uneasiness concerning the uncertainties surrounding the afterlife. The faith and preparation one makes will create the needed freedom to bypass the fears that dictate how death impacts one's life. If your perception is negative in nature then the fear of dying will intensify. However, if one sees death as an opportunity to belong to a place, absent of all the things that make life on earth miserable, leaving only those things that give us fulfillment with regards to all aspects of our lives, then embracing death will not be as devastating.

My dear unborn, it is not by the will of God that some men live longer than others but by the will of fate. It is not by the will of God that some lives are filled with pain much more so than others but by the laws of circumstances. Indeed, the Lord giveth but seldom does he take it away. I say this to you, my dear unborn, that your thoughts of death should be few, for both death and pain are invited guests that will make their presence known with or without your approval. Your preoccupation should dwell on life, and your life should evolve around God and the spirit of the Messiah.

My dear unborn, at some point in your life you will desperately seek to unravel the mystery of life itself. It will be a journey worth embarking on, one that must begin with the questions: "Why am I here?" "What purposes does my existence serve?" Without faith, the answer to these questions can take a lifetime of searching, but with faith only a second. Man exists simply to serve, and it was not by accident that man exists in this world but by the will of a Higher Power. It is by our will that we must choose whom we wish to serve. The spirit of the Messiah would hope that through his grace we would choose to serve God directly and indirectly. We serve God directly by establishing a one-on-one relationship with him, and indirectly by the many ways we treat our fellow men. Death and pain must also play a role in the manner in which we serve God. Both concepts must be at the forefront of our minds when we utter the name or principle of our Higher Power. My dear unborn, the word of God dictates that a man who does not practice or believe in the teachings of God or the Messiah places himself in the precarious position of facing eternal death in addition to eternal pain. Therefore, each concept is very much a part of our life here and the life after. The good news is that man is still in control with respect to how both death and pain can influence his existence in the afterlife. While he has some control over pain in this world, obviously, the degree of control over death is much more limited. Being concerned about death and pain in this world as well as the next are both legitimate concerns. But the fear should be geared mainly toward having to face both in the life after. While it is indeed rational to fear pain in this world, it is somewhat irrational and illogical to fear death since both death and birth are children of the same womb. One's mind should thoroughly be conditioned to the acceptance of both. Remember, the aging process starts moving us toward death seconds after delivery from the womb.

My dear unborn, I cannot teach you how not to fear death. It is not something one man can teach the other. However, I can show you what degree of consciousness has gotten me to the point, thus causing the fear to substantially diminish over a period of time. The essence of one's consciousness must evolve totally around the spirit of the Messiah and must be one with the enormous love he has for his father, the living God. In addition to a strong faith you must possess a strong desire that far outweighs other desires in terms of love and other physiological needs, then let it serve as a replacement for those things that would otherwise give you self-fulfillment. In short, you must be consumed by the love of your faith, a love so powerful and fulfilling that everything else becomes secondary in your life, a faith so loved and cherished that even death cannot shake the love of this faith.

My dear unborn, I tell you this: when a man gets to the point where the love of his faith becomes a shield, then the shield will also protect him from the fear of dying. This love gradually nourishes the faith and makes it strong as well. Still, to reiterate a point, do not be preoccupied with death, for if the process of thinking cannot change a situation, then it is unwise to influence the mind to that which may cause harm to the body. Death, like life, is a journey that ultimately you will experience. Therefore, let your focus be life when you are alive and death when you are dead. Only remember that as you progress toward your journey of spiritual enlightenment, concern yourself with getting to a point in your life where your faith and spirituality are rested on God's shoulders and your consciousness dwells in a state of nirvana. Remember that within the scope of God's master plan, all that matters is that you are wise to the essence of his love and humble enough to receive its illumination.

My dear unborn, while the sources of pain are many, there are none more devastating than the one that comes with poverty. Poverty slowly deteriorates the human spirit, redefines the individual to himself, and dissects the dignity in open view of the soul. But God did not create poverty, man did. Life is not hard because of God's unwillingness to help humanity but because of man's willingness to help only himself in most cases. God created heaven on earth so man's baskets would have fruits beyond their abundance. It is man through his greed who has turned the heavenly portion of his universe into a living hell for those who are unable to master the survival mechanisms needed for a convenient and comfortable existence. We can ask, however, why then does God allow this to happen? But imagine what our existence would be like if God were to step into our lives whenever things are going bad only to step back out when things get good again. How would we ever learn as a race the importance of progress after struggle or from a web of mistakes that have a tendency to make us stronger as individuals, or simply the essence of who and what we are because of a series of trials and errors that derive from our life experiences? It is indeed for this reason that man has been given so much control, which he tends to acknowledge reluctantly.

My dear unborn, a poet once wrote, "My destiny lies in the hands of God and not in the bosom of man." There is some truth to this verse, for although God helps shape our destiny, we must also embrace the notion that our destiny is also our responsibility in terms of shaping it and seeing its judgment. One's destiny is the embodiment of life experiences interfacing with self-acknowledgment and contentment at the crossroad where the strength of one's faith gives birth to self-acceptance. Frequently it is asked why some people live and others die. We then turn to God in amazement as to how he could have allowed all these things to happen, especially to the innocents. God gave man the promised land and with it a number of mechanisms and processes that when they function at an optimal level allow all variables to which they are connected to be able to operate smoothly. For example, the procreating process when worked correctly produces offspring who are physiologically sound, yet when it fails then a child can suffer from certain physiological defects. People have a tendency to blame God when these mechanisms and processes go awry. These mechanisms and processes were originally created in a perfect manner. If by some reason they do not give perfect results, it is because somewhere along the line they were messed up by man, who inadvertently turned around and blames God.

My dear unborn, people live and people die not by the will of God but by the will of the laws of circumstances, as stated earlier. Pain and suffering come to us all, not because God has forsaken us but because they are a part of the world in which we live. As long as man continues to be a part of this world, he is subjected to things of this world—the good, the bad, and the indifferent. It is irrational to exist in any world and not expect to become a victim of its inhabitants and mechanisms. God has better things to do with his time than to constantly set up roadblocks throughout our lives in order to make our existence miserable. However, make no mistake, he does test us occasionally. But when he does, it is for a particular reason. Still, only the children of God are tested by God—those who have consciously turned over their lives to him—but all are subjected to the constant temptations of Lucifer. Those who are children of Lucifer are not only tested by him but their everyday lives are so enmeshed with his that they routinely conduct themselves in a way that bears testimony to the philosophical ideology of Lucifer and his legions of demons.

My dear unborn, the Creator has a tendency to let his presence be known in our lives under certain conditions. The first is if you are a child of God who has literally asked him to be saved through his grace, and therefore ask him for his help in times of need. Second, God is intrusive in those souls' lives who have yet to know him or the Messiah. When individuals are ignorant or lack the basic knowledge necessary to make an informed decision about the living God or his Son, then he will make himself known to them by becoming a compelling force within their lives. Third, God will help those who are humble enough to recognize their sin and repent whether this individual has a relationship with God or not. In short, he will help anyone who asks, but his reply will not come without their repentance.

My dear unborn, many ways are made known to us of God's love. With all of these ways, one essential axiom remains. He will not trample on our rights to exercise free will regardless of what road we have chosen to follow. He will not turn away from us in our time of needs if we allow him to become a part of our lives or recognize him as the living God to whom all things and worship belong. We were not placed on this earth only to engage in self-serving idiosyncrasies but to become a godly assistant to others. Indeed, unless one is with the spirit of the Messiah, the journey one takes in life will begin and end with one's self only. God allows no man to walk alone unless he so chooses, and even then God quietly tiptoes behind them so he may catch them in the event they should fall.

My dear unborn, until mankind puts a face on evil, he will not be able to see it for what it truly is and possess the necessary insight into who its representatives are. Indeed, while God knows who these representatives are, he will not and cannot intervene, knowing that the cloak you wear also casts a shadow of the essence of evil. The pain that man is confronted with quite often is his own creation, not God's. Yet, because God is always in a position to alleviate this pain, regardless of its origin, more emphasis is placed on what he should have done or what he did not do. Little or no emphasis is then placed on the origin or causes for the pain. We do not take the time to embrace the notion of free will when things are going good in our lives, only when they are going bad. We do not embrace the notion that God created the process by which some things come about, and if we cause the process to be impaired, then he should not be held responsible for the outcome. A child who is born in this world as mentally or physically challenged was not created by God in this manner. He created the process, procreation in this case, but if a mother abuses her body with various chemicals and other factors that disrupt the procreation process, thus resulting in a child not being born correctly, then man, not God, is to be blamed. Hence all pain resulting from this experience should be unrelated to God.

My dear unborn, never allow a negative circumstance or experience to prevent the emergence of a positive outcome.. Reject all thoughts that have the propensity to create self-doubt, for true faith precludes us from knowing absolutes. The uncertainties that you will feel must be suppressed by the knowledge that in these times God will shield you from all negative consequences that came about as a result of your trust in him. Although at times you may convince yourself that he has forsaken you, be assured that he has not, and the struggle that you bear now will one day bear testimony to your survival. Man's struggle is incomplete without death and pain, for without these two variables such a struggle lacks merit and ultimately will become meaningless to an individual's quest. The true measurement of any struggle cannot be validated in the absence of death or pain, for with struggle comes sacrifices, and sacrifices cannot be pure in essence if they do not embody either pain or death as a primary ingredient.

My dear unborn, in recent years acts of terror have shaken our entire nation. On September 11, 2001, America was faced with unspeakable evil. Terrorists hijacked four airplanes and flew three of them into America's symbols of freedom and democracy: one building was the Pentagon and the others were the Twin Towers of the World Trade Center in New York City. On that day almost three thousand people lost their lives. Three thousand people were suddenly and unknowingly about to face judgment day, were about to stand in the presence of God and one by one defend their entire existence. As the nation shared condolences and struggled to extricate itself from this grip of evil, the one thought that constantly plagued my mind was how many of these individuals were actually prepared to meet God and the heavenly assembly. Tears flow down my cheeks when I think that out of such a travesty even one of these three thousand people who died might not have been prepared. Someone in his twisted mind robbed another fellow human being of the opportunity and time to prepare himself or herself to meet the living God who will decide that person's fate forever. This within itself saddens the human spirit. Lucifer has unleashed the spiritual demon that raises a nation's consciousness to the level that forces its people to rethink and reevaluate the way they will forever live their day-to-day lives. Man's first line of defense against such evil is his faith, followed by the true essence of his heart and soul. Therefore, let the love and forgiveness that are only a few of the traits within our hearts and souls shine through like the Son of God bringing light to the world. In these times of evil, we must still forgive the evildoers as a demonstration of our love for God if not for them. But let there be consequences, for to forgive does not relinquish us from our duties to render a learning experience that will ensure the following of appropriate behavior or standard of norms.

My dear unborn, being prepared to meet God is a lifelong journey, one that is reinforced daily by our deeds and our faith. Although this preparation is the most important thing in our lives, many fail to realize this. Many individuals are under the impression that preparation to meet God starts when one has decided to make a commitment to God, then seal it with some religious rituals like baptism or confirmation. But these are only formalities that are important but still secondary to what lies in the hearts of individuals, formalities that pale in comparison to what is actually necessary to the preparation for meeting God: a clean spirit and a pure heart. Remember that with each morning comes another chance to work on one's readiness to meet the Creator. This has very little to do with the church, but has a great deal to do with one's relationship with God. Be prepared!

THE SIXTH MONTH

19

TRIALS AND TRIBULATIONS

My dear unborn, having trials and tribulations as part of your life will define the sculpture of the iron from which your armor is made in times when hopelessness appears to be at the forefront of your existence. There are times when it will seem as if you are in the eye of a storm, developing a feeling of helplessness with no feasibility to stop or prevent the deterioration of your life. Frustration will ignite the temptation to run a race that you cannot win, a race against yourself, one that you will run for a while, only to realize eventually that you have never left the starting gate. Remember, trial and tribulation are the first steps on the ladder of pleasure, for in the absence of pleasure lies an emotional testing ground; a place where challenges are met and agony seeks reprieve from life's dilemmas; a place where the power within is nurtured and conditioned in a way that allows us to project the inner strength needed to gradually climb the ladder of pleasure and harmony to wholeness; a place that captures the inner peace that comes from bringing the mind, body, and spirit on the same mental playing field; a place that reflects the only aspect of human lives for which both leaders of the spiritual world, God and Lucifer, occasionally collaborate, a collaboration that serves to test the very limit of human endurance. Indeed, as cold and as painful as it may be, sometimes the character of an individual can only be ascertained when one's endurance is pushed to the limit and molded by the harsh realities of life. Whether we overcome the given obstacles or not depends on the true essence of our self as well as how we perceive the various entities around us. But the measurement of what we are derives essentially from a series of trials and tribulations that we experience during the course of our lives.

My dear unborn, a life without some form of trials and tribulations is not one worth living, for such a life will stagnate self-growth as well as stop a variety of stimulation that is needed to create excitement within the soul. The vision and perception of all life's problems will determine the consequences of each outcome, an outcome that can be positivistic or negativistic depending on your ability to control how you view and perceive the objects of your difficulties or dilemmas. This realization will give you the power over any problematic features that confront you. Avoidance is the enemy, and confrontation without procrastination is the key. When we avoid dealing with our problems, we do so because we are intimidated by the uncertainty followed by an overwhelming feeling of fear. The fear of knowing once and for all whether or not we are made up of more weaknesses than strength, the fear of finally succeeding at something and having no one or nothing else to blame, the fear of changing those things that make us acceptable in the eyes of our friends and loved ones, even though those very same things make us unhappy. These fears must be removed, for only by removing your fears can you embrace fully the issues that contribute to your sleepless nights, thus mending the void within your soul. Free yourself by freeing your thoughts and by drastically changing your outlook, not only on your problems but on your life as a whole. When you are able to free yourself from your thoughts and perception, then you must free yourself from the inner voice, the voice that tells you that regardless of how hard you try, you are still a nobody who is not trying hard enough; the voice that asks you why are you going the extra mile for trying to achieve the things you want when the result will always be the same failure; the voice that tells you that perfection is the only measurement to abide, and anything else is not worthy of your effort; the voice that tells you that unless he or she has the qualities of mom or dad, then any chance of love is slim or futile. The voice that cripples your movement prevents you from taking risks. Remove the blur from your vision, the blinders from your perception, and the bars from your mind. Keep the problems where they belong, not in you but in the world. "What does not exist in the mind does not exist at all." Therefore, create your own world and make it a part of your mind, then choose and become a god for all that exists in your new world. In your mind make it a perfect world for a perfect soul, leaving your imperfect body in its imperfect world. Unless your soul or spirit is used as a reference point for the things you do, then your problems will still exist even in this perfect world that would have been created by you. Any reference point that entails using the body as a starter will be the embodiment of imperfection regardless of how perfect you have made the world within. The body was born in sin and in sin it will remain until death. Therefore, let your focus be on the spirit until it is liberated by death for a much higher purpose.

My dear unborn, mastering trials and tribulations involves having the ability to create a perfect world in an imperfect world and choosing the source of your strength, spiritual or physical. It is easy to give up under the severe strain of trials and tribulations, especially when frustration and anger are at the forefront of all other facets that are designed to destroy your peace of mind thus creating a living hell on earth for you. But in this very moment rationality and reason must prevail, counteracting the frustration and anger that are generated by the arrival of the "x" variables. In times of trials and tribulations we are needed not only as champions in the circle of spirits, but also as warriors in the game of life. Never complain about the things you do not have or that which is wrong with your life. Never ask, "Why do things happen to me?" as if to suggest that they should not. Instead ask, '"Why not me, since I too am a part of the human race?" Once you accept that life in this world is not perfect, then you can go on from there with respect to making various choices and changes based on this obvious revelation. But it never ceases to amaze me that although many of us know this, we still complain about the unfairness of life; soon thereafter frustration follows. The limitations and expectations that we place on ourselves dictate the outcome of the trials and tribulations we face, regardless of what form they may come in. There are times when we escalate the nature of a problem by simply limiting ourselves.

My dear unborn, in your times of trials and tribulations when it appears that you are at the end of your rope, remember to always make a final stop on your knees. Take your burden to the Creator. Bring with you not a series of rationalizations for the unfavorable outcomes of your troubles, for all that is necessary are just two words: "Help me!" Do not dim the light of your success long before the foundation of any failures has been drawn in the sand. When you prevent the realm of possibilities from shining on your potentials, you have made yourself one with all the obstacles that await you, a union that will generate more negativities, merely because of the mind-set in which you have greeted the domain of chaos. Do not choose to limit yourself when neither God nor man has chosen to limit you. Remember that the world you live in belongs to you; hence, no one can give you that which is already yours. Claim it!

My dear unborn, indeed, claiming that which is already yours can be quite challenging, for there are those who will question your ownership and try to devalue your existence and the right to this claim. Unless you claim and solidify a place for yourself in this world, others will instill in you that even your very thought belongs to them and would have you seek permission for your right to exist. You will soon learn that unless you exercise great caution, an enormous amount of energy will be spent trying to convince others of your right to exist and belong to the world as they do. I tell you that a large portion of the trials and tribulations that you will face will consist of the desire to exercise the very right of your existence. But do not be timid or afraid to claim that which is already yours. Do not shy away from the battle that they will instigate, for God always fights on the side of the right.

My dear unborn, as human beings we have a natural tendency to gravitate toward each other, whether socially or because of interdependent necessity. We are compelled to constantly reinforce the type of bonding that makes survival a bit less stressful. This interaction serves a purpose that is borne out of necessity, but must be replaced whenever possible by solitude and isolation. Where there are people, there will always be trials and tribulations, for a person's problems will always be compounded by the forces of the world. Hence, eliminate some of these problems by decreasing the frequency of socializations. Being a loner is not tantamount to being lonely, and though there will be times when your body cries out for another, then you must lead your thoughts to the playground of your mind. A wise man seeks liberty from the mind; a foolish one becomes its prisoner. The fulfillment of your desires is inevitable; the experiences will come and the love you seek will be yours. However, place your solitude and isolation above all other priorities. Be one with yourself and learn to become your favorite friend, because the uncertainties that trials and tribulations bring leave an emotional scar, but seldom when solitude and isolation are your home and you are already your best friend.

My dear unborn, trials and tribulations can deprive you of nothing when nothing is the entire principle on which your world is built on. You will find out as you develop that most people spend a lifetime trying to avoid solitude and isolation, terrified of what they will have no choice but to confront, something for which socialization tends to serve as a remedy: the facing of themselves. You must master solitude and isolation even if it means getting in touch with your demons, for lack of insight into self is the feeding ground for trials and tribulations.

My dear unborn, your burden will appear to be more than you can bear when the weight of your troubles outweighs the weight of your faith. When you walk, follow the footprints of the Messiah, prints that are clear for the world to see and to lead you away from troubles, thus bringing you closer to challenges that will make you wise. The standards by which you evaluate the tribulations of others must be no greater than the ones you set for yourself. Empathize, don't sympathize, with those who are experiencing their share of trials and tribulations. Display no guilt when their cup runneth over, for no man's trials and tribulations are greater than the other. The ratio will balance out as the same in each individual's lifetime, the notion behind the concept of cosmic balancing.

My dear unborn, the temptation of searching for reassurance will be of paramount importance. The greater the troubles, the greater the need for reassurance. Many will comfort you, some under false pretense. Trust only in the Messiah, for his words are direct and true. Place your faith in him and him alone, for his gifts are without strings attached and his love always unconditional. The tribulations that you incur will be the measuring rod used to sort out those who have proclaimed themselves to be your friends. As you strive, strive with the knowledge that wealth and tribulations are the only two mechanisms by which one can judge the sincerity of those who would convince you of their friendship. Friends easily come with wealth, but in its absence, replaced by troubled waters, you will undoubtedly drink alone.

My dear unborn, the concept of social comparison gives birth to the notion that in times of crisis we selectively seek out those with whom we share a common similarity, whether it may be through some association by occupations, social status, or race. I tell you that the greatest gift you can give to this world is one of inclusion. Whatever you do in this world, if a part of it does not involve bringing people together even in some small capacity, then you must revamp the essence of your existence. Unification and integration should be at the heart of how you relate to others. Indeed, preserve your solitude and hold it dear. But as you cherish the moments of your isolation, so must you learn to appreciate the significance of setting aside a period of time when the primary objectives of relating to your fellow man is not only bringing them closer together but also to enhance and nurture the mutual respect for all. An entity who defines itself through its ability to bring people together will be feared, for those who strive on other's weakness will chastise you for this noble attempt. Integration and unification allow people to see that the things that keep them apart in most cases are the very same things that can bring and keep them together. Once this discovery is made, it is rather difficult to turn back the hands of time to a state of darkness, for once one is awakened to the truth it can no longer be distorted in one's mind. Truth is the enemy of fear. They coexist in the same domain but mask their appearances so that those who thirst for righteousness will still be able to choose without sacrificing any components of their free will.

My dear unborn, when the foundation of a house is built on a pillar of lies, then even the truth has no place to call home. Consequential thinking serves as an attempt to evaluate the degree or the extent to which to lie. Indeed, lying epitomizes an individual's unwillingness to embrace any given consequences resulting from the fabrication. One lies simply because one is afraid. Fear is the mystical component on which all lies are driven. It is the same fear that manifests itself when our security, social status, and life are threatened, but it intensifies when the probability of unmasking our persona, which we have spent a lifetime conditioning to be seen or perceived, is on the verge of being detected by others. Regardless of the rationale given for lying, it is counterproductive to any form of spiritual enlightenment, and as such sways and creates an imbalance in harmony, thus closing the doors to wholeness. Lying serves two purposes: to feed the element of fear and block the path of truth. Become one with the truth and eliminate the intimidation that comes with your fear, and the seed of lies that is planted within all of us will have no place to grow in you. In the world you are about to become a part of, lies and deceptions are associated with trials and tribulations if the light of God is not imprinted on your soul. But if you can feel the warmth of his light on your face, then you will delight in your trials and tribulations, for in them you will find an opportunity to win the struggle against yourself, a struggle that you must win if you are to embrace a legacy of greatness. I confess I cannot tell you if you will ever lie, for the intensity of your fears as well as your quest for the truth will reveal that only to you. I do not know that if your convictions and character are the baseline for all that is true in you, regardless of the circumstances, honor will prevail.

My dear unborn, there will come a time when the world will attempt to convince you that "time" is either your friend or your enemy, depending on the nature of your circumstance. You must decide for yourself if such is the case, yet you must know that time does not take sides. It is the one constant neutral element that has borne witness to the birth of the living God. They shared the same womb. Time listens to your troubles, shares your darkest secrets. It accepts unconditionally while opening itself up to all who have chosen to redefine its meaning. Time is rooted in a universal platform that lends itself to the mercy of man. The face it wears is the one man gives it by how he has chosen to live and the deeds that a given era experienced. Its innocence is untouched, and although man frequently tries to stain its purity, within the blink of an eye it is able to shed all the corruptions, the transgression, and life's iniquity. The past, present, and future are one in its eyes. Still, it allows itself to be measured, dissected so that man can fulfill the hidden need to distance himself from the forces of the world and the forces from within. As your existence evolves, your need to conquer the world will be great. Sometimes you will question yourself, wondering if your goals are within reach, worried that life might be passing you by as reflected by your age. Remember that whether you follow through with your goals or not, time will remain the same and your age will increase, regardless of whether or not you allow time to influence the goals you have set for yourself. I heard a young man in his thirties once say, "I cannot become a doctor because I'll be in my forties by then." What he failed to realize was that whether he became a doctor or not, he would still be in his forties within ten years.

My dear unborn, time offers countless opportunities to each of us regardless of our trials and tribulations. It readily accepts us, showing us a new horizon. It makes only one request, "Write a script in history that makes it proud." Needless to say that it has had its share of disappointment. Still, it will be your responsibility to do everything in your power to ensure that as long as you are alive, each moment in time will become a tribute to your existence, a reflection of who and what you are. Time must not only pay tribute to the way you live, but to your death as well, for once your name is written in time, it is written forever. Time, in essence, possesses the attributes that make it the one known factor of this world that is already a part of eternity. Do not allow time to severely influence your decision-making process or whether you should go left or go right. No! We are not in this world forever, but time is. Thus, it has us at a disadvantage in terms of measuring any aspect of our lives. The only way to equate ourselves with this powerful concept that is rooted in both heaven and earth for all perpetuity is to elevate our quality of life. If we dare to live in a manner that leaves room for no other explorations, at least not in this world, then time becomes measurable by our quality of life and not by its quantity, thus putting us on an equal footing. It is better to kiss the lips of death early with all of life's passions beneath you than to experience the bitter juices of life on the backside of time—forever. Find the source of your passions and live it. Remember, an incongruent self leads to unhappiness, and the mood of time is unchangeable; therefore, it is imperative that both self and time be true to one another if harmony is to be achieved.

My dear unborn, regardless of your trials and tribulations, regardless of your suffering, always leave room in your heart for another. Strive constantly to change the direction of the world by first raising the consciousness of your fellow men. Do this by taking them to a point in their lives where for once and if only for a moment they are able to help others think or feel positive about themselves. Second, penetrate the essence of their true nature, whether it is good or evil, by allowing them to gain insight into your own sense of self in hopes that they will emulate the primary ingredients of your character. Third, remain steadfast in your convictions and principles, thus allowing them to be your guide in the journey that both you and your unknown traveler will take, even in the absence of his or her resolve. Bear your burden alone until it becomes your desire to cast them at the feet of the Messiah. Each man has his own demons to bear and as such need not hear of yours, and yet your spiritual duty is to assist others in the extrication of theirs. As heavy as your cross may be to carry, reserve the strength to bear the cross of others when it becomes absolutely necessary. Be assured that the weight of your own cross will become lighter as you alleviate the burden and suffering of others.

THE SIXTH MONTH

20

REASSURANCE FROM GOD!

My dear unborn, in silent meditation you comfort me; in agony you soothe my soul; when I was confused, you reassured me. Yes! I will forever be your guiding light, and as you lay helpless in your mother's womb, I will protect you. When you lay asleep in your crib, I will watch over you, and your arrival will bring excitement to my existence. I will mold you in my image, wrap you in my strength, and supply a reservoir of nutrients for your self-esteem that will set your feet on the same plane as the Son of God. I will set before you a chalice filled with glory brought to you by a naked bride who has a fiery passion for an embrace. I will instill in you the arrogance to question the wisdom of the Almighty God and the curiosity to recognize the realities and illusions of the world, and the ability to know the difference. For only then, you too will know that the world we live in exists only in the mind of God and will cease to exist when the imagery it produces no longer sustains and entertains him. Indeed, this is not to say that God gets pleasure from our misery but rather to inform you that the absolute assurance that you need from me about your life can only come from him. When the wheel of life is set in motion and the direction it takes is like a roller coaster, money will let you down, people will let you down, but the bosom of God will await you with all the needed reassurance. Remember, he was there by your side in your mother's womb and will suffer with you throughout your entire life. He will cry when you are in pain, laugh when you are happy, and rejoice when death knocks on your door. Therefore, do not seek reassurance from me, for though no father's love can be greater, even the light of my love can be dimmed by circumstances. But his love will never fade, for he has already proven that pain and death are matchless against the love he has for the entire world. To the young, reassurance is sometimes optional, but to the "youthful decline," it becomes a necessity as various aspects of their life diminish.

My dear unborn, the reassurance we often seek from God stems from the obvious inadequacies we see in ourselves. We look to him for that which will make us whole. Yet, it seldom appears to us that we must first rid ourselves of our inadequacies before presenting ourselves to God. While it is true that God readily accepts and takes us as we are, he looks to us for resilience or the willingness to at least try and heal ourselves before turning our lives over to him. He has more faith in us than we do in ourselves. Many of the problems we take to him can easily be resolved if only we patiently look within ourselves for the answers. All that is needed to be whole is already within our reach; any needed reassurance stems from our own lack of faith in him as well as ourselves. It is ironic that we seek reassurance from God, yet in the same breath display actions that clearly indicate a lack of trust in him. Reassurance is built on a platform of trust. Therefore, it is illogical to seek reassurance from anyone for whom trusting them is a factor.

My dear unborn, remember that you cannot seek reassurance from someone you do not trust, and when you truly trust someone, you do not need reassurance from them. You will find that man is basically good, but only until life is fully able to develop and nurture him with elements of evil, then depending on his disposition, good or evil, one will rule over the other, placing a permanent face on that individual's presentation. Indeed, man's behavior, good or evil, past or present, has and will always dictate in what direction God will raise his hands on behalf of humanity. Do not be surprised if reassurance from

God is sometimes limited, for God exists not to resolve the problems of humanity, but to assist us in making our burden lighter through wisdom and the intelligence to use it wisely, with a promise of salvation for those who yield to his commandments. Unfortunately, many are under the impression that by praying, God must answer their prayer upon hearing their cry. Not true! It is arrogance to expect God to respond to our every whim. Mind you, nothing is wrong with arrogance as long as it does not exceed our humility. As adults, seldom do we expect our parents to resolve our troubles for we are grown, and as such we were taught by them that it is our responsibility to take care of our own obligations or suffer the consequences. Yet, with God we somehow develop the notion that there is no need to display these signs of adulthood but rather embrace another idea, one that states that since I was not asked to be born, my follies are your responsibility, and yours alone, thus testing the degree of God's love. The ultimate reassurance and guarantee that comes from God is simply that God will love us regardless of our circumstances or sins.

My dear unborn, the love of God makes it possible for him to forgive us for our transgression against him and humanity. Still, his forgiveness does not come easy, as many would think. As we ourselves sometimes find it difficult to forgive others, so does he. But the love he has for the world is so great that he is compelled to do so, for in the eye of God, man is still a "work in progress." Each pattern of behavior shown by man reveals and increases the degree of insight into his potential and capabilities. Indeed, God's omniscience comes from timeless encounters with man. For the things that man now does, God has seen many, many times before. This is not to say that God cannot foretell the future, only that the perception of the future is viewed quite differently by both man and God in terms of the past, present, and future. Man sees the future as what lies ahead, but God sees it as what will soon be repeated by man again. Therefore, the reassurance we get from God is rooted in the essence of time, a time that is not categorized by past, present, and future, but rather by the repetitiousness of man and the certainty that what he does, he will undoubtedly do again. Reassurance or not, man should live to serve God, and serve him well so that they may come to learn how to truly live. Unless a man lives in Christ, with Christ being at the center of his life, he will never know the true joy of living. The need for reassurance is indicative of weaknesses in one's faith, which usually shed light on some elements of mistrust. When the urgency for reassurance becomes a necessity, the doors to hesitation and uncertainty are best left closed.

My dear unborn, there are those who ask for reassurance from God, reassurance that he does indeed exist in hopes that they are not wasting their time serving a God that lives only in the mind of man. Yet, when faced with this reassurance from God, the splendor of it all so often escapes the very same people who sought it in the first place. Why? Because the expectations of this reassurance do not manifest themselves in some elaborate supernatural spectacles. Such individuals fail to realize that the heart of their faith is based on their lack of need for reassurance relevant to God's existence. They do not take into consideration the process that brings about a child in this world, or the majesty of an airplane soaring through the sky like a "chariot without wheels," leaves falling from the trees in autumn only to grace our presence once again in the springtime, or rain falling from the sky, replenishing reservoirs so we may continue to sustain the heartbeats of our souls. But most importantly, when I see the metamorphosis occurring in people's lives, a metamorphosis that takes them from a web of despair to a life of contentment and harmony, I know that the living God Jehovah is behind these wonders. Those who seek reassurance from God should bear in mind that the strength of one's faith is not measured by reassurances but rather by the absence of them. Indeed, God must and does exist, for only by his grace and his mercy have we been able to exist for so long without finding some way to become extinct. My dear unborn, when your faith is shaken because of lack of protection from those who now defile it in all kinds of unimaginable ways, do not turn your back on those who have temporarily lost sight of the truth. Pray for them and help them back to the path of enlightenment. In the event they are adamant about not wanting to serve or trust in God anymore, then I say to you that it is better to love them from afar than to risk corrupting your own soul by being in their presence. Selfish is not the man who recognizes the follies of his fellow men and chooses not to become a victim of it as well. Although it is the enlightened spiritual duty to assist and serve those who are in need, a man must know his own limitations. Hence, he should seek God's help when all other options are exhausted. When men seek God's help, let them remember that God has the "whole world in his hands," and each favor that is requested of him is one that is weighed by him concerning someone else who might be in more dire need of assistance. Therefore, in addition to your reverence, be mindful of God's insurmountable task and do everything in your power to alleviate as much as possible the stress that comes with solving the world's problems. In short, just as God looks out for us, it becomes our duty to look out for him. Man needs reassurance from God as much as God needs for us to believe in him. Man's belief system when directed toward God opens up all avenues that lead to God's kingdom. But without this belief, God knows that man's mind will forever be plagued with self-doubts and all its inadequacies.

My dear unborn, it is ironic but when all is said and done, both God and man seek the same thing from each other: reassurances. Both want to be able to believe what is known about each other: man seeks reassurance of the existence of God, and God seeks reassurance from man that he will believe what has been said by God about him. Yet, regardless of the reassurances that are given, only faith will determine the legitimacy of each other's belief system. As stated before, man must have faith in God, and God must have faith in man.

The Sixth Month

21

In the Mind of Rage

My dear unborn, I listen to a young man who appears to have all the answers, answers that cry out in rage and confusion about the social elements to which he has shackled himself all his life. Convinced that there is no place for him in this world, having no sense of belonging, watching as others embrace life to the fullest, he silently contemplates on what havoc he should reap to get the world's attention, if it's only for a second. As a child his grandmother taught him right from wrong, for although he knew his mother and father, they did not know him. He was nurtured by anger and groomed for our society by the parents of neglect. As he grew and grew he was torn between being a clown or becoming a tyrant. The choice was easy, for in his world there was nothing to laugh about. Death had become his daily companion, and guns and knives his only means of security. A long time ago someone did mention school, education, and all the wonderful things that society has to offer. But time has taught him that the world would only respect and listen to his rage. And that's all he has ever wanted, to be heard. His biggest fear is to put down his guns, for he knows to do that is to be ignored. He does not know how to reach out; no one taught him that it was okay to lean on a fellow human being because all his life they have been leaning on him. Entrapped by his own twisted views of everyone around him, he continues to plan his next temper tantrum, which always results in another body for the mortician.

My dear unborn, over the years this young man has mastered sleeping with one eye opened, watching and waiting for the grim reaper with guns and knives for his pillows, nerves of steel for his cover. Occasionally, he gazed at two lovers in a magazine only to have flashbacks with his first experience with love come rushing through his mind. He was taught how to make love by his stepfather and sometimes by a distant cousin at sixteen, both of whom would visit him late at night while his grandmother lay asleep. Yet he could not understand why he was perplexed by the mere gesture of the opposite sex's flirtatiousness. Confusion engulfed his soul as he pondered desperately, tormented about which gender he should be reacting to sexually; after all, his cousin was of the opposite sex but his stepfather was not. Lost in no-man's land he stopped for a bite to eat, but the taste of his food is spoiled by the whispers and the eyes of unwanted spectators. Welcomed by a nearby street corner, he attempted to finish his meal, realizing that the taste had returned. He walked up and down his block the opposite side of his home, praying that for once the smell of alcohol or drugs would not greet him at the door when he gets home. Suddenly, he crossed the street, but his thoughts were interrupted when a shot whistled past his ears, finding its mark in a parked car before him. Knowing that he could not outrun a bullet, having no choice, he dashed to a nearby condemned building in hopes of drawing danger away from his home. He hid behind some dirty garbage cans, his heart pounding like roaring thunder in his chest, as he listened intensely as his chasers hurled things around, trying to know his whereabouts. Finally they left, and he breathed a sigh of relief because his life span had just extended another day. His close encounter with death opened his eyes for a minute, and a new reality kicked in. He vowed to relinquish his life of drugs and crime, a promise he had made before, each time he had a brush with death.

My dear unborn, hours later he was awakened by an old familiar sound, the sound of hunger, as his little brother came crying to him for something to eat. He turned to his grandmother, but the look in her eyes told the same story: no money, no food. He picked up his gun and swore to himself that this would be the last time. Soon thereafter he was back with food and a mother was left without a son, a son without a father, and a wife without a husband. He leaned over and kissed his little brother, glad once again he was able to stop the ache that lurked in his brother's stomach. His grandmother asked, "Were these foods expensive?" He responded underneath his breath, "You have no idea." He hid his gun as he made another promise never to touch it again. Soon his promise was reinforced by his grandmother telling him how much he means to her and wanted him to do right by stop selling drugs and associating with friends with no future. He hugged her and promised to obey, but not before listening to her telling him about being two months behind in the rent and eviction notice just days away. He left the house as he pulled his shirt out of his pants. A stranger walking by noticed the gun handle sticking out. "What the hell are you looking at, man? Who's gonna pay my grandmother's rent?" Later on that evening, another daughter lost a mother and a husband lost a wife. He returned with a bag full of money and gave it to his grandmother. She kissed him on the forehead. "Thank you, my lovely child." He started to walk away. "Remember, you promise to be good." "I know, Grandma, I promise."

As he walked idly by the street, he gazed all around as if he was behind enemy lines in wartime. He held his gun tight in his waist as an old beat-up truck pulled up beside him. "Do you want a couple days work, young man?" asked the truck driver.

"Hell, I don't need to work," replied the young man.

"Are you independently wealthy or something? Tell me your secret so I don't have to get up every morning," said the truck driver.

"You just don't know how to get over on the white man, that's all," said the young man.

"I thought the best way to get over on the white man was by working and getting what you want out of life," said the truck driver.

"Hell no, you must be crazy! You got to collect welfare and let them pay for it, that's how," the young man replied.

"I feel sorry for you because the white man is getting over on you and you don't even know it," replied the truck driver.

"If you were a strong black man who takes what he wants when he wants it, you wouldn't be talking trash like that," said the young man.

"Maybe that's the problem right there. You need to consider yourself a part of the human race first before you think of yourself in terms of your own race," said the truck driver.

"What do you mean by that?"

"Simply that you should try being just a man first, then a black man second. You have a lifetime to look forward to with regards to being black. But unless you become a real man first, you'll be dead before you reach twenty-five, and that's no lie," the truck driver explained.

"Look at you. You're driving around in that old beat-up truck hustling for a few bucks. Is that what you call being a man?" asked the young man.

"Yes! Because I am working for my keeps, and this old beat-up truck is mine. But even more important, I can put food on my family's table without having to rob or kill anyone," replied the truck driver.

"Old man, you better move on before you get hurt, because unless you can feel me socially, economically, or psychologically, you can't tell me a damn thing."

"Listen to you. You have a brain in your head, but rage in your heart," replied the truck driver. "Come and put in a few days work with me and start earning your keeps."

"I have something to earn my keeps right here," said the young man as he showed the truck driver the handle of the gun in his waist.

"I guess every beast has to rock and roll with the devil before he can waltz with angels," replied the old man.

"I'm no beast. I'm just a guy who is trying to feed his family. A guy nobody listens to unless I have a gun in my hands, a guy who knows that people will always think he's a punk unless he shows them that he's no punk, but a brave man who takes what he wants from society."

"Young man, humility is the father of courage. You can be a great man or a great criminal, but at least have the integrity to be true to yourself about the reason for your decision."

Alphonso pulled the gun from his waist. "Who the hell you called a beast anyway? You don't know me!"

"That's where you are wrong, young man. I know your generation very well, a generation consumed by rage and breathe nothing but hate until someone takes time to show them the way."

"I'll pop you right now if you don't shut your damn mouth up."

"You do that, young man, and you ruin your entire life."

"See how much you know, old man. Nothing can happen to me. I'm a juvie, and if I get caught for popping you, within two years I'll be back on the streets, that's the law. And if you call me 'young man' one more time, I swear I'll pop you right now. My goddamn name is Alphonso."

"Okay, Alphonso. But does that give you the right to kill another human being? Because you are a juvenile and won't do much time?"

"Hell yes. I can pop you right now, like I have done others and the law probably won't know about it. And so what if they find out? I'll be out for my twenty-first birthday. They know they can't try me like an adult." Alphonso was taken aback by the old man's responses.

"Do what you must, but at least let me say a prayer before you pull the trigger."

The old man closed his eyes as Alphonso struggled within himself, tormented between going left and coming right as he listened to the old man's prayer.

"Merciful Father, Jehovah. Finally I'm coming home to Your kingdom, a place I have worked my entire life to reach if ever I'm found worthy. Judge me now, Father, as in my final hour I relinquish my place in Your kingdom to Alphonso. Forgive him for what he feels compelled to do as l am compelled to denounce my love for You and all the heavenly staff if Alphonso is not allowed to be seated in my place at Your table. If the shedding of my blood will help him find peace, then let my blood pour like a river's stream and my love for him wash him from this evil act." The old man opened his eyes to find tears dripping down Alphonso's face and the gun trembling nervously in his hand.

"No one has ever given up anything for me before, much less a place in heaven, a place my grandmother is always talking about. I don't believe in heaven, but not my grandma. Even when we are starving, she be saying the Lord will provide, he always does. I wanted to tell her that he is providing alright, but why does he have to use me to do it all the time? Every time I rob or kill someone, I say this will be the last time. But a couple days will pass, and Grandma would tell me that she does not know where the next meal is coming from but the Lord will provide. And sure enough I go right back out on the street to get the money. She don't understand that every time she tells me about no food in the house or money for the rent and about other bills, it's a message that I have a responsibility as the man of the house to go out and get the money any way I can. It's funny. You know, old man, you talk about heaven and she talks about heaven, but I am on my way to hell and she has no idea that she is helping me get there. When I pop somebody I don't see their face. I see hers telling me how much we're in need, So, you go ahead, old man, and ask God back for your place in heaven if he exists. I won't pop you."

"I meant it about the job, Alphonso. It's steady work and you don't have to do what you are doing anymore."

"How much money would I make?"

"I could start you off with $7.50 per hour, and if you work hard you'll be making $10 in no time."

Alphonso laughed out loud. "You gotta be crazy. I make what you're offering me in two weeks in just one score."

"Yes, Alphonso, but at what price? You're not a bad young man, just a misguided one. At least give it a chance, and if you don't like the job and how you feel, then you can quit with no questions asked."

"People have been using me all my life, so why should you be any different? Besides, why would you want someone like me around, a cold and heartless monster?"

"Alphonso, maybe you have been so busy taking from people that you never stopped to take the time to see that there were people out there who really wanted to give freely. You talk about being cold and ruthless. That's okay, Alphonso, but use it the right way. You see, being cold and ruthless within the boundaries of the law makes you a shrewd person, but being cold and ruthless outside the boundaries of the law makes you a criminal. Lose your gun and let your mind be your weapon."

"But nobody listens to me without a gun."

"Then make them listen, Alphonso. But you gotta have something to say, boy, either through your actions or your words. But make them listen. I noticed you put the gun back in your waist a while back; but here I am listening to you, and so will others if you give them a chance."

"You still want me to come and work for you?"

"Yes, Alphonso, I would be honored."

"Okay then, man, I'll try it for a while."

The old man went inside his pocket and took out five one-hundred-dollar bills. Alphonso's eyes popped wide open. "I told you that I was not going to rob you, man, so what's this for?"

"This is your first paycheck, and here's my card with my address. I know you will show up to earn it."

"What to stop me from just splitting and don't show up for the job?"

"Nothing, Alphonso. Nothing at all except yourself."

"Don't sweat it, man. I'll be there bright and early." Alphonso walked away, but the old man was not finished with him yet.

"One more thing, Alphonso. If you really what a chance to live your life, then you must confront your worst fear."

"I'm not afraid of anything, man."

"How about losing your grandmother's love and approval? Is that not why you always try and make a score when she gets depressed about the bills and other problems she's going through? It's time to tell her, Alphonso. Tell her about how you feel about all the pressure but most important what you have been doing to get the money to support the family. Atonement begins with confrontation, then forgiveness. If you are serious about starting over, then you must put a stop to all the pressure she has been laying on your shoulders without being aware of it. Then the forgiveness will come later."

"Who's going to forgive me? Most of the people I capped are dead."

"God will forgive you, Alphonso, but first you must learn how to forgive yourself. You may not believe this, but to use your own words, I've capped a couple people during my time also, you know. But thank God I don't have to live like that anymore."

Alphonso found the old man's comment quite funny and laughed aloud in an unstoppable fashion. "You? No way, man. You couldn't cap anybody."

"Never judge how tasty a pig will be by how much mud he has in his sty. I was young just like you once, and I grew up right down the street at the corner of Benning Road."

"That's close to where I live. I just live on the other side of Bladensburgh Road."

"I did not finish high school but I started Anacostia High School; later I worked hard and got my GED. Now I have my own business. So you see, Alphonso, if I can change so can you."

"But you are one of the lucky ones who was able to get out of the ghetto."

"I know, Alphonso, and that's why I am trying to offer you the same opportunity, the same way someone helped me to get out. What do you say, do you want to give it a go?"

Alphonso looked at the money in his hands. "Hey, man, if you are willing to take a chance on me, why shouldn't I take one on you?"

"You are going to talk to your grandmother, right?"

"I will, and don't worry, I will be at work tomorrow."

"I know. I'll see you then." The old man drove off.

Alphonso whispered quietly beneath his breath, "Thank you. See you tomorrow, bright and early."

My dear unborn, the dialogue between the old man and Alphonso has just depicted a generation in rage, a rage that transcends all racial barriers, a generation that refuses to play host to the system, a system that gradually sets up obstacles to further intensify the anger and frustration that quite frequently results in learned helplessness, thus feeding the stigmatization that nothing this generation does will bring about any meaningful consequences or changes. Since little is being done to nurture the relationship between society and this new generation in rage, we must ask ourselves why the astonishment when some variation of this rage reaches into our backyard and inflicts damages to our loved ones or to ourselves. When we weep for this generation, and we must, then we cannot forget to weep for ourselves, because ultimately we will be the receptacle of this rage.

My dear unborn, the old man captures Alphonso's attention by suppressing his own fear and finding the courage to display an act of love in the face of adversity. The sign of true trust between them came when the old man was willing to sacrifice his place in heaven, thus giving it to Alphonso even as he was about to take the old man's life. Indeed, to reach this generation in rage, we must be able and be willing to lay it all on the line. We cannot live in our own little corner of the world, playing it safe from a distance by sending a few dollars here and there. Time and ourselves are the two most important things we can give to a troubled youth. Unless they can see that someone is truly willing to make a sacrifice that entails giving up a portion of themselves to make a difference in their lives, then nothing one says to them will penetrate their armor of rage. In their world, trust is not built on promises but by actions. All their lives they have been lied to, deceived, and exploited, frequently by their own family or someone they hold dear. There is very little one can say to them to win their trust in order to facilitate change. However, a small act of kindness can plant a seed of hope in a garden of despair. One has to surrender to both fate and faith in relinquishing this kindness.

My dear unborn, fear and the illusion of power are the two worst elements one can bring to the table when attempting to establish a rapport with a member of this generation, for in their world this is viewed as a sign of weakness, thus opening you up to vulnerability that you may or may not have in your psyche. Warmth and reason will face them to confront the irrational and illogical perceptions of their subjective world and society and serve as a nurturing tool that can be quite effective when used with firmness and kindness. Firmness, not authority, for if you are seen as an authority figure, you are inviting a power struggle. If you are in a power struggle with a member of a generation in rage—a power struggle that you are not 100 percent sure that you can win—you will lose any hopes of having a relationship with them if that was your intent. And even if you win, you would have lost because their respect and possible compliance would have derived from fear, and fear is the essence of their world.

My dear unborn, when Alphonso told the old man he was getting over on the white man by not working, he voiced a powerful statement of fact that is seen as a major axiom in his subjective world. It has nothing to do with Alphonso being industrious as many would probably think. What it has to do with, however, is defiance, not only against the white man but against the entire world. It is easier to blame the white man for all his troubles than it is to blame himself. Blaming the white man diverts attention from his own inadequacies and keeps him from focusing on the most important issue, himself. The greatest misconception is the belief that when a statement is made about the white man that it is only about the white man. For some strange and diluted reason, "the white man" is just another name for society in their world. Unfortunately, not knowing this, the white man personalizes any such statement and reciprocates with inadequacies of his own. When there is a meaningful dialogue between members of the white race and a member of a generation in rage, the so-called antisocial personality, frequently there is little or no anger between the individuals themselves, the conversationalists. But society takes on a different color when historical biases and hatred are at the forefront of many of the circumstances that govern the daily lives of the disadvantaged.

My dear unborn, the old man spent time slowly confronting and breaking down Alphonso's irrational beliefs about the white man by asking him questions about his own thoughts. This is an important step, because unless you can make a member of a generation in rage see a picture of his own thoughts, little or no communication will occur to the extent that change will. The irrationality of their thoughts must hit them dead smack in the face, from which hopefully realities will kick in alleviating them of any variation of denial and other pseudo-defense mechanisms that are seen as coping devices. But to do this, one must also be willing to embrace the hard truth about the world of a generation of rage. In short, don't tell these young people that everything is hunky-dory in their world when it is not. It will be seen as a sign of disrespect and naivete by them. Because they are angry does not mean that they are stupid, and any attempt to treat them as such will be met with deep resentment and contempt. Show them that you understand or are trying to understand what is going on in their world by first listening to what they have to say, then summarize what you think you have heard, then ask them if your description of what they have said is correct or not. This gesture will indicate that you are really making an effort to try and understand what's going on both in their world and in their head. Keep in mind that quite often what's in their head is a reflection of what they think is going on in the world. But when we plant a seed of hope in a garden of despair, what we get can depend on what type of fertilizer we choose to use. Hope is the one element we must leave with them and impress upon them to believe in. Regardless of whatever else we do, we must never surrender our fight for their souls. Hope to believe that things can get better; hope to believe that redemption is at hand regardless of what they might have done in the past; hope to believe that they too can become an important asset to society, thus having a sense of belonging. They hope to believe that one day they too will find their niche in the world in which they live. Hope should always be offered as a light at the end of the tunnel.

My dear unborn, the old man was also able to teach Alphonso by showing him that he too had something in common with him. He too was able to identify with his life in some small respect. Indeed, unless one is able to identify with a member of a generation in rage socially, economically, or even psychologically, as stated by Alphonso, any attempt to establish a rapport with a member is like Armstrong trying to explain what it was like to walk on the moon to a person who does not know what a moon is. I am not saying that one has to be like them at that given moment, but there must be some similarities before any serious thought is given by them of taking you seriously. In this world, it is inevitable that you will meet such an individual, a member of a generation in rage. When you do, remember to greet them with hope, that is, if you are not at the end of the spectrum of one's rage and fury.

THE SEVENTH MONTH

22

THE EPIGENETIC PRINCIPLES OF LIFE VS. THE EPIGENETIC PRINCIPLES OF THE UNIVERSAL ORDER

My dear unborn, when your prayer is left unanswered or you grow angry because you believe God somehow refuses to intervene on your behalf, remember the concept of free will has bound him to rules that even he must follow. Unlike most of us, at times, he is a prisoner of his own creations, one of the many prices he must pay for being omniscient. Remember always that each individual's life intertwines not only with each other but also on a much larger scale, the universal order of things. God has insight into each of our lives from the beginning to end, and while we are not privy to this type of information about our own lives, and instead must wait and live it day by day, this abundance of knowledge makes it difficult for him to sometimes intervene on our behalf. Indeed, one single intervention on his part can result in a domino effect of a series of circumstances and consequences. The epigenetic principles of life state that each individual from birth to death must go through certain experiences in life. It also states that the outcome of each experience drastically impacts the outcome of the next experience. In short, the success of each experience depends on the one before. These experiences range from life changing to building the foundation of one's wisdom, what is known as learning experiences.

My dear unborn, the epigenetic principles of the universal order are similar in nature. It states that things are placed in their own respective order within the universe, and each order when altered for any reason drastically influences the sequences of this order. Once the chain of events has been altered depending on the laws of circumstances, the dynamics within the universe change, and when this happens it changes everybody's life as a whole depending on what predicament they find themselves in. Hence, one of the primary reasons as to why life is so unpredictable for each of us and will always be is because very rarely two or more individuals affect the universal order in the same manner.

My dear unborn, let us assume for a moment that God does not hold free will in such high regard and therefore frequently intervenes in our lives as a matter of practice, knowing full well that each intervention will drastically change the next body of experience within the epigenetic stage of an individual's life. God would ultimately become responsible for every chain of events that occurs within our lives, and an assignment of blame would be warranted for experiences that were not completed to our satisfaction. Keep in mind that God would not be intervening in our lives based on what we think but rather based on how he thinks. The outcome of each epigenetic experience would be an outcome based on God's vast experience rather than our own limited one, which is based primarily on trial and error. The experiences of each individual would then become God's, for it is he who would be manipulating the laws of circumstances to provide the perfect possible outcome of each scenario. Indeed, the absence of free will tends to ignite a slippery slope to control. Any interference in man's experiences by God, randomly or otherwise, changes the course of that individual's existence, which in turn changes the existence of another individual that may totally be unrelated. When an experience is shaped by a divine power, he must shape the outcome of that individual's other experiences as well, and when this happens, the line that leads to free will becomes blurred.

My dear unborn, the success of each epigenetic experience is relative to each individual's existence. For most of us, it involves a spiritual growth that leads to contentment and the maturity of the psyche as well as an openness to all things. Indeed, the lack of frequent intervention into our lives by the Supreme Being paves the way for man to be in control of his own destiny, but more importantly, it provides us with a fighting chance in dealing with the outcome that stems from the influences that the laws of circumstances have on the universal order of things. In short, it raises man's cosmic consciousness.

My dear unborn, when God intervenes into our lives, no matter how small the intervention, in actuality he is changing the entire course of our existence and indirectly molding all the other lives that we touch. And although the realities of life can be harsh to the point where the innocents suffer and children die, we must allow our faith to sustain us and reserve our judgment of God. Sometimes, however, man seems to forget that God also has free will. We have a tendency to take for granted that we have turned away from him, and that he has gone at great length to promote the reunification of souls. Man's arrogance has led him to believe falsely; he thinks God owes him something, and as such God must clear all obstacles from man's path. Man seems to believe that simply by asking for forgiveness, it is then incumbent upon God to extend this forgiveness into some tangible act of charity. What seems to escape us is the notion of free will that God also has, a will that does not always transform itself in acts of mercy or charity, but also acts of sternness and firmness. It is his will to say no at times regardless of the catastrophic circumstances we may find ourselves in. An act of denial or refusal to assist us in our tribulations does not demonstrate in any way that he loves us any less.

My dear unborn, we sometimes hold very unreasonable and unfair notions about God. One of these ideas is that if bad things happen to us or our loved ones because of some perceived lack of intervention on God's behalf, then he is not deserving of worship. Furthermore, the lack of intervention depicts a God that is not in tune with his people, or it must be some sign of punishment from him. We seem to forget that as much time as we say no to God by way of our actions he, like us, possesses the same free will to say no, not this time. You ask, "So when did I ever say no to God?" Every time you say yes to something that is counterproductive to his teachings through your deeds and thoughts.

My dear unborn, the epigenetic principles of life, when run smoothly with the universal order of things, give way to a body of collective experiences that serve as a nurturing source to our existence. The circumstances that man finds himself in sometimes can be the deciding factor as to whether or not the experiences of his life can be successfully completed without drastically altering the link that connects him to the universal order of things. Each man is connected to the way things are placed within the universe. The changes he experiences during his existence with respect to the way he deals and anticipates the laws of circumstances can be the deciding factor in terms of whether or not his connection to the universal order of things will be weakened or strengthened. When a man is not in sync with the laws of circumstances or the universal order of things, he leaves himself open up to the worst possible scenarios that life has to offer. A man who has successfully mastered the art of anticipating the laws of circumstances and its association with the universal order of things is a man who has been blessed with wisdom beyond his years.

My dear unborn, God must not be blamed for man's transgressions against man. He must not be blamed for the world man has created and the wickedness that emerged as a result of man's creations. Do not view any tragedy as a test from God, for the heart of man is transparent to God, and he has no need to confirm that which he already knows about man. Tragedies should be seen for what they are, things or man being manipulated by the laws of circumstances in relation to their places in the universal order or sequences. Tragedies are the end results of these manipulations. The hands of God are and will forever be stainless of the horror that confronts man daily. The success of each epigenetic experience of man's life depends on man's ability not only to fully comprehend this notion, but also to show prudence in dealing with the entire phenomenon of the epigenetic principles of the universal order as well. Both concepts are a major part of the foundation on which man's entire existence stands. Unless each epigenetic experience is successfully resolved to one's satisfaction, it undoubtedly will affect the next experience that is in line for that individual. The unresolved experience will then resurface at some later date, thus providing the individual with the opportunity once again to deal with it satisfactorily. Therefore, it is usually better to handle the experiences in one's life because not only will they impede the next experience the person will face, but eventually circumstances will dictate that you face this same unresolved experience again and again until it has been resolved.

The Seventh Month

23

The Two Types of Eternities

My dear unborn, life after death can either be the beginning or the end of the soul that you possess, a soul that unknowingly will have the decision to choose between the two types of eternities. No! I am not talking about hell or a variation as the second type of eternity. Still, the first type of eternity that I speak of is the infinity behind God's love to return man back to a state of grace and the constant struggle to help man find his redeemable qualities—the ability to be able to see the world through the eyes of many, while never losing one's spiritual identity, a perpetuated regurgitation of the soul in an ultimate quest to find redemption. Souls that are judged not to be damned, yet lack the spiritual attributes to reside with God, will be offered this first type of eternity, an eternity that involves timeless birth and death, followed by continuous confrontation with God. The nature of the confrontation? To hopefully guide the individual closer to the holy circle of light. The great sadness, however, is that with all of God's guidance, the freedom to take heed and exercise the instructions still depends on the individual. Indeed, free will, God's grand gift to mankind, can also lead many astray when left unchecked to the point that how and where man spends eternity is of his own making and choosing.

Reincarnation is not a way of life for the soul; it's an option, the first type of eternity. It is for those souls that with all the guidance, with all the good intentions, and with all the drive or desire still are unable to fulfill the criteria needed to rejoin God's holy circle of light. Reincarnation is for the souls that are not bad enough for hell but not quite good enough for heaven. It is the first type of eternity for many individuals whose souls will forever wonder but somehow never seem to be able to find a place in the spiritual realm because of follies committed in this world. These souls are able to develop a sense of belonging on a temporal plane, yet strangely enough not within the spiritual realm. It is not that they are antagonistic or defiant within the spiritual realm, but like so many of us in this world they are misunderstood and have often found it difficult to conform in a manner that makes them at ease with themselves or their environment. In his wisdom, God embraces this spiritual uniqueness and returns these souls to a world that they can feel a part of for eternity, or until these individuals have become worthy. Indeed this type of eternity is not problem-free like the other type of eternity, the rejoining of the holy circle of light back in God's kingdom. One could also argue that spending eternity in this manner is hardly fair in comparison to spending eternity in a problem-free world. The focal point, however, is "hope without the possibility of condemnation." The process of reincarnation still provides hope for those souls that are able to overcome their spiritual defects and become worthy for God's kingdom, while not depriving them of an opportunity to obtain the second type of eternity, the rejoining of God's holy circle of light.

My dear unborn, reincarnation is not a sentence that God arbitrarily passes down; it is a choice presented to each soul with all its ramifications. In the final analysis, the soul that is being judged must make the decision regarding its own destiny with respect to eternity. The choice given is not between going to heaven or being reincarnated, but rather being reincarnated or returned back to a state of "nothingness," back to the dust from whence we came. There are those who would have you believe that the Creator has already created a place equivalent to purgatory, a place where man can stay in limbo and struggle to redeem himself. God does not have to create such a place, for one already exists. The world we live and die in, this world, is the only purgatory man will ever know.

My dear unborn, the challenges that an individual will need while going through the process of reincarnation will be provided by life's demands. If indeed there is such a place as purgatory, it is here in the world you already exist in. If man cannot find redemption in this world, he will not find it in the next, unless it is given through the grace and mercy of God. Eternity is for those who have found redemption or are on the verge of discovering it on their journey. The two types of eternities share the same destiny, a destiny that entails giving those who have lived in Christ a chance to live forever. While the means by which this is accomplished is distinct between the two concepts of eternities, the merciful God has made it possible for man to claim the gift of salvation, if he can conquer his worst enemy, himself. Those who do not seek God's kingdom by way of Christ must do so by way of God's mercy and grace.

My dear unborn, the gift of eternity is still a matter of choice. The idea of living forever, as strange as it may sound, does not appeal to all people. This in no way is indicative of a lost or sick soul or even a distraught mind, but what it does represent is that of a limited vision. The inability to foresee or visualize the kingdom of God, the fallacy of doing a comparative analysis between this world and the one they cannot see or imagine, and false attributes of the kingdom of God based on the known attributes of this world . . . these are just a few of the notions that are embraced by some individuals who have chosen living a life in this world with no intent or wish to be a part of the life after. As stated earlier, even eternity is a matter of choice. In short, if an individual has successfully met the criteria and therefore is deemed worthy to enter the kingdom of God but chooses not to exist for eternity, such is right of this individual, one that will be granted. It is not within God's character to compel anyone to do anything against his or her will, much less making a decision that will impact their lives forever. The kingdom of God has no locks on its doors. Even in eternity man is free to go as freely as he is allowed to enter. The essence of eternity does not consist only of infinite immortality, nor is it only about giving praises to the Almighty in worship. Indeed, God does not grace individuals with everlasting life simply to have subjects pay homage to him forever. Eternity exists as an effort to return man back to a state of grace. It exists as an effort to reunite man's soul with the holy circle of light, inadvertently emerging, becoming one with God's. Eternity is God's way of providing the opportunity for man to know and live the existence that was intended for them before man became exposed to sin. The harmony and peace that were meant to be a part of man's life forever but eluded man because of his iniquity and having been born in sin is still at hand. It is God's wish and hope for man to have this peace and harmony, even if it takes an eternity to get it to them.

THE SEVENTH MONTH

24

IN THE MIND OF GOD

My dear unborn, people have a tendency to believe that the outcomes of their life experiences are attributed to what God might or might not have been thinking at a particular time. There are countless numbers of atrocities that have been done in the name of God or religion. Yet the greatest wrong of all is the justification that we offer to ourselves when we have brought some element of danger to our fellow men, regardless of the transgression. It is bad enough that people behave like wolves toward each other, but to possess the audacity to make God a conspirator by telling themselves that the deed is part of God's plan or his will, as a form of justification, surely tests the limitation of God's mercy. Man seeks knowledge of all kinds, yet seldom takes the time to decipher what truly lies in the mind of God.

My dear unborn, man has scrutinized religious relics and teachings over a period of centuries only to reach one main axiom: that the path to God has many directions. The Muslims have their path; so do the Christians, the Jews, and other variations of Eastern spiritualism. Regardless of the distinctions between the religions, one tenet remains basic amongst them, and that is there is some greater force or being than ourselves to whom all men must one day give total accountability for their actions. Everything else is in accordance with their own faith in terms of what they embrace ideologically. Man must exert more energy in an attempt to understand God's mind, but we must first struggle to understand our own, for the human mind is only an extension of the mind of God. Once we truly understand the potentials of our own mind, only then will we begin to gain some insight into the mind of God. Being created in the image of God includes obtaining a part of him that makes us able to gain access not only to his mind but to his soul. In truth, to gain better understanding into God's mind and soul, all we need to do is to become more familiar with our own.

My dear unborn, the mind of God entails a multidimensional frame that consists of a small piece of all human minds, a frame that allows God to see and know what lies in our minds long before we do. To see what lies in the minds of men is to know what lies in their hearts as well. Very few men have learned to embrace the true potential that comes with being given a piece of God's mind. I have seen young children who have never been taught create masterpieces within their areas of interest, and in them the mind of God glows like a halo around their heads as they bear testimony to what a small piece of God's mind is like.

My dear unborn, you ask how can man be a part of evil when his mind is a part of God's. But in response I will only remind you that man does not entertain evil; he is confronted by it and must therefore choose for himself if he will allow it to devour him or pass him by. Although the Messiah possesses the mind of God, that did not preclude him from being confronted by Lucifer. Why then should man be any different? The more man sets out to accomplish a meeting of the mind with God, the more insight man will have into the manifestation of his own imperfections. Evil does not always derive from Lucifer.

My dear unborn, indeed, it has become extremely difficult for man to read God's mind since man seldom follows the wishes of God anymore. Man will only discover what truly lies on God's mind when he is able to unmask the darkness from his own mind. God relishes the time when man's mind will be so in tune with his that the need for words will no longer be a necessity for communications, and the linkage between heaven and earth will once again be seen clearly in the minds of man as before. I tell you that the closest man will ever get to the mind of God is through meticulous reexamination of his own mind, or by standing in the presence of an innocent child. There will come a time when man will be able to harness the potential and capabilities of the untouched regions of his mind. When this time comes, he will see for himself a reflection that will cast an image of the mind of the living God. It is not by chance that man is unable to tap into the full capabilities of the mind, for to do this is to be able to see into the mind of God. It is by the will of God, a God who recognizes that man's fall from grace has made it impossible for him to be able to handle the powers that would have come from such accomplishment.

My dear unborn, I do not presume to know what lies in the mind of God, but I do know what lies in the mind of man. As such, it has prepared me with an alertness to God's mind. Recently a man asked why do bad people have everything with respect to material things and people who serve God have nothing and always seem to be struggling to make ends meet? He seemed angry with God when he asked the question. I told him that God has his disciples and Lucifer has his; both reward their disciples in their own way. Lucifer subscribes to rewards relevant to man's desires and weaknesses often by giving him all the earthly things he wishes because he has nothing else to offer except a place beside him in hell. But God rewards his disciples with eternal life and heavenly wishes. He knows that the things of this world will not last and does not like to create the illusion of health and prosperity. So he takes care of our needs and hopes that our spiritual growth will not let us indulge too much in the things we want, things in many cases that are designed to corrupt our souls. This is not to say that God wants his disciples to be impoverished; quite the contrary. But he wants us to maintain our focus on the things that are truly important. The things that define the essence of wealth in the eyes of God are not those that define wealth in the eyes of Lucifer. Man having earthly wealth is not a priority for God if it means leaving man's spirit in danger of not being a part of God's kingdom. Wealth and riches that do not include faith and spiritual edification are an illusion that will not last; it is the embodiment of Lucifer's gift, one that creates envy in the eyes of the spiritually deficient. Do not measure your wealth by the abundance of your earthly possessions but rather by the extent of your relationship with the Creator and the amount of lives you have influenced on the path to righteousness and spiritual growth. Remember, to truly unravel the mystery of God's mind, look to your own and then the children.

THE EIGHTH MONTH

25

FACING ADVERSITY SPIRITUALLY

My dear unborn, it is easy to say to another that adversity must be met with dignity and that the decision we make must follow a moral code. But the truth is, each of us must strive for our own perfection when it comes to dealing with adversities of any form. While the personal fiber of that individual is paramount to the way in which the person copes, no one can dictate to another the degree of dignity he or she should put forth in order to be politically correct amongst their peers. Indeed, one should strive for perfection but never delude themselves in actually becoming perfect. Doing things in accordance to a certain moral standard is a wonderful thing, but when dealing with certain adversities, man cannot afford the luxury of always doing that which is morally upright. Remember, the moral compass of a man cannot exceed the true essence of his character. Therefore, when you are blessed with spiritual enlightenment, your self-awareness will guide you along moral guidelines, not the issues themselves that might come up.

My dear unborn, lack of emotional homeostasis frequently runs parallel to adversities. However, this should seldom be the focal point during such times. But since it does influence the decision-making process, the consequences of these decisions will still play a role in your life during the aftermath of the adversity. Hence, it is critical that some type of stability remains in the decision-making process so you do not suffer from any adverse impact after you are through coping with the adversity. As stated earlier, one cannot concern oneself with perfection during adversities, and morality must be kept in perspective. Indeed, in resolving or dealing with adversity, one must be guided by convictions and principles, and if one is spiritually enlightened it is enough for the measurement of any moral yardstick or criteria. An enlightened individual is not guided by moralistic issues but rather by a spiritual arrow that directs itself not at the heart of social taboos and expectations, but only by the approval of the Messiah. Hence, adversities should be approached from a spiritual standpoint, not from an emotional, social, moral, or politically correct one. Two thousand years ago the Messiah was seen as an entity diametrically opposed to being politically correct socially, politically, and even morally by the majority, and yet we know today he was right with respect to keeping his focus only on the spiritual standpoint.

My dear unborn, with any adversity the impact is only as effective as your thought process allows it, and what you tell yourself during this process. When faced with adversities, you must ask yourself why does it affect you the way it does. Question your feelings as well as the thoughts behind them. For example, a man lost his wife to cancer. Ten years after her death he finds himself crying daily and has become so depressed that he lost his job and has no interest in any other aspect of his life. His kids, however, have gone on with their lives and wonder why their father could not do the same. The kids dealt with their mother's death by acknowledging that she was a good mother, that they loved her and will always miss her. The father, however, started to do a self-analysis of what he could and should not have done while she was alive. Hence, he indirectly blames himself for failing to measure up in certain areas of his relationship with his wife, thus tormenting himself daily.

My dear unborn, remember, when you are faced with adversities of any kind, if you are looking for a reason to blame yourself or hold yourself responsible, chances are you are going to find one if you look hard enough. One should learn from adversities but not become a prisoner to them. Regardless of why adversities occur, it is up to an individual to use them to strengthen the human armor that we all wear to protect ourselves. Learn from it if you can but do not wear it on your sleeve as an excuse not to deal with life's demands or as an incentive to retreat into your own world so as not to deal with life and all the unpleasantness that comes with it.

My dear unborn, in dealing with adversities, people must choose to deal or not to deal with it. Sometimes they choose suicide as a means of dealing with the pain from the adversity, but suicide ends all pain so by choosing to end the pain from the adversity in this way, the decision is made to end the pain of life inadvertently in its entirety. In making the decision, they engaged in the line of thinking that there must be an alternative to the pain of this world. The belief in heaven or a better world besides this one is usually a strong incentive to leave this world. People do not commit suicide because of the pain of this world alone. They commit suicide because there is promise of a better world besides this one. People who believe in heaven or utopia are much more likely to deal with adversities by committing suicide than those who do not believe in either. If there is no life after this one, then the person is more willing to stay in this world and cope and find some way to deal with adversity. The fact that there is an alternative to this world makes it a little easier for people to leave it, assigning a permanent solution to a temporary problem in most cases.

My dear unborn, absolution in death is the one forbidden request according to most religious teachings. Even if people are likely to commit suicide, some may not because it is considered a sin, and in death there is no way to ask for forgiveness for taking one's life. But if one makes a conscious decision and the circumstances are justified not by man but by God, then no punishment will be attributed to the taking of one's life. Therefore, no absolution in death is a myth, one of man's greatest misguided presumptions. Only God, not man, not the church, can decide what sins will be forgiven and under what circumstances. Christ came into this world to do a job, a job that included dying for man's sins willingly, a planned death for the noblest of reasons, and one that was justifiable in the eyes of God, his Father. Are we to assume that God would not judge us or use the same level of insight when it comes to us, his other children? Are we to assume that God can in no way relate to human suffering simply because he is not occasionally plagued by the frailties of human idiosyncrasies? Nonsense! God wishes that we will have great respect for our lives and would hope that our sufferings are bearable. But in the event not, it is not beyond his comprehension and mercy when our sufferings become too painful that we should seek to end it by means of suicide.

My dear unborn, facing adversities with dignity is not as important as facing them spiritually. Dignity in this context implies being functional in a manner that meets your approval as well as that of your peers. But facing adversities spiritually implies a commitment on the part of an individual to allow God to intervene with respect to the adversity, and render whatever solutions, relief, and healing that he deems appropriate under the adverse situation. It involves total surrender to one's faith and the knowledge that comes with knowing that regardless of the nature of the adversity, with God's help it will not become emotionally crippling or spiritually draining. Indeed, maintaining one's self-respect during the course of any adversity is more than just a general concern, and rest assured that when you approach adversities from a spiritual perspective, self-respect and interpersonal sensitivities are as much a part of the equation as faith itself. As long as one remembers that while God does not create adversities within our lives, he does seize the opportunity to use them to test various aspects of our character to the ends that it will reveal certain revelations about our true nature, not to him but to ourselves—the true human nature, not the mask or the persona that we spend almost all of our lives creating so that we may live with ourselves or be accepted by others, people who—regardless of what we do—still see us in a manner that question why we would consider any type of association with them in the first place, people who regardless of how hard we try, we'll still fall short of their expectations.

My dear unborn, the revelations that usually emerge from these adversities serve only one purpose: to allow us access into our own psyche, giving us the type of learning experience that will ultimately lend itself to some greater purpose within our lives or the life of another with whom you will one day come in contact. The ability to face adversities will become twice as difficult if the reference point one chooses to use in coping with the adversities is not a spiritual one. Without a spiritual involvement, the resolutions are cognitively limited to the efforts of man with little or no attempt to initiate the process of channeling to and from the Messiah that which will once again make our lives complete during the aftermath of the adversity. The primary ingredient that is necessary for the process of this channeling would have been lost without the spiritual involvement. Spiritual involvement is the key to God's kingdom and should be the embodiment of your faith.

THE EIGHTH MONTH

26

THE ENLIGHTENED

My dear unborn, the question of why anyone should strive to become spiritually enlightened is as complex as they come. Yet, while I can only shed light on what it is like for me, I do hope that for all those who have chosen to follow the path of enlightenment that the underlying principles are similar. Before a garden of paradise can be created, sometimes the weed of destruction must be destroyed; so it is with the mind, body, and spirit. To be enlightened is to carry all three entities through a rebirth process, allowing them to die, buried in the abyss of darkness clouded by ignorance only to be resurrected in an illumination rooted in wisdom and cosmic consciousness. One must shed the three entities of all their superficial attributes by relinquishing their connections to the earthly ties that serve as a substitute for the essential spiritual elements that are needed to fill the void within one's self.

My dear unborn, the journey must involve embracing and harnessing both the positivistic and negativistic learning experiences that stem from making the choices that ultimately make us more prudent about the entities of the universe. Indeed, these learning experiences often dictate not only our level of prudence but in actuality become the essence of the shield which emerges when the mind, body, and spirit come together as one, serving as the ultimate defense against the entire world. For when one is enlightened, the combination of these three entities operating in total unison is the primary protection one has against all those things that have a tendency to enslave a person as a whole, things which are relative to each individual, depending on his or her desires and weaknesses, but will become blatantly more obvious as one's relationship with the Messiah deepens and one remains on the road to spiritual enlightenment.

My dear unborn, remember always that spiritual enlightenment is about knowing God, but only through the Messiah, because man's sin forbids him to ever enmesh his soul with God's, but not with the Messiah. Therefore, it is only by becoming one with the spirit of the Messiah that man can hope to become one with the spirit of God, but only after the soul has been totally liberated from its sinful body. Hence, as long as man continues to exist within his body he must seek and can only obtain the zenith of spiritual enlightenment through the grace of God by way of the Messiah. There are those who will argue that their relationship existed with God long before Christ came along and therefore see no reason to alter it and refuse to pay tribute and reverence to the Messiah. Remember this: just as God is and always will be alpha and omega, so is Jesus Christ. The fact that God chose not to introduce his Son to the world until he was ready to do so should not prevent any man from giving him the same degree of reverence and love. While it is admirable with regards to only recognizing one's relationship with God and desire only to serve and worship him, such notion stems from a foolish heart, one that is hardened by Lucifer's refusal to remove the cognitive blinders so that one may see and come to know God through Christ. Indeed no matter how great one's love is for God, one cannot truly love him without first loving his Son, for to deny Christ is to deny God.

My dear unborn, to be enlightened is to master the art of humility and possess the ability to exercise it in the presence of great exaltedness without the need or compulsion to hide behind one's pride, ego, or rationalizations. It is the daring of one's self to embark on a path of righteousness and goodness when one is confronted by evil and the ignorance that forces man to display wickedness toward one another. Being enlightened is to find the beauty in things and places where others have failed to see them. It is the ability to foresee a small glimpse of God's master plan for the world as well as decipher a minute fraction of the wisdom that comes from his mind, through one's spiritual connection with the Messiah. Although the enlightened is set apart from those whom have yet to see the light of God, filled with compassion and love they are drawn to man's darkness in order to save him from himself by bringing him forth from that darkness. The enlightened seeks neither to persuade or to convince but rather to engage your mind in hopes that through your own insight you too will discover the one essential axiom that will set your feet on the path to spiritual enlightenment: without God in one's life, the life one has will never be as fulfilling as it was meant to be.

My dear unborn, the spiritually enlightened is in a holy union with the Messiah, a marriage between two souls that has been ordained by God, a marriage that will one day become a part of God's holy circle of light, after man has left his sinful body and is judged to be worthy. As stated earlier, spiritual enlightenment is not about being religious, for many people are religious and are still cloaked in darkness. It is not about making a large contribution to the church of your choice in order to justify having your enormous wealth. It is not about being the first to volunteer when your church pastor calls on you. It is not about starting up a church charity. Although the deeds of man reflect his conscience, the conscience is fluid and yields to the ways of the mood, and yes it does give insight into man's soul. But it is the unpretentious heart that will truly reveal the essence of man's spirit and not the underlying motives for his deeds.

My dear unborn, being enlightened is more than the unraveling of one's personal fiber or the laying of a foundation for salvation through redemption. It is a commitment to imprint one's footsteps in the lives of all those whose paths you have crossed. The enlightened has a spiritual duty to do everything within his or her power to enrich the lives of those they have shared bread with figuratively and literally.

Remember, resisting the temptation to convince or persuade is paramount to the success of revealing what spiritual enlightenment is all about. Spiritual enlightenment must never be misplaced, for when the bellies of children cry out in pain, the mothers and fathers of these children are not at the height of Maslow's hierarchy of needs. Therefore, any attempts to enlighten another must be measured against that individual's physiological idiosyncrasies as well as spiritual.

My dear unborn, the road to spiritual enlightenment can be blocked by the simplest of obstacles. Before you can assist another on the road to spiritual enlightenment, you must assess not only these obstacles but the individual's sense of priorities with respect to God, economics, and the "x" variable. The "x" variable is a desire or weakness that gives the individual a false sense of security and somehow has managed to become a significant part of the person's life. When the enlightened does something to enrich the lives of others, he or she is also enriched. Although adults have a tendency to be more challenging because of the many experiences that they have acquired, many of which are toxic or counterproductive to the quest for spiritual enlightenment, the effort to share in their journey can be quite fruitful. Indeed, these adults set the tone for future generations and ultimately will provide offspring that, if taught well through modeling and with unwavering convictions, can create utopia on earth. The closest man will ever get to God on earth is being in the presence of a child. Therefore, whether we are enlightened or not, one should always try to mold his/her mind in the image of a child. Children, unless possessed by some demonic entities, frequently represent the spirit in the purest of forms, as pure as it is able to get on earth. Except for their lack of wisdom because of their innocence and lack of experience, children are in a position to serve as examples for what is truly needed in order to be enlightened enough to one day see the face of God. A new baby's spirit is coming directly from the presence of God. However, the spiritual energy that generates from a newborn baby substantially diminishes over a period of time as a number of different experiences are accumulated. Some of these experiences taint the spirit, allowing it to lose its effectiveness in terms of possessing attributes that are necessary to continue nurturing the bond between one's spirit and the spirit of the Messiah.

My dear unborn, as an enlightened soul, regardless of your feelings toward friends, relatives or significant others, you must make it a general practice to treat each person using the same criteria that you would like others to use concerning you. This is much easier said than done, because when feelings run high and you just cannot seem to forget the things that were done to you, then it is more than a possibility that you are inclined to allow those feelings to set the criteria that will govern how you do behave. Being enlightened is not and will never be a substitute for perfection, and it is a gross misjudgment for anyone to assume that it is. Perfection is an attribute that is best left to God; with this being said, keep in mind that even the enlightened is fallible and is capable of acting foolish. Therefore, one way of dealing with getting past these feelings is through projection-identification. Treat each person in terms of behavior as if he or she is the Messiah. Genuinely see the person and your behavior toward him/her as being done for the Messiah and him alone. This will take away the sting as well as eliminate some of the temptation that goes along with doing something for a person whom you may still have some ill feeling against, because after all, you would have now been doing it for Christ himself.

My dear unborn, it has been said that for "evil to triumph all that is necessary is for good men to do nothing." The spiritually enlightened are obligated to eradicate all elements of evil whether it directly or indirectly crosses one's path. The more one becomes spiritually enlightened, the more one will be severely challenged by demonic influences that will manifest themselves in a variety of forms and under several inconspicuous circumstances. In some cases, the meditative state of the enlightened will be bombarded by these demonic influences on a daily basis, leaving the individual to doubt his own state of spiritual enlightenment. During this phase, it is essential that the enlightened bond even more with the spirit of the Messiah in order to strengthen his/her faith and have an ally in the fight against Lucifer.

My dear unborn, in addition to self-doubt, guilt for experiencing these trials and temptations will set in, but as long as one remains steadfast with respect to faith and refuses to give into these temptations, rest assured that all is well. There is nothing wrong with being tempted; the devil will always do that, but giving in to these temptations gets us in trouble. There is one positive side to these demonic influences: They place the enlightened in a position where they must bond with the spirit of the Messiah, even much more than usual, in order to get the devil off their backs. Frequent meditation and prayer are vital in defeating these demonic influences, but even more important, one must never lose faith. There are those who believe that having a deep faith is an indication that all of one's troubles will soon be over. But for those of us who have experienced otherwise, we know it is only the beginning. The devil has no need to tempt sinners for they are already right within his grip. Only those who are trying to get out of a sinful realm or have strong convictions in serving God find it absolutely necessary to recapture their focus. The more the faithful resist, the more frustrated and determined Lucifer becomes, until the faithful get overwhelmed and give in. Indeed, for this reason it is imperative that more frequent prayer and meditation become a daily routine until the devil's influence gradually ceases to exist. It is foolish arrogance to think that any one person can rid himself/herself of these demonic influences alone. Lucifer has been practicing the art of deception and evil since the beginning of time. Therefore, without the help of God or the Messiah, the devil will devour us without mercy, for that which he cannot possess he destroys. A piece of advice: if you must do battle with the devil, never do it alone.

My dear unborn, being enlightened is not a "rite of passage" to the kingdom of God but rather an acknowledgment that one is vigilant in the struggle to become a true warrior in the battle between good and evil, and that one has made a commitment to embrace the gift of life in a manner that will pay homage to the Messiah and our Heavenly Father. To be enlightened is one of the greatest gifts God could bestow unto man, and yet it comes with a price that could make one wonder whether or not it should really be considered a gift after all. The concept or notion of being spiritually enlightened carries with it a danger zone, which when interfacing with one's wisdom and vanity can lead to serious consequences. Sometimes the spiritually enlightened are not only blessed with wisdom but also with the intelligence to decipher the laws of circumstances as well as the psyche of his/her fellow men. This asset, a blessing from God, almost falls on the borderline of being prophetic with respect to the enlightened's development of insight into the human psyche. Indeed, one would think that being blessed with such ability is always a good thing. And yet it has the tendency to cause the enlightened great concerns and rightfully so. This ability, when left unchecked, can become quite precarious to the self as a whole, for it is a great responsibility for any man to be able to see even a small glimpse of what lies in the heart of men. Once what lies in the heart of men is made known to the enlightened, especially if it is evil, the enlightened are then faced with the responsibility of having to do something about this newly obtained information. Failure to take any action by the enlightened will weigh heavily on his/her shoulders, thus resulting in guilt and frustration. If and when some action is taken by the enlightened with regards to this evil being, he or she must also prepare to deal with the individual's response. A response that is pending on the issue involved is more likely to be negative in nature. It should be reiterated clearly that being enlightened does not in any way make one omniscient. Instead, it provides the mind-set where the enlightened more often than not are able to successfully anticipate the psychological promise behind an individual's predicament as well as some foreseeable events that might occur as a result.

My dear unborn, the state of spiritual enlightenment embodies an all encompassing, multi-faceted projection of thoughts and code of conduct that is based on the love and expectations of God and the Messiah. It is not only one major paradigm of school of thought nor does it lend itself to only one absolute axiom. Indeed, the spiritually enlightened have an open mind and a welcoming embrace for any entity of the universe that reflects the smallest representation from the Creator. There are times when man struggles with his conduct as well as his thoughts, for fear that the parallel between man's wishes and

God's is so far away that to embrace one and not the other will leave a void within one's spirit. But when every fiber in your body is telling you to engage in conducts that are wrong by God's standard and right by man's, you must reach deep within your soul and muster up every conviction and love for your faith. Execute this love by standing firm for righteousness as commanded by the Creator, then trust in him that the consequences for your convictions will not result in a betrayal by your faith. Remain in sync with the spirit of the Messiah and use him as a guide for everything you do. Do not fear the tyranny of men, for with God by your side no one can make the light within you go dim, except you. Remember, the flame that comes with being spiritually enlightened was not lit by man but by God. It gives off a heat of truth that will forever serve as a protective shield around you like God's holy circle of light.

My dear unborn, live your life without limits and without restrictions, but live it responsibly. Never forget that everything happens for a reason, whether God has alerted you to these reasons or not. Engage inconsequential thinking on a daily basis and a willingness to face the accountabilities for your convictions and principles. Know that the world will not always be kind to you or those who have chosen to adhere to your words. But to paraphrase a verse once written by a poet, if the Son of Man in all his majestic glory was only accepted by few, then who are we to be accepted by all? As you struggle to devise or discover the purpose for your existence, remember that each man's destiny is shaped by predestination by birth or by fate. Learn the difference then choose, for the notion behind both concepts is relative to each individual's existence.

My dear unborn, a father's hopes and dreams are incomplete without signs of emulation from his children to share in his destiny or the intent to travel in a similar path as they journey to their own horizon. The path of my destiny may not be of your choosing but, my dear unborn, I am compelled by my love for you to raise your consciousness to the best of my abilities regarding the mechanisms of my own destiny. Long before I was baptized by fire with respect to life's trials and tribulations, every inch of my destiny was molded by fate. The direction of my life was driven by one predicament after the other. It was as if I had no control over my own life; fate was dictating my every move. When I made plans to go left, fate took me right, and when I made plans to go right, it took me left. My destiny and I were not one; it was being controlled and shaped by fate, the offspring of the laws of circumstances, while my psyche and I struggled to deal with the incongruency. It was then I realized that if ever I am to be the master of my destiny, it was critical to become one with fate and totally in sync with the laws of circumstances. Over a period of time my life was no longer subjected to predestination by fate. Fate was no longer in control of my life; I was. Indeed, I was so in sync with the laws of circumstances that its ability to influence my life in any way had drastically diminished. Soon, fate was not dictating whether I go left or right but had become my messenger, alerting me in advance of all the obstacles that were ahead of me or that I am about to face.

My dear unborn, I am no longer a by-product of predestination by fate. The laws of circumstances or its offspring no longer control my destiny. I do. The idea of being in control of one's destiny is an enormous responsibility. It involves ensuring that the purpose to one's existence becomes a reality. Each individual has a duty to take the life God has given him/her and bring it to a level of self-actualization. But first, the purpose to that life must be discovered, and doing this can be a process within itself. Hence, I have solicited the assistance of the one entity who has lived a life on earth and knows what it is like to suffer in order to fulfill his purpose and his destiny, the Messiah. The moment he was introduced into my life, I became a child of predestination by birth. My entire existence was no longer a crap shoot, following a pattern of chance day by day as most people live, a life filled with uncertainty and one that lacked any real fulfillment or joy. Instead, I was now spiritually enlightened. My life had meaning, and the path to my destiny was laid out step by step by the Messiah himself. Every single life experience now had meaning and a reason behind each direction it took. While being in sync with the laws of circumstances was still very much a part of my life, it was not out of necessity, but rather out of choice, my trust and my faith in God and the Messiah with respect to the fact that the unfolding of my life was being done based on the script that They had written. I was able to achieve this by taking the free will that God had given me at birth and replacing it with faith. In short, I asked him to take my free will and use me as an instrument to do his will, thus making my free will secondary to his will. Once I relinquished my will and accepted his will as the primary force that would shape my existence, this action cemented my thought process as well as how I live my life to the new notion of predestination by birth.

My dear unborn, attribute all that is good to the Supreme Being and all that is bad to the laws of circumstances. Man's reluctance to embrace probabilities and possibilities of anticipated outcomes before projected occurrences will constantly frustrate his effort in coping with the elements that surround his existence. This is not to say that both God and Lucifer do use opportunities provided by the laws of circumstances in their own way and for their own unique purposes. Remember, evil is only the manifestation of man's imperfections, imperfections that usually arise out of situations and events that are triggered by the laws of circumstances. God and his heavenly assembly influence certain aspects of our lives but only to a degree, a degree that depends largely on our relationship with him. On the other hand, Lucifer and his fallen angels influence certain aspects of our lives whether we have a relationship with him or not. One is intrusive and the other is compliant, responding only to our wishes. One wants you to hate yourself then take out your hatred on the world, and the other wants you to love yourself and seek strength from him in dealing with the forces that are not within the realm of your control. But it can be said that fate, the offspring of the laws of circumstances, has two masters, God and Lucifer. The circumstances that are created to bring you misery, torment, and discontent derive from the mischievous creator, Lucifer. The circumstances that are created to test one's abilities, unknown potentials, and the essence of one's character by providing unexpected challenges derive from God. Wise is the man who takes the time to decipher the origin of each predicament with respect to the two masters who frequently use the end result of the laws of circumstances.

My dear unborn, it is very easy to lose faith in humanity. After all, we bear witness to so much of the follies of our fellow man, it makes us question our own humanity. Each day we are exposed to so many circumstances where man is at the heart of misery. Indeed there are countless reasons that we should no longer believe in each other. I used to think that the height of spiritual enlightenment is loving, trusting, and having faith in God. But then I discovered that it was learning to love, trust, and have faith in each other. Somewhere along the line people have lost their humanity as well as the ability to believe in each other. People have allowed life and a few dark souls to convince them that it is of little importance. People have substituted their belief in each other for belief in God and somehow managed to convince themselves that this gesture is all that matters, thus conveniently forgetting that God's entire testament to humanity has been about teaching us how to live with each other. Man's love for God is best demonstrated through man's love for each other. One of the greatest gifts one can give to God is the gift of humanity. Sadly to say, it is difficult to give something which most of us have lost.

My dear unborn, man's salvation is a precious thing, and although it is bestowed upon him through the grace of God, it is incumbent upon him to maintain it by remaining in God's good grace. Once salvation is given to man, man must do that which is in accordance with God's teachings in order to maintain it. This is one of the many reasons that the hearts and spirits of man are constantly being examined by God, just as they are constantly being tempted and tested by Lucifer. Indeed, while salvation is given unconditionally by God, one's worthiness of it is proved through deeds, the degrees of one's faith, and the nature of the relationship one has with God. No one of these factors alone will render proof of the level of worthiness needed to provide the proper maintenance of one's salvation. Repentance is not an absolute concept, for the temptation and revisitation of sins are forces that make it a fluid phenomenon unless great care is initiated to uphold its resilience. Man may obtain salvation after his repentance, but the structure of this repentance is subjected to change with each sinful act thereafter. Indeed, the avoidance of sinful acts by individuals holds one's repentance status in a stationary and steadfast position still subjected to alteration or mobility, whether negative or positive through means of action or inaction. In short, man's deeds dictate the status of his repentance, which in turn validate or invalidate the legitimacy and sincerity of his salvation in addition to his faith and the extent of his relationship with God. God may grant an individual salvation after one's repentance, however, if that individual then turns around and becomes a murderer, robber, thief, etc. These sinful acts without forgiveness have now changed the status of this individual's salvation drastically to the point where its legitimacy becomes in question. Still, God did not take back this individual's salvation. But through his deeds, this individual would have invalidated his own salvation, thus rendering it useless as a key to enter the kingdom of God. Remember, my dear unborn, that no single ritual is a guarantee that one day one will be seated next to the King of Kings in the afterlife; nor can it guarantee a life without misery, pain, and suffering in this world. Although salvation is given unconditionally, it must be maintained. Indeed, being spiritually enlightened does not ensure a perfect life, but it does ensure a blessed one, and that makes all the difference.

THE EIGHTH MONTH

27

THE LOVE THAT DEFIES REASON

My dear unborn, in the absence of any true faith, it is only logical that some may wonder why God permits the things to happen in this world as they do. This is a question with some subtlety concerning the legitimacy of God's love. As mentioned earlier, things that do happen in this world cannot be attributed to God because the concept of free will limits the extent of his involvement unless otherwise asked by a person. I suppose one could always argue that since he has the power to drastically alter events he should still get involved, for by not doing so ultimately he does permit these things to happen. By "these things," I am referring to all the catastrophic and unpleasantry that exists within the world. But rest assured that had it not been for his small involvement in the world, mankind would have ceased to exist centuries ago. But involvement or not, he will forever be blameless, for the fruit that comes from man's tree of despair was planted only by man, not God. The feasibility exists that as time goes by, one day you too may find yourself wondering about this matter, and it is for that day that I am addressing this issue. Behold a vision, a vision of a kingdom without darkness, with illumination as dazzling as the sun, whispering wind leaving behind a climactic euphoria as tiny pebbles of sand sparkle like diamonds at the bottom of the ocean. Rainbows like shooting stars leap from north to south as fresh scents of fragrances delight the nose, while softly played music soothes the wings of the doves as both man and beast relax in harmony. A pictorial bliss greets the eyes in every mansion, mansions that stand tall in stature like the Taj Mahal, as echoes of praises ring out in melody in reverence to Jehovah and the sweet name of Jesus. Pain, famine, offsprings of misery are laid asleep, unable to resurrect from a deep death, leaving behind the timeless beauty and the life-force of eternity.

My dear unborn, suddenly, all the exuberance and jubilation that transforms this kingdom to a place worthy to be called God's home was still, silence was everywhere, and a great emptiness filled the souls who stood by as they struggled to overcome this indescribable sadness, a sadness that was generated by the question: who will die so man might live forever? The broken silence gave birth to a roaring yet quiet voice amongst their midst as God laid out the conditions for the task at hand. A gentle tap come on the shoulder from a beloved son who declares without hesitation, "I will, Father." "The world you'll enter is a far cry from this one. In it there are those who will despise you for proclaiming yourself to be my son and for having been the light that will pierce through their world of darkness. It's a world filled with wickedness and reprehensible transgressions, one where selfishness and greed rule the hearts of many, frequently blocking the path to compassion and love; a world where the weak is at the mercy of the strong, and the voice of justice is silenced by the deeds of injustice; a world where the tolerance of man's differences is blinded by man's intolerance to accept their own uniqueness. Yet, with all its troubles, it is a world that possesses the very essence of what we stand for, the preservation of all spiritual connections which ties us together forever.

"The heart of their world lies with the need to believe in some power greater than themselves. Still, because you will not be able to wear your crown in all its splendor, they will struggle with what they need to believe and rationalize this belief into disbelief. They will see and yet they will not see, for the naked eyes alone cannot pierce the boundaries of the spiritual realm. For this reason, one must see with their spiritual eyes in order to bear witness to your birth. In the end they will crucify you, but your death will set them free."

My dear unborn, soon the Son of Man arrives, dies, is resurrected, fulfilling the dreams of the prophets. But I wonder, would any man besides God make such a sacrifice with his own son, regardless of the reason? Can any man love another that much? And, if so, is this love not beyond reason? I struggle daily to the point of tears to understand such a love, desperately trying to be worthy. Still, I fall short daily and, in frustration, even get angry with myself. Regardless of how you live your life, always try to be worthy of God's love, even if it is deemed beyond reason. Yet, it is because it is beyond reason as to why you should hold this love in such high esteem. A man must always pay his debt to friends, relatives, and even society when warranted. A man died that we may have life; it is a debt, one we must pay. The way to pay this debt is by returning the love to others, that Christ died for. Start by loving yourself, forgiving yourself, and by making a commitment to truly love others. Let your love show, for by doing this you would have demonstrated first how much you love God. I do not claim to understand God's love. I wish I did. I do know that the worst type of ignorance is the one that comes from having too much knowledge. Never let it be said that your father is guilty of such an ignorance. Therefore, adhere to the little wisdom that I have shared with you, my dear unborn. Know within your heart that any man who is willing to sacrifice a son for another in hopes that one day both souls will join each other in unity is not only a master gambler but deserves to be worshiped, if for nothing else, for his faith in human nature. Remember, when your faith in human nature is shattered, seek comfort in the knowledge that your Creator has already demonstrated his faith in you by offering his precious Son as a means to an end Remember, no matter how much you have suffered, your suffering pales in comparison to that of the Messiah.

My dear unborn, God's love will only appear not to have defied reason to those who have little or no faith or have no idea what love is. Eternity is not forever for those who are beyond redemption, and with the death of God's son, the Messiah, this transformation has changed the course of man's destiny. God no longer has to spend time searching for ways to convince man of how much he loves him or that he even exists. He instead absolves himself from his tedious effort by turning the table, thus allowing man's belief system to determine the nature and direction of his destiny. The death of the Messiah relinquishes God from all future obligations or responsibilities concerning man's fate forever. He no longer has to seek out earthbound generals, like Moses and Elijah, prophets, or even pastors in order to convince man of his existence and love. Indeed, with the sacrifice of his Son as well as his deeds he has empowered all men to become the master of their own destiny, whether they want to accept this responsibility or not. The empowering factor is relatively simple. Believe in the Messiah and live forever or travel beyond redemption and see for yourself that eternity will not be forever. Still, I must wonder if the death of Christ impacted God in the same manner as it did with Christ's disciples and his many followers. How can it I asked myself, when because of his infinite wisdom and power God knew that Christ would soon be seated at his right hand in a glorious manner? The disciples and Christ's many followers, however, were not privy to this type of knowledge and therefore did not have the certainty even with faith that Christ would rise on the third day following his crucifixion. They were still pondering whether or not he was the Messiah. Indeed, his death must have been a shock with crippling emotional effects. This rationale makes perfect sense and even begs the question as to the legitimacy of Christ's death, or so it seems until one extrapolates a little further and realizes that Christ was also flesh and blood. Hence, even if God sought comfort in knowing that soon his son would be with him, no father, God or otherwise, could withstand the horrific manner in which Christ died. Such death must have eradicated the slightest joy that God might have had from the certainty of seeing his son again.

So, my dear unborn, when you think of Christ's death and the devil tempts you into believing that Christ's divinity softened the blow to his crucifixion, take a hammer and a nail. Then see yourself sending the nail in your hands and feet. You will know that the blood that Christ shed as well as his tears and pain were that of a man who chose to put his divinity temporarily aside in order to bear the agony that would bind all men together in one form or another forever.

My dear unborn, as stated earlier, with the death of Christ God no longer has to part the Red Sea or do any other miracles in order to let us believe in him. Yet, each morning, if one looks closely, there are so many miracles all around us. Whether we see them as such depends on our faith. Any man who thinks that God's love does not defy reason is ignorant of the depth of God's love. I would say to this man or woman: bring me your flesh and blood, one for whom your love knows no bounds. Then give us your permission to use his organs, heart, liver, kidney, etc. in order to save the lives of strangers. Let us do this with no questions asked, no money in hand, no monument built, only the satisfaction for being pure in heart. Do this and I assure you your love, though magnificent, will be seen as one that defies reason. Man will never really deserve the love of God or the sacrifice that he has made until man learns to love his fellow men in such a way that it too defies reason.

THE NINTH MONTH

28

THE CHURCH

My dear unborn, let no man tell you what church to choose, for a church has only one purpose; it is a place where one assembles in order to pay tribute to God and the Messiah. I do not see it as a place that is needed constantly for worship, and seldom do I see it as a necessity for the introduction to God or the initiation of faith. A church is or ought to be a place where people who love the Supreme Being and his Son can come together on a special day or days, regardless of their faith or religious denomination, and pay tribute and reverence to God. Indeed, during this time one could also be introduced to the love of God, but an individual does not need a church in order to worship or in order to establish a relationship with God and the Messiah. I say "God and the Messiah" because one cannot come to know one without having to know the other, and those who believe that they can pay reverence to the Father and not the Son are suffering from a critical and dangerous delusion, a delusion that leaves their soul in a precarious position. The purpose of the church is not so much to worship, but to provide an opportunity where the children of God can share their burden, lean on each other, seek strength from each other, and more importantly remember the sacrifices that Jesus made and for whom. A church is a symbol of the remembrance of the crucifixion of Christ as well as the everlasting love that God has for man. The worshiping of God or the introduction to God can be accomplished anywhere at any given time, and without the aid of any special building.

My dear unborn, man's introduction to God started by his willingness to accept that he does exist, and man's worshiping of him began long before the realization that he existed, depending on what type of person he truly is. People every day worship God even though they do not believe in him. You see, it is not necessary to believe in God in order to worship him. But the road to spiritual enlightenment and self-awareness becomes clearer when one acknowledges that the principles that govern one's life can be attributed to the Creator. For example, if the life you live is one of decency, love, compassion, and mercy, etc., yet you are an atheist, you are still worshiping God, whether you like it or not. The mere displaying of these gestures to others is a manifestation of a symbolic reverence to God. While you may not believe in God at the time of your behavior, he believes in you and takes your behavior as a sign of honoring him. When you claim to worship God yet your actions are bigotry, anger, betrayal, etc., you are really worshiping Lucifer whether you like it or not. The beginning of man's love for God comes from the heart, which manifests itself in deeds. Hence, the deeds of man go a long way in worshiping God. Once an individual is introduced to God's love, it becomes the foundation of his worship, a worship where church is not an essential variable to its completion, for God's love can be felt and accessed on the sea, in a forest, anywhere. The true church lies within the structure of man's heart, not in man-made buildings. Once you have established a relationship with God, the manner in which you have chosen to worship him is entirely up to you and not that of the church. Keep in mind always that the true church of God lies within you and not in a foundation of bricks and stones. A church made of wood, stones governed by a set of bylaws, is sometimes used as a means to control or restrict individuality in worship. As uniquely as we were created by God, so must it be with the embodiment of our worship, a uniqueness that is quite frequently dimmed by the church's need to promote and enforce conformity.

My dear unborn, the bond between the church and its congregation is seldom based on a give-and-take relationship, but rather on the type of relationship where the giving is done mainly by its congregation. It is very rare when a church, regardless of its religious beliefs, allows its congregation to use the facility without the need for some type of payment or financial stipend that may camouflage itself under some other disguise. The church must be maintained. However, when the emphasis is placed more on the budget than its congregation's spiritual need, then something is wrong. It is astonishing to discover that churches today are used as a vessel to bring in the type of wealth needed to allow one to live the lifestyle of the rich and famous. Messengers of God are now manipulating the minds of their congregation to bring in millions of dollars, often by allowing people to feel guilty about the amount of money that is being tithed. These pseudo-messengers of God put themselves on the same level as God in order to convince people that when they fail to give to the church, they are in actuality failing to give to God. The church in some cases is no longer a resting place for the holy spirit; it is a mockery, a pulpit for those who are seeking control and power through manipulation, which eventually trickles down into finances. The only church an individual needs to visit, maintain, and nurture is the church within oneself—the place where all of one's goodness resides, the place which reminds us of who and what we are when life's demands are on the verge of changing us into something that by nature we are not. The church within us is the most sacred of all. Although the man-made church is also a temporary resting place for the Holy Spirit, it is seldom visited by this entity because we do not keep it clean. So assemble if you must, especially on the day of communion, but only in remembrance of God and the Messiah. Let the time that would otherwise be spent listening to the stories that are used to initiate an emotional appeal by the man-made church be spent making the one within you truly worthy of the resting place for the spirit of the Messiah, for with each story usually comes another gesture that involves money.

My dear unborn, there are those within the church who will try and convince you that they are given the power to serve as a bridge between God and man. I tell you that only the Messiah has earned the right to grant absolutions. Therefore, share your confessions with no man except to him who has paid the ultimate price for your transgressions, and let he who claims to be granted with this power seek absolutions for his own demons. Do not be fooled by their gentle manner and look of sincerity, for they come to you in long robes of color in hopes of learning your innermost secrets and with a promise to remove the stain from your soul, not knowing that the absolutions they give are without merit and are as empty as the foundation it stands on—empty because only the Messiah and his Father have the power to grant absolutions. These people who claim to grant absolutions are without merit because Christ, through his death, has more than earned the right to decide who will or will not be forgiven for their sins. But no man on earth has earned that right, and each act of absolution that is granted by man is one more stain on that person's soul that has yet to be forgiven. Indeed, since the absolution that is granted by man is false and without merit, the sin for which the person seeks forgiveness still remains. Although the person is still of the mind-set that his or her soul is free from this sin, in actuality it is not. Therefore, when you seek absolution, seek it from the Messiah and not from man, for it is he whom has paid the ultimate price for your sins, not man.

My dear unborn, the church lacks passion when it comes to conveying the necessary and needed information relevant to God versus the laws of circumstances. For example, it would have you believe that during one's journey through life, one lives or dies by the whim of God. The conditioning of this notion by them leaves no room for the truth concerning the laws of circumstances. As such, they have committed a grave error in judgment with respect to allowing the children of God to think that God uses his power over life and death like a slave master who whips his slaves arbitrarily for no good reason. They constantly neglect to inform their worshippers that seldom does death manifest itself at the will or request of God. Instead, congregations are conditioned by the church into believing that God's power over life and death somehow makes him responsible for all living things that cease to exist regardless of the circumstances. Like adding salt to an open wound, they then insist that death as a general practice usually serves some greater purpose, a purpose that they themselves do not know and vehemently suggest that as children of God we do not have the right to know nor should we question God's wisdom or seek to find out what these purposes are. The church would have us believe that curiosity and concern on the part of God's children is tantamount to having no faith or lack of it, somehow giving the impression that presumptuousness is a sign of disrespect. It is important to trust in God always for he is privy to information relevant to our future that we simply do not have. Indeed, this trust is an essential ingredient for the basis of all faith. Yet, God gave man free will for a reason, one being to exercise our ability to seek answers to questions concerning things we find interesting, troublesome, or curious.

My dear unborn, diseases claim human lives every day, something that has been going on for centuries, and it has nothing to do with God arbitrarily taking human lives. Traumatic occurrences are all a part of human suffering. It is burdensome, sad, and even unfair, but it stems from principles governed by the laws of circumstances, and once again has nothing to do with God. God does not relish the idea of constantly putting up roadblocks in our lives, a life that is already fragile and unpredictable because of so many unknown variables. God does, however, test individuals, but he also has spent a great deal of energy and time delivering individuals from evil. The church has little or no insight into the laws of circumstances, so it spends all its time assigning the blame from life's tragedies to God and his master plan, a master plan that does not involve making human lives miserable for sport or convenience. Yet, the church attributes so much of human suffering to God's higher purpose and further claims that questioning that purpose is ungodly. As mentioned before, the church seldom subscribes to the laws of circumstances because of lack of knowledge into the universal order of things as well as lack of faith on the part of the church—that once individuals continue to probe and ask questions, if these questions are not answered then one's belief in God will be weakened and so will the individual's faith. The church apparently does not have enough faith in God that he will find some way to answer man's questions and bring some form of relief to human suffering. Another important reason that the church does not promote cosmic consciousness is fear. The church preys on human suffering and tragedy as instruments of punishment served by God for not conforming to its ideologies. This notion is similar to the brimstone and fire theory. Somehow, by making people afraid of going to hell, they will conform and do what is necessary so as not to feel the wrath of God, thus making the church in full control of its congregation and the manner in which it thinks.

My dear unborn, all answers you seek can be found within the greatness of God's love. Therefore, any entity, church or otherwise, that finds it necessary to use fear or the wrath of God as a means to get people on the path to spiritual enlightenment does not walk in the shadow of the Messiah. The church has failed to realize that where there is mutual respect there is no need for mutual control. Terror, regardless of what form it manifests itself in, has no place in the quest for spiritual enlightenment. Remember always that if God's love cannot melt the harshness of humanity in any given circumstance, then the dreaded fear of his wrath should not be a contingency. It is love and not fear that will bring man to the bosom of God. When the church equates love and fear as the same criteria on which to introduce man to the greatness of God's love, it is guilty of a terrible sin, for it is recklessly sending the message that if God cannot win you with love, then he will win you through intimidation by fear. When this is done, the church without knowing it also tramples on the concept of free will. It should be man's choice and not the church's that ultimately decides the avenue that must be taken to God and spiritual enlightenment.

The Ninth Month

29

The Metamorphosis of Love

My dear unborn, the interpretation of love by a spiritual being must maintain its essence, an essence that brings one as close to agape as possible. For while love can be a real and powerful emotion, its intensity is only as real as the level of interpretation that is placed on it. There is no greater love or joy that one can experience than that which comes from God, a love so pure and true that it has become the landmark for an entire universe. God's love is pure because it is given unconditionally and at a great cost to himself, the sacrifice of his only son, the Messiah. In a world that is constantly struggling to find love, it is astonishing just how few actually know what love is and the incredible amount of misinterpretations that are offered as its definition. This misinterpretation that I speak of is not rooted in a conceptual premise, but rather in the misinterpretation of feelings and misguided associations. True love does not come from knowing a person; it never has, but rather from a spiritual connection that transcends all earthly experiences. In the world in which we live, we have a tendency to see or relate to love as passion or stimulations guided by sexual appeal or outer appearances. Freud said decades ago that "anatomy is destiny," realizing that the way people look will ultimately determine how far they get in life. Sadly to say, this observation about the human race has not changed. Indeed, our concept of love seldom revolves around our spiritual attributes. The true sadness, however, is not that we fail to see love beyond anything that gravitates toward sexual impulses and physical appearances, but that we have become our own stumbling blocks with respect to the type of love that we seek. This is not to say that there are not many of us who are fortunate enough to find true love, only that most of us find ourselves being attracted to the wrong indicators in people: The type of indicators that surround physical appearances and sexual impulses. Quite frequently these very same indicators spontaneously attempt to transform our feelings that will produce the type of love that is sought, but we vehemently manipulate the indicators in order to ensure that the love does not move beyond its superficial aspect. We do this subconsciously, totally unaware of our intent.

My dear unborn, it should be made clear that a love that is based on sexual impulses or physical appearances can transform itself into something pure and real if the individuals involved do not manipulate it into something else. People who find themselves with such a love will soon find out that their sexual energy has diminished and the focus on their partner's appearance is not as important once the transformation of their love begins. Those who lack insight will interpret this phenomenon as lack of interest by their partner or even begin to view the lack of sexual interest by him/her as some physiological anomaly, but in actuality the superficial aspect of their love has metamorphosed into something more pure and true. For example, have you ever noticed how God's love, which is the greatest of all love, lacks sexual energy or physical criteria, yet it remains the purest of all love? Love is an entity that will take on a life of its own regardless of what form it manifests itself in. The problem is frequently that it does not get a chance to function autonomously because of our interferences and manipulations. Because love involves a spiritual connection, seldom does it need any manipulations from us. Still, unable to help ourselves we always try to assist in its transformation, thus resulting in the type of love that lessens the quality of a relationship once it is formed. One of the greatest myths about love is that it changes from time to time depending on various circumstances. A husband and wife loved each other but somehow are convinced that they hate each other after a nasty divorce. When love is the embodiment of any relationship, it remains constant forever and cannot be altered by any situation or circumstances. It is so pure in essence that it transforms itself into a spiritual type of agape with or without our assistance or intention. Yet, we often become the main obstacle in preventing this process simply because we do not comprehend the nature of the process with respect to the transformation.

My dear unborn, I once saw a couple in my office who was terrified of the possibility that they might have been falling out of love with each other. The presenting problem of this couple centered around the fact that the husband in question had lost much of his interest in sex with his wife. After five years of making love at least twice every week, the wife was upset that her husband must not have been finding her attractive anymore. Still, she was deeply confused and puzzled because he was still as affectionate, romantic, considerate, and even more loving at times. But his interest in sex had diminished to a point where she became suspicious of the idea that he might have been having an affair, thus getting his sexual need met elsewhere. Admitting, however, that he was not that type of man who would betray their vows in that manner, she became even more distraught. She reported that while they still enjoy sex occasionally, in most cases he just wanted to cuddle while telling her all the things that make her special. But the absence of frequent initiation of sex by him leaves her questioning his sincerity. The husband said that he did not see any problem within their relationship and would be willing to take Viagra, even though he did not think it was needed. This gesture was necessary in order to convince his wife that his love for her was real because, like most people, his wife associated true love with sexual energy. The more sex one has, the more individuals seem to be convinced that the love is real. In many relationships, the diminishing of sexual activity has a tendency to give the impression that either the love is not there anymore or it is fading within the relationship because of some other serious underlying issues. In general, we have a tendency to associate the degree of love with the degree of sexual activity.

My dear unborn, while it is tempting to associate love with the degree of one's sexual activity, remember always that sometimes the decline of this sexual energy usually involves the beginning of a transformation necessary to embrace the type of love that is built on the foundation of God's love, agape. A passionate love that involves frequent sexual activity and foreplay must be allowed to metamorphose; indeed, without this transformation the love will eventually fade away and die. The fear or inability to embrace this transformation will kill the chance of having a nurturing relationship. Beauty fades and passion dies. The metamorphosis of love within a given relationship takes time and in no way minimizes the importance of sexual energy. Sexual energy decreases over a period of time in all human beings, and although this does happen naturally and is usually accepted without concerns, it can be quite problematic in relationships. It becomes a problem not because it is, but because individuals are led to believe that lack of sexual energy or activities in a relationship is indicative of some inadequacies that are in need of correction if indeed a relationship is to thrive. Individuals are conditioned that true love manifests itself in relationships, which is set by a social standard that involves frequent sexual activity, and its absence connotes a dysfunctional relationship. When the transformation of love experiences no obstacles, it sets the tone for a relationship where the love gradually becomes liberated from the residual desires and needs of the flesh, a love that taps into the energy of the spirit, bringing both individuals face to face with agape, the type of love that God intended man to have for each other. Once both parties in the relationship embrace agape, they are more inclined to be in harmony with God. Sacrificing the pleasure of the flesh in order to be in harmony with God is often a necessity. The need for sex regardless of the legitimacy of its purpose is still an obstacle to being in harmony with God if it becomes the dominant force in one's life.

My dear unborn, the flesh was not designed for our own personal pleasures and amusements; even procreation is secondary to its true purpose. The flesh serves a higher purpose, which is to allow God to evaluate man and all his intricacies. The flesh provides an opportunity for God to probe the darkest region of man's soul as well as to test the endurance of the human spirit. If man had iron for a body, there would be no way to examine his capabilities except through his deeds. But the vulnerability of the flesh allows man to draw on his inner strength along with his faith in order to deal and cope with life's challenges. Indeed, the functions of the body and the way it is utilized are indicative of what type of soul it possesses. God judges the soul based on what the body does or does not do. While it is described as the temple, as we all know from experiences, it seldom behaves or is revered as such. Man seems to always find new ways to corrupt the flesh in an effort to find new thrills and pleasure. Remember, the Son of Man does not focus on the flesh as much as he does the spirit. But he, above all, knows just how fragile and susceptible the flesh can be.

My dear unborn, it was recently stated that love is constant; indeed it is, but it should be made clear that love is constant only when it goes through the metamorphosis. When love has successfully completed the transformation, it remains constant and will not disintegrate regardless of the circumstances, adverse or otherwise. However, a love that has failed to metamorphose, thus lacking the ability to transform into something more spiritual and meaningful, will emerge into the "illusion of love." The illusion of love engenders two fundamental characteristics. First, individuals are engaged in a relationship where the love is based on attraction. These attractions usually involve physical and superficial attributes, ranging from looks, the type of car a person drives, how much money the person makes, etc. Here, the parties within the relationship express their love for each other by taking cues from each other's body. The stimulations, desires, and arousing mechanisms all stem from their primordial urges, and in the absence of any spiritual connection. Second, the illusion of love during a given relationship will compel either one or both individuals to seek power and control over the object of their attraction. This means, of course, that since the attraction is with each other, a power struggle will take place or one of the parties involved will be the dominant force within the relationship. In most cases, this leads to abuse by the person who has the power and control, which eventually gradually deteriorates the illusion on which the love was built. Once this happens, the relationship ends. In short, individuals who do not allow their love to experience the metamorphosis leave themselves open to the possibility of having that love becoming an instrument of destruction, whereby both parties within the relationship will bear witness to the slow and often painful deterioration of its existence until all that is left is the nothingness on which the illusion of love was formed. When a love goes through its metamorphosis, the individuals within the relationship realize that the essence of their attraction is based on love as opposed to having a love that is based on attraction. Here, the expression of love is not shown by the bodies, but rather by the strength of the spiritual connection between the two individuals. The emphasis that is placed on this type of love is more abstract and intangible in nature, and yet the pleasure that comes from all five senses cannot be compared. The bond between both souls clears the path for harmony, leaving a heightened collective body of senses to bathe the individuals in cosmic ecstasy that has no emotional baggage or residual toxicity from a spiritual deficiency. Indeed, sexual intercourse that is based on the illusion of love is short-lived because the energy shared during the moment of passion comes only from the individuals' bodies. This same experience when shared by individuals who are spiritually connected releases energy from the spirit that stays with them even if they find themselves no longer together. In addition to its longevity, each moment of passion produces a clarity within the relationship that makes it more likely to last. For example, sexual intercourse between spiritually connected individuals enhances the relationship and allows them to see the best in themselves and their relationship. In the absence of any spiritual connection, sexual intercourse serves as a prompt and a coping mechanism to assist the parties within the relationship to deal with each other or to fill a void, thus compensating for something that is seriously lacking in the relationship or the individuals themselves. As much as it is possible to know oneself, extend the quest to knowing one's loves as well.

The Ninth Month

30

My Name is Still Gandhi!

My dear unborn, in a world that is harsh and constantly requires a struggle just to survive beyond one's mere existence, individuals are sometimes placed in positions to do things that are counterproductive to their spiritual growth. The need to be true to the principles of our spirituality sometimes clashes with other pragmatic needs that are necessary to the survival of our family and ourselves. I have looked into the eyes of those who battle with this dilemma and come away in tears, for what I have seen in their eyes illustrates the suffering that their hearts endure when being faced with these decisions. Sometimes the search for reconciliation is a futile one, for the basis of this struggle embodies a presumptuousness that one of great spiritual richness cannot forego, and for them it is especially hard for they know that there is no greater sin than a presumptuous sin. When one renders what is to Caesar unto Caesar and what is to God unto God, one cannot help wondering whether or not one's faith is not somehow being compromised in the process, especially when what one gives to Caesar is something God frowns on. Yet, in many cases to reject an offering by Caesar is to endanger a means of provision for our family. Should we really reject this avenue that is being offered by Caesar at the risk of our self and family, when time and time again both faith and fate have brought us to the same crossroad, a crossroad where opportunity and necessity intersect, thus providing a foundation for not only the survival but the sustaining of the stability of our spiritual, psychological, and economical existence? Indeed, the strength of our faith can be stripped away by the hunger and the tears of our loved ones who lack basic foods or economical consistency that is essential to prevent the tyranny of poverty.

My dear unborn, never allow yourself to shun another human being whose struggle to provide for his family has made it impossible to walk in the same path as the Messiah. Rather hold a candle to his footsteps as you share bread with him. Do not question his faith or his love for God, for in times of hunger the suffering of a man's family far outweighs his faith. This is not to say that he has lost it, only that he has placed it in suspension until his faith in God has expanded his blessings, thus allowing him to regain his focus on all that which is holy.

My dear unborn, during my visit to India I came upon a holy man who traditionally traveled hundreds of miles in order to bless the city of New Delhi annually. It was by mere fate that our paths had crossed. There I was sharing the little money that I had to those who were asking in front of my hotel. It was very little indeed being dispersed to the many whose hands found their way to my face. I had only a five-dollar bill left to give, but before I could, I saw this man who apparently was much older than most of the people in the crowd. He too was begging. A boy said to me, "He is a holy man who came to bless our city; give it to him." I was astonished and moved by the young man who desperately struggled to get his hand in my face as an effort to capture my attention. Yet, when I had finally focused on him, preparing to relinquish my last five-dollar bill, he pleaded with me to let the holy man have it instead. The holy man whose hands were also a part of the crowd seemed relieved when the boy begged that the money be given to him. When the holy man took the money, he put what seemed like a Hawaiian wreath (lei) around my neck. In that instance I saw more pain and shame in his eyes than I have ever seen in any one person's face for having to ask and compete for the five-dollar bill. Having to beg in this manner had killed a small part of his soul; of this I was certain. Yet, regardless of how he felt, he took the time to anoint me with holy oil and offered words of blessings. I wanted to say to him, it is okay; we do what we must and sometimes if we are lucky it does not change the essence of who we truly are. I wanted to say, I too have done things of which I am ashamed. I wanted to say that even Gandhi had not led a perfect life. I wanted to say that God understands the choices we are compelled to make sometimes. I wanted to say at that moment what I thought Gandhi would have said: "Regardless of what I have done with respect to the survival of myself and my family, my name is still Gandhi." But instead I let him walk away, for by allowing him to take the money so freely, I had done enough.

31

FALSE PROPHETS

My dear unborn, they claim to be able to foresee the coming of the times, to possess the ability to unmask the revelations of man's destiny and set their feet on the path to self-discovery. They are the prophets of modern times. They do not travel the path of the Messiah; instead they are here to do Lucifer's bidding. The price of their spiritual insight is high. It calls for your worldly possessions and the opportunity to share your innermost thoughts, thoughts that once shared will only serve to strengthen their hold on you. Be aware of these self-proclaimed prophets for they come in many forms—as psychics, clairvoyants, and even as clergy who claim to be messengers of God. They will befriend you, console you, then contaminate the essence of your spirit with the falsehood of their predictions. Do not be mystified by their speculations, for Lucifer is not without power, the type of power he offers to them as a gift in order to seduce them and obtain their loyalty and obedience. Although some of these false prophets are unaware that Lucifer is the prevailing force behind their insights into the human soul, they must and will still be held accountable by God. Remember, a man cannot do Lucifer's bidding at night and attempt to sit at the Messiah's table during the day. A man who chooses to walk a particular path in life must do so boldly, with no regrets, no fears, and with acceptance of all the consequences that come by the nature of his travels. My dear unborn, harden not your heart against those who do Lucifer's bidding so they may quench the hunger of their children's belly. Judge no man for the path he has chosen in life, but rather invite him to sit at your table that he may sup with you. Ease his soul with kindness and the burden he endures with compassion, for at the end of the day comes another, and with it, the facing of himself and the emptiness within. Remember, my dear unborn, that no man ever truly escapes the essence of his own heart or the ingredients of his character. Therefore, it is imperative that one always extend an olive branch in hopes that for him one day there will indeed be hope. You cannot introduce someone to spiritual enlightenment by treating that person as an outcast, and since no man has earned the right to judge another, the love we have for the Messiah must also be shown to those who have not yet become conscious of God's everlasting love. The motives behind the individual who comes to you under the pretext of being a prophet must be examined whenever possible as carefully as time and circumstances would permit. Indeed, this is not to suggest that there can never be a scenario under which an individual camouflaging as a false prophet is acceptable. But rather, we must embrace the notion that unless a man walks in another man's shoes, he can never really appreciate what that man has gone through. Therefore, if one is to influence a false prophet into seeking the path of spiritual enlightenment, one must discover the propelling force behind his or her action or the underlying reason for the pretext. It is the enlightened spiritual responsibility to do everything possible to introduce another human being to a higher level of consciousness regardless of that individual's past deeds. In the process of doing this, resistance is inevitable. Still we must persist but never at the risk of our own state of nirvana.

My dear unborn, a new prophet emerges daily, meeting the demands of a society desperately grasping for answers, answers that if examined closely can be found within the depths of their own souls. Yet, because of lack of faith and impatience they are quick to genuflect to the first person who comes along and offers them a sign of hope. Were there no demands for these individuals who proclaim themselves prophets, they would cease to exist. But as long as man continues to look for answers and hope in all the wrong places, there will always be false prophets like psychics and tarot and palm readers, just waiting to fill the minds of their victims with worthless and shortsighted predictions, and miracle healers who have yet to possess an ounce of faith and whose empty promises in all likelihood have caused more harm than good. When the deaf still cannot hear, the blind cannot see, this glimpse of hope that has been offered to them by these false prophets is much more painful than one could ever imagine. Pain is at the heart of every deception. Whether it manifests itself now or later depends on the nature of the situation. False prophets seldom think of the impact of their predictions, only of the profits to be gained. A man must define himself as early as possible. Unless a man defines himself, others will do it for him. Do not allow anyone to define you by imposing their moral codes or ethics. Assess whether one's moral codes serve to manipulate your existence or restrict your spiritual liberation. One's spiritual philosophy does not always have to coincide with one's moral codes or ethics. Decipher for yourself where one ends and the other begins. False prophets prey on the weak with respect to those who lack a firm sense of self. They frequently will try to impose their morals and ethics by slowly conditioning you to think that it is from that reference point which your thinking must emerge while they attempt to stroke your ego and unravel the links that hold you together. As they gradually condition your mind to readily accept their suggestions or so-called predictions, they are also molding you to trust them by using subliminal cues and other means. Unless one is totally comfortable within himself with respect to self-esteem and confidence, persuading such an individual will be like taking candy from a baby. This is not to say that the world lacks any real and genuine psychics or healers, only that there are more false ones as foretold by the real prophets who walked our earth centuries ago.

My dear unborn, there was a time when prophets and healers possessed powers and communicated directly with God. Those people were constantly in a state of grace. Their sense of spirituality and devotion were unquestionable. Their only reward was the act itself, whether it was delivering a message, informing others of changes that were about to be made by God or just lifting someone's burden. The only profit was the act itself; nothing of material value was needed. If it was offered, it was refused by these people who sometimes viewed it as an insult. Preying on the weak or misusing their gift would be seen as sacrilege. But it is quite easy to prey on the weak when one does not have the gift of a prophet in the first place. Since the entire scenario is based on falsehood, I am unable to protect you from all elements of danger, thus keeping you safe, the duty of a parent. Although you have yet to be born, these dangerous elements keep me awake at night, but I have also learned that when an environment is inescapable, arming the individual who must face the environment with enough coping skills and wisdom can be a useful weapon. Therefore, I tell you that when someone claims to have all the answers, chances are they were not given to that person by God. He alone has knowledge of all things. Therefore seek your answers directly from him. Remember always that the elimination of all options is God's way of asking you to choose him instead. When you thirst for predictions about your future or destiny, look within and not outside of yourself. When uncertainty and self-doubt are at the heart of any issue, rely on your instinct as the final decision-making process. Never become attached or like anything or anyone to the point that it makes you place the love that you have for God secondary to that thing or person; trust in God always. Treat all friends as potential enemies, and all enemies as potential friends. When the beast within starts to dictate your behavior toward your enemy, then substitute that person mentally with the image of the Messiah or God, thus allowing your feelings to gradually change. Place no limits on yourself unless God has placed them on you. Listen to the voice of God and not the voice of the church. Know the difference! When the devil presents himself to you, regardless of his disguise, see him for what he is. Let your relationship with God dictate the measurement of your faith and not your obligation to the church. Practice the art of humility with strength and firmness so they who would confuse humility for weakness will put this delusion to rest. Give freely and secretly so your pride may know that your action serves God and not the glorification of man or self. Remember always that the life you live will bear witness at the day of judgment. It has been said that sometimes the end justifies the means, but this never applies to matters of the soul. You cannot rock and roll with the devil in hopes of waltzing with the angels, just as no man can serve two masters. Each choice one makes in life becomes a part of the root that will determine the fruitfulness of one's existence. Shield your heart from everything except love. When a romantic experience fails to actualize to its fullest potential, it is only because both souls were meant to travel a different path. Show no signs of regret. True love is constant, and although two hearts are no longer together, the love once shared is locked in time forever.

My dear unborn, subvocal taunting can be an adverse condition of the human spirit. There are two variations: (1) constant negative influences aim at criticizing God, the Messiah, and your relationship with the two entities; and (2) serving as a direct channel for the instinctive component, which offers insight both good and bad about life and human nature. The closer one gets to a state of nirvana or its sublevels, the more problematic subvocal taunting can become. It can be especially problematic for someone with a form of psychological dysfunction. Frequently, people with mental health difficulties assume they are hearing voices and respond to them thinking they are getting directions elsewhere to do things that quite often can be dangerous. For example, they may get instructions from the voice to kill another person, or claim the voice from the radio or TV commands them to jump off a bridge when in actuality what they are responding to is voices from their own subvocal cues, which can be so powerful that they overwhelm the individual's entire thinking process. In many cases, medication is required to suppress what even doctors assume are voices, not knowing what they are medicating is the individual's own thoughts echoing from the individual's mind. These false prophets use the same subvocal cues to project ideas that may be relevant to an individual's life, then proclaim them to be predictions. Subvocal cues are such powerful forces that some false prophets genuinely believe that their suggestions are really from some deep spiritual connections that they have with entities from the afterlife or another world. These individuals, however, are in a small class with respect to the overall occult, because unlike the others they really do believe that their predictions derive from unknown entities that are working with them as opposed to the other false prophets who make the conscious decision to deceive their believers. Subvocal cues can be a nightmare for the spiritually enlightened. The closer one gets to God and the wisdom he offers, the more subvocal taunting one endures. It is like having a little voice in your head constantly criticizing and mocking all aspects of your spirituality in the worst way possible. Self-doubt and self-incrimination can be attributed to some of the causes of subvocal taunting, which cause the spiritually enlightened to question his devotion, his love, and his commitment to both God and the Messiah. One's faith is tested on all levels, but this faith will allow you to defeat the daily taunting. Constant praying and daily meditation will eventually allow you to conquer this phenomenon, just one of the many means Lucifer uses to weaken the human spirit.

THE BIRTH

32

THE ONE PARDONED SIN!

My dear unborn, besides the Ten Commandments, there are still many rules that God insists and expects all men to obey and live by. In essence, some of these rules are spoken, yet many are unspoken. Remember always that there are no greater or lesser sins. God judges all sins and renders consequences using the same criteria for all. There are times when because of extenuating circumstances, the criteria he uses are subjected to certain alterations, but all sins are held in the same esteem. A man guilty of stealing a loaf of bread will receive the same degree of God's mercy as a man who premeditatively plots and kills his wife in order to collect the insurance money. But sins are not the only Persian flaw that serves as a threat to man's salvation. Rather, man's arrogance will be the eternal death of him.

My dear unborn, although many will disagree, remember that the one sin which is arbitrarily forgiven by God without man even asking is the one that is associated directly or indirectly with man's desire for women. In short, fornication, adultery, bigamy, etc., are all pardoned by the Supreme Being, especially if these acts resulted from man's unwillingness to lawfully approve polygamy. All sins that are related to man's weaknesses to control his sexual desire toward women are automatically pardoned sins, especially when the circumstances are such that men are forced into monogamy. God is the same yesterday, today, and forever. He does not think that man should have many wives one day, then turn around and change his mind to one woman for each man the next. Man's imposition should not be confused with God's wishes. God knew when he created woman that man would find it often difficult to control his desire. This one element of weakness in men puts woman on equal footing with them, regardless of men's physical make-up. In God's eyes, women need this leverage in order to survive in a man's world. This is primarily one of the reasons that men, to this day, are not still controlled or disciplined enough to regulate all their sexual desires to the point where women are not an essential variable in their lives. The inability to accomplish this has left men with both feelings of hate and love toward women. The hate comes from not being able to prevent the feelings of need that are drawn out by women's sexual appeal, regardless of how macho or manly they try to be. The love comes from giving into the natural instinct that projects a feeling of completeness when they are with the woman they love. All men are possessed by both feelings of love and hate for women, even the one they eventually marry.

My dear unborn, because all men are possessed by feelings of love and hate for women, the nature of a relationship between a man and a woman will be determined by which feeling is the dominant force within the man, in other words, which element—love or hate—was nurtured more by certain experiences within his life. If, indeed, he had a loving mother or many pleasurable relationships with women before actually being married, then the probability of him having a good relationship with his wife is high. However, if the hate was nurtured more, then that man will become a negative force within the relationship, which will manifest itself in the mistreatment of his wife, or women in general. Most men's self-confidence lies in their ability to control the nature of their surroundings, Therefore, when a woman comes into the picture, men also feel the need to control, not realizing that where there is mutual respect there is no need for mutual control. Still, the inability to control their desire or sexual urges for women triggers an underlying anger in them. Guilt then kicks in for not being able to control something as basic as themselves, and when this happens frustration also sets in which feeds the love and hate mechanisms that are constantly working within their psyche. The frustration intensifies even further when they cannot control acting out on their desires. It is then that an individual with an irrational or unstable mind is inclined to initiate rape, an act of aggression against women. By this time, the hate is the dominating force within the man. He gets angrier for feeling less than a man and for not having the ability to control himself or his basic needs, which further create resentment toward women.

My dear unborn, all sins that relate to women directly or indirectly are pardoned by God, except when any part of the sinful act is not consensual by both parties. Rape is not pardoned by God automatically because anger is involved, because in some sexual relationships between couples anger or some variation of it serves as a stimulant. As such it is not pardoned because it is not consensual and it has to be. Indeed, further frustration comes when men convince themselves psychologically that they are fighting a losing battle and as a result join the priesthood, become a monk, or convince themselves that they find the same gender (other men) much more suitable for their sexual needs. The idea that woman is the weaker sex is an illusion, just as the idea that all Christians who practice humility are weak. But it is an illusion that is vital to the stability of man's ego and their ability to somehow feel superior. Remember, a man who has to convince himself that he is better or stronger than others is the weakest of all men. Yet, there is a part of man that has the need to convince himself that woman is still the weaker sex. Men seem to have a hard time reconciling with the idea that with all their strength, physical and otherwise, and perception about women's status in a male-dominated world, they somehow lack the control necessary to override their desires. Armed with this knowledge, which often manifests itself in women's behavior at times, men's anger and frustration reach its peak when they are reminded that they lack the simple control needed to control their body. Indeed this realization tends to feed the love/hate relationship that all men have for women.

My dear unborn, very few men are disciplined enough to resist their urges for sexual gratifications. But the truth of the matter is that it has nothing to do with being weak. Even in the face of true love and grave consequences, they have the propensity to still choose sexual gratification with someone they think they desire over what is prudent in a particular circumstance. They are inclined to do this because men are given an innate mechanism that regardless of how hard they try, they simply cannot say no to persistent sexual overture with someone whom they find attractive. Indeed, this is not a rationalization for adultery or promiscuous behavior, but rather sadly to say the hard truth, the type of truth that women are unwilling to accept in most cases. After all, how can love profess to exist when faithfulness is not a part of the equation, especially since it is at the heart of the holy institution of marriage? This is not to say that all men are cheaters, only that they possess the genetic predisposition that if placed in a position where they can engage in sexual interaction with someone they find attractive, they will do so. If they are married, they will still engage in this type of behavior, especially if there is no chance of the truth being discovered. In short, men cannot resist sexual overture from someone they find attractive if the engager is persistent or they think no accountability will be given. Therefore, whether he asks for it or not, this sin is automatically pardoned by the Supreme Being. Men should at all times be very firm when confronted by someone they find sexually attractive but cannot or do not wish to act on these urges because of other commitments or involvements. This way the engager hopefully will stop the persistence. For the sake of their spirituality, they should also avoid being in the type of circumstances that might feed or increase the opportunity for sexual misconduct on their part. It is not only sexual behavior by man that is pardoned by God, but behavior in general that stems from the association with women and their utilization of sex appeal.

My dear unborn, I was once shunned for my views on the one pardoned sin, and in defiance I asked, "Where are Sampson, David, and Solomon at this moment—men who in one way or another betrayed God's wishes simply because of the influence of a woman. My questioner did not answer, but I told him these men are sitting on the right hand of the Messiah, for God judges no man whose actions stem from the manipulation or influence of a woman. He does this not because he thinks man is weak and is at the mercy of woman, but because he understands that the same thing makes men strong is the very same thing that makes them sexually irrational: their innate need for conquest. It was never God's intention to restrict man in terms of how many women he may have, and still wishes that a man should have as many as his heart desires. However, a man who chooses to have many women must be true to them and hold them sacred equally in the eyes of God. The women must know about each other, and there can be no deception in an attempt to have more than one. There was a time when men were allowed to have many wives, and although in some parts of the world this is still true, in the Western world the idea is frowned upon. A spiritual being does not dwell on his desires for women or any other gifts. Still, he must be true to his own nature and meditate on the weaknesses that would otherwise make him strong. A man should not devour as many women as possible in order to satisfy his libido because his behavior is pardoned by God but rather see this as an opportunity to remain true to himself, his loved one, and to his Creator. It is not always wise to partake in certain behavior simply because we can. The restraint shown under these circumstances is a much greater test of our discipline. If an enlightened individual cannot be satisfied by one partner, then the problem is much larger than this enlightened individual. The road to happiness, sexually or otherwise, does not rest on anyone except you, the person who may be searching for the happiness. No emotion can take the place of the space reserved for God. Remember always, no emotions can take the place of the space reserved for God.

My dear unborn, the need for intimacy with another individual other than a loved one seems to take top priority regardless of the degree of love one has for a loved one, in many cases. Yet, this in no way should cast a poor reflection on the individual whose need for intimacy with this person outside their relationship remains strong, although it does run contrary to the way a person in love ought to behave. After all, when two people are together for a substantial amount of time, their minds develop a natural curiosity after a while in order to see whether they are still desired by others as well. The romantic love people once had for each other over a period of time transforms itself into much deeper feelings of attachment. Their bonds in most cases are stronger than they have ever been, and yet the need to be noticed and to be intimate even with a perfect stranger still continues to be the focal point of their preoccupation. Feelings of desires for each other, though they exist, are replaced by feelings of companionship. The sharing of thoughts and quiet times becomes paramount to the couple and sex actively engaged in with an emphasis on cuddling and emotional tradings. Betrayal is never a part of the equation, and yet it does find itself on the mind of one or both of the couples, though it is difficult to believe without leaving a dent in the couple's love for each other—that is, until the truth becomes known to the one who has maintained his/her truthfulness to the vows taken on the day of wedlock. Betrayal is never a split-moment decision by any of the parties within a relationship. Before betrayal comes a preoccupation with sexual fantasies, an evaluation of past relationships, an assessment of physical attributes both of oneself and one's partner, a nostalgic travel down memory lane, and finally a summary of past conquest of the opposite sex. Next comes a plan by the potential cheater with respect to ways on how to manipulate their loved one, friend, employer, and time in order to ensure that if the opportunity does provide itself, there will be little effort or risk to see it through. Soon one or both members of the relationship have broken their vows, and yet, unless the truth is known, their love for each other will still remain in tact.

My dear unborn, the love shared by these couples is nothing but an illusion based on the years of delusions of wanting to love and be loved. But it is an illusion, for true love is pure in essence and as such cannot be supported by betrayal, infidelity, or that which runs counter to spiritualism. Even with betrayal or infidelity, while rooted in sin, this person will be pardoned by God. Why? Because this type of love, like most aspects of life as stated before, is an illusion that can only become real from moment to moment. Regardless of how long people are together, a man and woman sharing this type of love are sharing a love that lacks substance and a real sense of purpose. In short, such a love exists from moment to moment and can only remain real to the couples if it remains in this mode. In these moments, one member of the couple can easily go off with another individual whom they feel can supply them with a single element that has been missing from the years of being together with their partner. During this moment, the person they have chosen will expand their illusion, providing the missing piece that was not offered or could not be seen.

Chances are that the thought that might have been lacking in this long-term relationship might have been just hidden because of the toxicity of their souls. As such, they attempt to find it in someone else, not knowing that what they seek so desperately is not real. But their love is only given the perception of reality simply because of the many years of sharing the same delusion together.

My dear unborn, how could God not pardon such an individual or individuals? This illusion of love does not apply to all but, sadly to say, to many. God forgives this type of infidelity and intimacy because the love on which it is based is an illusion. God cannot judge an act that derives from an unreal premise. Indeed, it would be like punishing a magician for making a rabbit disappear from his hat, lost to the eyes forever. The Creator, therefore, will not penalize one for an act that lacks the ingredient of reality. Since the love shared by the couple for however long they might have been together is unreal, even though they themselves may think otherwise, carrying out an act of intimacy with someone they desire for the moment is, as they would say in the legal arena, grounds for dismissal by God. However, the tendencies and propensities to carry out such an act provide God with something even more important. It gives him tremendous insight into the character of such an individual and sets the tone for how he will indeed judge that person on other issues whose platforms are rooted in reality. One might have escaped the consequences for cheating on a loved one, but the seed that has been sowed by cheating will wreak havoc on one's character in the eyes of God. As any good attorney will tell you, once your credibility has been shattered in the eyes of those who judge you, you might as well rest your case, so to speak. You would have just won a pyrrhic victory with respect to the scenario on love that has been discussed. Indeed, you would have managed to escape the consequences for your sexual behavior because God would have pardoned you, but you would now open up yourself for more consequences based on other issues.

THE BIRTH

33

HEAVEN IS NOT MY REWARD

My dear unborn, many Christians and worshippers of all kind live to worship God primarily for one reason, and one reason alone: to one day be with him in his kingdom, to have eternal life. They sway their hands in church and drop a large offering in the church plate that one day they might find themselves worthy enough to enter God's kingdom in order to live forever with him. But I wonder whether or not these same people would be in church praising and worshiping God if the prospect of going to heaven and living forever did not exist? What would happen if life now is life forever? Would so many people still be praising God? From what I have seen, I doubt it very much. People are selfish and seldom do anything unless they can get something in return. Unlike God, they do not engage frequently in unconditional behavior, for it is an art that very few are able to master. But I tell you this, my dear unborn, when you come of age, choose your faith and choose it wisely. Give without the expectation of receiving, and let those who receive your offering know not from whence it comes. Be the star of your destiny. Detach yourself from all worldly possessions by forbidding them to possess you. Let your flesh share in its pleasure if you must, but keep your spirit separate from all its enticement. Love God for the life he has given you now, and though he has promised you life eternal, focus only on the one you must endure now. Although he will fulfill his promise, true freedom comes from having nothing to lose. Love your faith and your God; do so with the expectation of receiving nothing except the breath he has given you each morning. By doing this, you would have made your heart pure and your spirit liberated. Therefore, embrace the gifts God has offered now, gifts that many worshippers are unable to see because they have tunnel vision that leads straight to eternal life. The truly enlightened does not live for what might be but for what is. He sees the kingdom of God not as a reward for his service and loyalty to God but rather as the home of his soul, a soul that will one day return to the place of its birth. As such he has nothing to lose in terms of fearing that after death he will not see the face of God. A man knows the direction of his house blindfolded; so is it with the soul in finding its place of birth, the kingdom of God.

My dear unborn, it has been said that God never gives an individual more than what he or she can bear, just one of the many rationalizations man has made for God for which he is profoundly grateful, I am sure—as if God should somehow apologize to us when we manage to make our lives a mess. It is quite amusing how man turns his life upside down, then attributes his misery to God, after which he finds consolation by reasoning to himself that the misery will not go beyond a certain point. Why? Because God is in total control of how much misery he will allow man to experience, as if life was not difficult enough without God deliberately putting up obstacles in our path, or that God has nothing better to do. Man will always have a need to blame someone for his troubles, and God is as good a person as any. After all, everything is within God's power to rectify or make whole, which makes him a perfect scapegoat for all of man's troubles. But know this, my dear unborn: Man is at the root of all the troubles he bears, and whether he chooses to blame himself, God, or the bogeyman makes no difference, for the answers to his troubles still lie with him. When you arrive at the height of spiritual enlightenment, the one clear axiom you will realize is that the face of God will be seen by all, but the full extent of his majesty only by few. Regardless of the essence of a man's soul, it must be returned to its place of birth. However, whether it remains there is another story altogether. Eternal life is a gift unworthy for the spiritually enlightened. It is a luxury that is special not because it is eternal but because it offers the opportunity to exist for once in a world without evil. For me, being vanquished into oblivion after having seen the face of God is much more than I deserve. No man has truly lived if after his death he is not worthy to see the face of God. For many enlightened individuals, having eternal life is the greatest reward they could ever receive. But for me I am not worthy to sit at the same table as the Messiah, much less my Creator. To reiterate a scenario: if I am offered the choice of not seeing God's face and living forever in his kingdom versus seeing his face for a second or two and then ceasing to exist for all eternity, I would gladly choose the latter. Indeed, I have already tasted life and although eternity has its attraction, it pales in comparison to behold the sight of the living God. This is not to say that the standard that I have set for myself should be yours as well. For a son who has yet to be born, you have resurrected a joy for which no words have yet been created. What one perceives as a reward and the value one places on it is relative. Yet, I have always known that heaven is not my reward.

My dear unborn; everything about God intrigues me from what he looks like to where, when, and how he came into existence. But in time I suppose those answers will be made known to me. I must be content with just accepting his existence, and through his grace, mine as well. And yet I feel as if there is a void within my soul for not having some of these answers. There is honor in all living things, whether it be man or beast. But the preservation of life and honor should not exceed one's willingness to surrender the very same life in the face of a just cause. A cause is just not because many ordained it to be so. It is just because it falls in line with one's principles and brings honor to the self without being a traitor to one's object of loyalty. The life that one goes at great length to preserve should not be a hindrance in sacrificing for a just cause, for a child of God never dies. He sleeps only to one day be risen up at the appropriate moment like a phoenix from the ashes. Therefore, while death or dying can often be the price one pays to enhance a just cause, it can also be said that it elevates the momentum of the cause as well. However, unless one is certain that change is inevitable because of the sacrifice, the price is much too high because only the living can actively influence change. The dead are at the mercy of fate or inevitability. Being a martyr is about fate deciding the worthiness of your sacrifice to a cause. But being amongst the living is about you weaving the basket that will hold the fruits of your own destiny. Individuals who said that they will readily give their lives for a cause are subconsciously relinquishing their responsibilities and duties on to those who will say to their enemies "they are in for the fight of their lives." One chooses to surrender gracefully by projecting the idea of becoming a martyr while the other chooses to endure the hardship until his fate is determined by the laws of circumstances. Regardless of how you choose to influence a just cause, alive or dead the only certainty is to ensure that the ideals you fight for belong to you with respect to your convictions and principles. This is a critical thing because the problem with fighting for a cause is that individuals sometimes get confused about the reasons as to why they are fighting, People have died for causes simply because the majority told them it was the right thing to do.

My dear unborn, learn to pick sense out of nonsense. Never lose your identity or ideals to the words from another man's tongue. You have only but one life; therefore, this obligates you to make sure that if you must lose it, the sacrifice can be justified by you and your loved ones. There is no disgrace or dishonor in your heart failing to hear the sound of reason from the voice of those who yearn for justice. For the driving force behind that which moves you may be utterly different from that which moves them. Therefore, listen to the drums of your own heart and let its rhythm guide you toward your destiny.

My dear unborn, heaven is not my reward. My true reward lies in the face of God, but to see the face of God I must become a part of his kingdom. Heaven is a place that is relative to each individual's desires and fantasies; it is a concept of each man's expectation and perception tied in with God's own as well. Man's life embodies being in a constant state of disbelief as he struggles to reconcile his system of disbelief with his faith, thus making him less susceptible to embrace the spirit of the Messiah. Therefore, no matter how hard man tries, he will never be able to grasp even a small vision of heaven. And if by some miracle he does, he will not be able to comprehend what he sees. I find it profoundly troublesome that in such a society as ours, there are those who still accept the notion that the creation of all things somehow just manifested all by themselves without any assistance by a Supreme Being, and upon further extrapolation, that there are those who cannot bring themselves to believe that the same entity that created the world in which we live today could and has also created another one that epitomizes utopia. They do not believe because they live in, as mentioned before, the mind-set or conscious state of disbelief, thus lacking the spiritual edification that is needed to bring them closer to God. The realm of beliefs or the circle of faith is a by-product of the spiritual realm. One needs a spiritual eye to truly understand what is being seen. It encompasses everything that is of this world but can only be unmasked and deciphered by one who walks in the light of God. It allows a child of God to see the good, righteous, and spiritual side of all things. It holds a light to our steps as we continue our journey with God and the Messiah. The concept of heaven will always be a fleeting notion to those who live in the state of disbelief. These individuals are the doubting Thomases of modern time. They can witness a miracle today and convince themselves tomorrow that this miracle did not exist. Their negativity is like poison to the enlightened. Yet the enlightened's duty is to try and get them close, if he or she can, to the realm of beliefs but never at the risk of his or her own salvation. For me, heaven is not enough for reasons that have been mentioned before, but for others heaven is not enough simply because they do not believe in the concept of heaven. Therefore, they choose to exist in this realm of disbelief and as such expect all things rewarded and consequences to be given to them in this world and this world alone. Throughout their entire lives, they live a life that stands on the foundation of emptiness, lacking any true fulfillment, for without a spiritual aspect to one's existence there can be no real fulfillment in this world or the next.

My dear unborn, in order to grasp the concept of heaven, visualize for a moment all the things in this world that are at the source of all the misery and discontent, then imagine for a moment a world without them. By doing this you would have yet to scratch the surface of the true nature of this spiritual realm. Heaven is more than just a place; it is the spiritual marriage between the souls of man and the soul of God. It is a heightened consciousness that forgoes all boundaries, allowing each entity to embrace a new world where law and order are innately maintained without the need for any societal regulating bodies, a place where no one has to stand guard, and yet order is maintained merely by the various entities' collective consciousness. It is a world where the art of perfection is skillfully mastered and the quest for spiritual enlightenment is a daily occurrence, as entities with nothing to prove still struggle to become Godlike. It is not a place where one can sit idly with nothing except to indulge in leisure and fulfill all their fantasies. There are those who think that by going to heaven, all their troubles will be over. They will not work or engage in any challenging endeavors. "Easy street" is the way one individual describes going to heaven. I tell you this, my dear unborn, it will take great discipline to be a part of God's kingdom, the discipline of the spirit. No longer will man be able to use being human as an excuse for failing to strive for perfection. And although man would have already been judged and found worthy to be in God's kingdom, conflicts will still be an issue. But the resolutions will be swift, just, and final.

My dear unborn, from birth to death, man has received more blessings and rewards from God that far exceed his worth. Indeed, so have I, for because of his grace, dying will be easy, for I have lived. And yet he openly invites man to live with him for eternity. A man must know his worth regardless of what else might have eluded him about himself. For this reason I am reluctant to accept God's invitation to heaven. Instead, I have chosen to be ground back to dust and return to the perpetual nothingness from whence I came. Heaven cannot be my reward, because to accept would be to drastically exalt the value of my existence. But to see the face of God for a moment would be a just reward, for only then would my soul be prepared for the eternal emptiness that lies ahead. Man must remain true to his faith at all times, that in the end, his existence will bear testimony to his death. My soul will not be sustained by the heavenly light of God's kingdom forever. Yet my faith is an active faith. It soothes me in times of hopelessness and despair, and reminds me that where my ability to cope ends, God begins. Remember, my dear unborn, that God's assistance to man is at its peak when man has surrendered either to himself or to God. Man's darkest hour or biggest failure is God's grand opportunity to highlight the depth of his love for him, a love that knows no bounds and seeks only to liberate man from that which imprisons him. Quite frequently that which imprisons man is that which he loves most and values least.

My dear unborn, the value of a man's existence must not be rooted in the level of his productivity within a given society but demonstrated in his inherent propensity to love and embrace those who need it most. God does not care whether you are a doctor or a lawyer. The accumulation of wealth and credentials is of little importance to the Messiah. While they may do something to boost man's ego, they matter less to God. However, take a homeless person to your home and give him a hot meal after you have allowed him to shower; travel to a new place and become overwhelmed with the joy of being able to ease a beggar's suffering. Do this for the glorification of God. Then you would have captured the attention of the Messiah. A man must know his purpose for embarking on the quest for spiritual enlightenment. Some seek spiritual enlightenment to remain in the good grace of God, others to pay tribute to the Messiah. I choose the latter, but in the process of doing so I have realized in my attempt to pay tribute to the Messiah he has paid tribute to me instead. My mind, body, and spirit have experienced the type of metamorphosis that could only have derived from the Son of God. Yet through it all, I remain steadfast in my desire to exist in his shadow. Now I know that unless a man discovers a way to become one with the entities of the universe, thus acquiring insight into God's creations, the metamorphosis of the mind, body, and spirit, which is necessary to comprehend the mind of God, will not be achieved. The quest for spiritual enlightenment without the knowledge of God ultimately will lead one in the wrong direction. Remember, to understand God is to understand one's self; to understand one's self is to know one's destiny. Know your destiny, my dear unborn, and let the governing of your life be guided by the expectations of God and not man.